Deep Ellum
and
Central Track

Where the Black
and White Worlds
of Dallas Converged

Deep Ellum
and
Central Track

Where the Black
and White Worlds
of Dallas Converged

Alan B. Govenar
and
Jay F. Brakefield

University of North Texas Press
Denton, Texas

The paper in this book meets the minimum requirements of the
American National Standard for Permanence of Paper for Printed
Library Materials, Z39.48.1984.

Permissions
University of North Texas Press
PO Box 311336
Denton TX 76203-1336
940-565-2142

Library of Congress Cataloging-in-Publication Data

Govenar, Alan B., 1952–
    Deep Ellum and Central Track : where the black and white worlds of
Dallas converged / Alan B. Govenar and Jay F. Brakefield.
        p.   cm.
    Includes bibliographical references (p.   ) and index.
    ISBN 1-57441-051-2 (alk. paper)
    1. Popular music—Texas—Dallas—History and criticism. 2. Afro-
Americans—Texas—Dallas—Music—History and criticism. 3. Deep
Ellum (Dallas, Tex.)—History. 4. Dallas (Tex.)—Social life and customs.
I. Brakefield, Jay F., 1945–   . II. Title.
ML3477.8.D35G68   1998
781.64'09764'2812—dc21   98-21458
                                               CIP
                                               MN

Design by Accent Design and Communications

Contents

Acknowledgments

This book owes much to the legacy of Deep Ellum we first heard in the music of those individuals who started their careers there and were still performing in the 1980s. These include Bill Neely, Buster Smith, Herbie Cowens, Jesse Thomas, Sammy Price, Eddie Durham, Alex Moore, Marvin Montgomery, Jim Boyd and others whose names we never knew but whose sounds stirred our imaginations in our first discussions about collaborating on this book. We first met at the Alex Moore funeral in January, 1989—Alan delivered a eulogy and Jay was covering the event for *The Dallas Morning News.*

Over the years since then, we talked to all the people we could find who had any first-hand knowledge of Deep Ellum. We are especially grateful to Dr. Robert Prince, Dr. Emerson Emory, James Thibodeaux, Bill Callahan, C. W. "Gus" Edwards, Walker Kirkes, Ted Parrino, Masha Porte, Eddie Goldstein, Isaac "Rocky" Goldstein, Louis Bedford, Theaul Howard, Quince Cox, Rubye Cowens, Jay McShann, Ernestine Putnam, Nick and Anna Lois Cammarata, Anna Mae Conley, Lucille Bosh-McGaughey, and Johnny Moss.

While we depended heavily on primary sources, we also relied upon many people and institutions which provided us access to unpublished manuscripts and resource collections: Eliana Pittman, Greg Jacobs, Zella Sobel, John Slate at the Texas African American Photography Archive, Geraldine Dunbar and Gaylon Polatti at the Dallas Historical Society, Jeanne Chvosta at the Dallas Museum of Art, the Dozier Foundation, Juliet George and Rose Biderman at the Jewish Community Center, Jimm Foster and Carol Roark at the Dallas Public Library, the Hogan Jazz Archive at Tulane University, the Institute of Jazz Studies at Rutgers University, and Kay Bost at the DeGolyer Library at Southern Methodist University.

In addition, we have benefited greatly from the input of other researchers and readers: Kip Lornell, David Evans, Paul Oliver,

Chris Strachwitz, Kate Seago, Sumter Bruton, Chuck Nevitt, Tim Schuller, Kevin Coffey, Danny Williams, Donald Payton, Allan Turner, Craig Flournoy, Larry Powell, Hank Wackwitz, Doug Seroff, Lynn Abbott, Thomas Riis, Christopher Wilkinson, and Tommy Löfgren.

Our wives, Kaleta Doolin and Debbie Brakefield, and our families, offered moral support and advice at times we may have thought the task at hand was insurmountable, knowing as we did that we should have started this book twenty-five years ago (if we had only lived in Dallas).

Introduction
Deep Ellum in Fact and Fiction

Deep Ellum has been mythologized beyond recognition. Misconceptions about the area abound, principally as a consequence of the lack of solid historical research. *The WPA Dallas Guide and History,* for instance, states: "This Deep Ellum is the survival of the Freedman's Town settlement of former slaves established after the emancipation proclamation of June 19, 1865, growth and permanence of which was enhanced by the location nearby of the terminals of the town's first railroad in 1872."[1]

No documentation for this assertion is provided in the *Guide,* a valuable but flawed document researched and written by the Federal Writers Project. Completed in 1940, it was not published in book form for more than fifty years, though many researchers read it in manuscript form at the Dallas Public Library. Among those researchers was the widely respected Dallas historian A. C. Greene, who wrote that "Dallas became a mecca for former slaves, and several Freedmen's Towns, as the black communities were known, sprang up on its outskirts. One black community, called Deep Ellum because it was located along the farthest extension of Elm Street, created a separate universe and ultimately contributed more famous artists to folklore and music than did white Dallas."[2] Likewise, William L. McDonald stated, "The freedman towns that evolved in Dallas County just after the [Civil] war included . . . the Deep Ellum district, which reached its zenith in the 1920s and 1930s."[3] And Southern Methodist University's Darwin Payne said, "'Deep Ellum,' that part of Elm Street just east of Central Avenue, had originated after the Civil War as a 'Freedmanstown.' Construction of the H&TC Railroad depot nearby had encouraged its growth and permanence."[4]

Indeed, several freed slave communities *were* established in and around Dallas after the Civil War. The one called Freedmantown was a short distance north of Deep Ellum, in the historic area of the city now called "State-Thomas." This community extended to the eastern edge of Deep Ellum, near present-day Baylor University Medical Center. But Deep Ellum itself does not seem to have been a freedmantown.

The area has long been associated with music. This aspect of the Deep Ellum myth has considerable legitimacy, as we shall see, but its musical heritage has in many ways been obscured and distorted. Larry Willoughby reported that:

> . . . the hidden and forbidden clubs and speakeasies along the northern part of Elm Street were the center of the blues and jazz action. The area was seething with music—jazz combos, jump bands, bebop and boogie-woogie pianists, blues and jazz vocalists, and street-corner guitarists. It was a magnet for musicians of every racial and cultural background, and therefore, symbolically and in vivid musical reality, Deep Ellum was the most visible example of the interaction of cultures that defines Texas music.[5]

Willoughby had the broad outlines right, but he succumbed to the temptation to exaggerate and romanticize the musical activity, not to mention significantly confusing several eras. Bebop, for instance, wasn't born until the 1940s, long after Dallas's black night-life scene had moved away from Elm Street, and few non-black musicians played in Deep Ellum because of the segregation of the time. For that matter, nightclubs in the modern sense didn't really exist in the twenties and thirties. The night-life entertainment on Elm Street and nearby portions of Central Track was presented in dance halls, theaters, cafes, "chock houses" and "soft-drink stands" where bootleg alcohol was served. Writer Dave Oliphant describes Deep Ellum as a red light district and repeats an interviewer's misquotation of Buster Smith: "Ella B. Moore's theater" became "the L. B. Mose theater" because of Smith's heavy Texas accent.[6]

The neighborhood has inspired other florid prose, such as this description from columnist J. H. Owens, "Old Ironsides," writing in a black weekly newspaper, the *Dallas Gazette*, in 1937:

> Down on "Deep Ellum" in Dallas, where Central Avenue empties into Elm Street, is where Ethiopia stretches forth her hands. It is the one spot in the city that needs no daylight saving time because there is no bedtime, and working hours have no limits. The only place recorded on earth where business, religion, hoodooism, gambling and stealing goes on at the same time without friction. . . . Last Saturday a prophet held the best audience in this "Madison Square Garden" in announcing that Jesus Christ would come to Dallas in person in 1939. At the same time a pickpocket was lifting a week's wages from another guy's pocket, who stood with open mouth to hear the prophecy.[7]

Compounding Deep Ellum's aura of mystery, the very origin of its name is uncertain. But from its beginnings as a Wild West saloon district near the railroad station of the 1870s, this part of town was far from the center of Dallas life; hence the "Deep" designation. "Ellum," on the other hand, was a phonetic spelling for a colloquial pronunciation of Elm, by African Americans or Eastern European Jews, or both, who did business there and lived in neighborhoods nearby. Likewise, it's not certain when the two words were joined into one phrase, "Deep Ellum." Some veterans of the area say they've heard it all their lives, while others swear they never heard it until the 1980s revival of the area. It doesn't seem to have appeared in early Dallas newspapers. There is a reference to "Deep Elm" in a 1918 edition of *The Chicago Defender*. Certainly, however, the term was in wide use by the time of a

November 18, 1925 *Dallas Morning News* article headlined, "Hidden Nooks: 'Deep Ellum' Has Its Renown, But After All It Is Merely the Darkies Parade Ground." Readers were informed in an overtly racist tone:

> "Deep Ellum" is the Broadway of the Dallas Black Belt. Venture up there any Saturday night and you will see thousands of Negro merry-makers parading the streets in the gay life of a care-free race. Venture a little farther into the Black Belt and you will find that North Central Avenue is the Coney Island of the Negro district. It is on "de tracks" that the Negroes go to have a good time. Thousands of them parade the Central Railway tracks in the evenings and it is there that most of their amusements are staged.

It can be difficult to define precisely what Deep Ellum was. Visual representations of its earliest street life are scant, aside from a 1922 photo of streetcar track being laid on Elm Street, several photos of Jewish shopkeepers, and a couple of images of blacks walking along Central Track. In 1932, Dallas artist Otis Dozier completed a painting called *Deep Ellum*, which shows African Americans carrying watermelons past a pawnshop. No paintings or photographs have been found to give any sense of the musical activity that occurred in Deep Ellum and Central Track.

There are, however, several photographs of musicians who started their careers in Dallas and were, to varying degrees, associated with Deep Ellum and Central Track. Some of these are publicity stills, while others come from private sources. For this book, many people made available their collections, including Alex Moore, Marvin Montgomery, Walker Kirkes, Ted Parrino, Rudolph McMillan, Louis Bedford, Eddie Goldstein, and C. W. "Gus" Edwards. Additional images are reproductions from *The Chicago Defender*, as well as from numerous public institutions: the Dallas

Public Library, Southern Methodist University, the Jewish Community Center of Dallas, and the Texas African American Photography Archive at the 5501 Columbia Art Center.

The WPA Guide, in a section called "Deep Ellum: Harlem in Miniature," states, "Deep Ellum is the colloquialism used by both Negroes and whites for the congested Negro shopping district and amusement center lying on both sides of Elm Street between Preston and Good Streets, and the section about it for two or three city blocks to the north and south. The police department regards the real Deep Ellum as that area between Central Avenue, where run the all-but-abandoned railroad tracks, and Hawkins Street to the east in the 2500 block."[8] Surviving white merchants and their families say the real Deep Ellum was a few blocks of Elm Street, and really just the south side of the street, at that. But as the *Morning News* article and the *WPA Guide* indicate, nearby Central Avenue, or Central Track, could be considered a part of Deep Ellum as well. Businesses owned and patronized by African Americans lined the H&TC tracks from Freedmantown, or North Dallas, south at least to Main Street. These included shoe-shine stands and cafes, which often featured gambling, drinking and music, as well as dance halls and movie and vaudeville theaters. A few of these businesses spilled onto the north side of Elm near the railroad crossing, which could help explain why white merchants felt that only the south side was significant.

It is also important to remember that many street names have changed since the WPA book was written. Preston Street no longer exists—and should not be confused with Preston Road. The former Preston Street is now Central Expressway at street level. And Good Street has become Good-Latimer Expressway.

White merchants may have made a distinction between Deep Ellum and Central Track, but it is clear that the African Americans who frequented both the businesses along the track and those on Elm did not. A strong indication of this is found in a poem, "Deep Ellum and Central Track," published in 1936 by the African-American folklorist J. Mason Brewer, who once taught Spanish at Booker T. Washington High School in Dallas:

Talk about Harlem ef yuh wants tuh,
An Lennox Avenue
But Ah got sumpin' now, Baby,
Ah kin talk about too.
Harlem's got hits browns an' hits yallers
And sealskin mamas in black.
But 'tain't got nothin' on Dallas,
Deep Ellum and Central Track.
Harlem's got hits gin and hits whiskey
Uh li'l penthouse o' two;
But Ah'm still telling you, Baby,
Dallas got sumpin', too.
Now hit mought not be no apartment
Mought be uh 'shot-gun' shack;
But de gals sho makes you 'member
Deep Ellum and Central Track.
Done been all eroun' yo' big State Street,
Uh way up dere in Chi;
An hits uh pretty good hang-out—
Baby, dat ain't no lie.
Gals up dere do de snakehips,
On de streets fuh uh fac';
But gimme my gal an' de Jig Saw
Deep Ellum an Central Track.[9]

In effect, Deep Ellum became known as the "black downtown" of Dallas. As lawyer and former judge Louis Bedford, an African American, says,

Deep Ellum was centrally located. So, since people came from every section . . . you didn't have shopping centers and all the satellite places to go; it was right down there. So, it seems logical to me that if whites had a downtown section that was convenient for everyone, blacks would need the same thing.

People rode streetcars, wasn't a whole lot of cars. People had to come to town anyway to pay their utility bills and things of that nature. They had to come to City Hall; they could walk a few blocks. If they wanted to have a bite to eat and they had no place to eat because of the segregated atmosphere, there was Deep Ellum. They had to go to the restroom, there was Deep Ellum. It was someplace central where people could go. It was the heart. There were people living in Oak Cliff, people living in South Dallas, people living in North Dallas, but Deep Ellum was the core.[10]

Deep Ellum was not a neighborhood, strictly speaking. Few lived there, at least after the turn of the century. It was a business district—more accurately, the confluence of two business districts, one white (mostly Jewish), one black. When we talk about Deep Ellum, we're really talking about Deep Ellum and Central Track, as Brewer did. For brevity's sake, in this book, "Deep Ellum" will include Central Track, formally called Central Avenue.

The white-owned stores on Elm served both black and white patrons. On Saturdays, Deep Ellum evoked the State Fair of Texas, thronged with people shopping for furniture, groceries, clothing and other staples at reasonable prices. It was in a sense the outlet mall of its day. Many places, pawnshops in particular, stayed open late on weekends. Deep Ellum has also been called "a few blocks of New York City plunked down in Dallas," complete with some merchants living in or above their stores.

Although Deep Ellum was never officially a red-light district like Fannin Street in Shreveport or Storyville in New Orleans, it was a place where such vices as gambling and prostitution flourished, often in return for payoffs to the authorities. Black musician Sammy Price, speaking of the teens and early 1920s, said there were plenty of Deep Ellum drinking establishments run by women called "landladies." Asked if whites were seen around these places, he replied, "If there were any whites down there, they were running a foot race."

"In Deep Ellum, there was an alley called 'death row' where someone would get killed every Saturday," Price continued. "And there was a stool pigeon for the police, and his name was 'Yellow Britches.' If someone came into town that he didn't know, he put some chalk on the back of [the stranger's] pants so that the police could identify and arrest him."[11]

Pawnbroker Isaac "Rocky" Goldstein, speaking of the 1930s and 1940s, exaggerated the murder rate even more: "There was a killing every day. There were fights on the corner of Central and Elm all the time, and they had these holy roller women trying to convert these guys."[12] In fact, in 1936, Dallas had 102 homicides; seventy-nine were black-on-black crimes. Despite the hyperbole that pops up in such personal reminiscences, Deep Ellum was certainly prone to the violence that follows poverty, drinking, prostitution and gambling.

The area's biggest retail establishment was Sam Dysterbach's department store at Elm and Pearl streets, run by a second-generation Deep Ellum merchant, whom blacks sometimes referred to as "Sam Dustyback." Goldstein recalled that the store still had hitching posts out front and a nineteenth-century system of pulleys to move money around the place in a basket. Dysterbach was prosperous, in part because of lucrative contracts to sell uniforms to everyone from the police department to high school bands. He sold to farmers on credit and gave food away at Christmas.

Like many others, Goldstein remembered a legless man called Wagon Willie who got about on a skateboard. "He came in one day and said, 'Mr. Rocky, I need ten bucks; hold my wagon for me.' I says, 'OK.' I give him a ten, he's going out of the store, swinging his body. I say, 'Willie, come on back here. You owe me ten dollars whenever you got it. Take your wagon with you.' I couldn't see him moving his body like that."[13]

According to several accounts, Wagon Willie was a skilled gambler and pickpocket who bootlegged out of his home on the edge of Deep Ellum and once went to prison for stealing a car and driving it to Oklahoma. Willie wasn't alone in pawning odd items. Goldstein said one woman hocked her mother's ashes.

White singer Bill Neely recalled the area in the 1930s. He'd pick cotton all week in McKinney, then hitchhike into town and make for Deep Ellum. One of his regular haunts was a place he called "Ma's"—probably Mother's Place in the 2800 block of Elm— run by Lucille Cortimillia. "Ma's apron was so slick, even the flies slid off," Neely said. "She wore a .38 caliber pistol, and when she said 'hop,' they hopped. And the kind of people who went there weren't much better: gangsters, gamblers, people like Raymond Hamilton, Baby Face Nelson and Bonnie and Clyde." One night at Ma's, Neely recalled, he was singing when a man rose and told the noisy crowd to shut up. A hush fell over the place. The man was Raymond Hamilton, a member of the Barrow gang.

By that time, Neely said, Deep Ellum had become legendary for its music, gambling and street life, but also had degenerated into "a skid row, where all the hobos landed. It was where the drunkards and winos and people trying to roll one another hung out. There were all kinds of people: cowboys, Mexicans, blacks and down-and-out farmers."[14] Deep Ellum generally seemed to attract people who were offbeat. Rocky Goldstein once employed the black sheep of a wealthy Chicago family. The man was such a skilled salesman that he would often take a watch from the shop with him and sell it to another patron in the cafe where he ate lunch. The man eventually died of a drug overdose in his room at the run-down Campbell Hotel down the street.

Goldstein also recalled a salesman who was covered with tattoos, including one of a pig. He would pull out one of his body hairs and hand it to someone, saying, "Here, I'm giving you a hair out of the pig's ass." When things were slow, he'd strip to his underwear and do a handstand in the middle of Elm Street.[15]

The strip along Central Track featured not only offbeat characters and gambling, but prostitution as well. Women would sit outside on posts along Central Track, selling themselves for a quarter (in the twenties). Several walk-up hotels such as the Powell became notorious by the 1940s. "If you weren't movin' in that Powell Hotel," recalled Willard Watson, who later achieved fame as a folk artist, "them bedbugs would be movin' you."[16]

Black historian Dr. Robert Prince recalled the area in the forties, when selling *The Dallas Express* would gain him entree into the joints along the track. He remembered the gamblers and the women. Among the characters was a dark, muscular man called "Blue" who served as the lookout, or "good eye," in a gambling joint, and a gambler called "Six-Toed Willie."[17]

Anna Mae Conley, born in 1919, attended J. P. Starks Elementary, which backed up to the tracks in Freedmantown, before she went to Booker T. Washington High School. "It was a long ways. But to get there, all we had to do was walk out Central Track. And we did that. Most of 'em, from the time they started high school until they finished high school. But after I had gone down Central Track about two months, I could see all those bad places. Now nothing was happening during the daytime, but you knew what was happening. And I found another way to get home. I came out Ross Avenue and came on to St. Paul, or either I walked to Ervay." Ms. Conley's friend Lucille Bosh McGaughey, born in 1918, recalled that this route took them down San Jacinto Street near the high school. According to McGaughey, white prostitutes sat in the windows of houses and lured men, who would pay them fifty cents.[18]

During its heyday, from the early part of this century through the late twenties or early thirties, Deep Ellum was filled with contradictions: It was a business district that became legendary for violence and sin. As the song "Deep Ellum Blues" says, one went "down" on or in Deep Ellum, down to a world where people broke the accepted norms of behavior. Deep Ellum was a real place that provided a variety of services, legal and illegal, and came to represent the uncertainties and dangers associated with the growth of Dallas as a city. Indeed, several prominent business people and companies got their start in Deep Ellum.

As firsthand accounts attest, Deep Ellum once really did ring with music, from the street blues of Blind Lemon Jefferson and others to the orchestras that played in the theaters. Some musicians who played in Deep Ellum had quite an impact. Jefferson was the first country blues singer to achieve commercial success as a recording artist. He became very popular in his brief recording career and influenced a wide range of musicians, including another Dallas guitarist, Aaron "T-Bone" Walker, and Mississippian B. B. King. Jazz saxophonists Budd Johnson and Henry "Buster" Smith moved on from Deep Ellum to jazz centers such as Kansas City and New York, where they played major roles in shaping swing and then bebop. The black music played in Deep Ellum was also a force in the development of Western swing, a musical connection that has not previously been documented.

Deep Ellum, then, was a crossroads, a nexus, where peoples and cultures could interact and influence each other in relative freedom. A lot of interesting people filtered through an area of just a few blocks centered around a railroad crossing. Along Central Track and in North Dallas, African Americans created an amazingly rich, layered society.

In this book, we investigate what Deep Ellum was and what it meant, socially, historically, musically, and as a kind of metaphor for the underside of the city of Dallas. We explore the growth of the area, focusing on the groups of people who migrated there and the business activity and cultural life they generated. Music encouraged the interaction between cultures, especially with the advent of commercial recordings and radio. By the turn of the century, diverse styles of blues, jazz and early country music were popular in Dallas and were being performed in the downtown theaters, on the sidewalks, in medicine shows, and in juke joints and chock houses along Central Track. Insofar as Deep Ellum is a metaphor for the interplay of these groups, our treatment is wide-ranging and interdisciplinary. To establish the overall significance of Deep Ellum, we examine its relation to the broader context of Dallas history and to the settlement patterns and commerce of

African Americans and Eastern European Jews. In so doing, we elaborate on the lives and careers of extraordinary people and seminal musicians in addition to the proliferation of diverse cultural styles, including blues, jazz and country.

Given the lack of substantive documentation of this period of Dallas history, we found it necessary to bring together disparate sources, including oral history, scholarly articles and books, and anecdotal evidence. Many of these sources were identified in the vast collections of Govenar's nonprofit organization Documentary Arts, and its Texas African American Photography Archive. We assessed the relative merits of each source on a case by case basis. Articles and books were checked for their accuracy; in some cases we discovered errors that had been repeated so often that they were assumed to be fact, such as the Freedmantown origins of Deep Ellum. Oral history and anecdotal evidence were authenticated through city directories, maps and other public records. Of necessity, we integrated these accounts to present the most comprehensive description of people and events. In instances where primary and secondary sources simply do not exist, we were forced to extend the bounds of our discussion beyond Deep Ellum proper, to incorporate relevant information about other areas of Dallas and Texas history. This also helps to provide a context for the events we describe.

Deep Ellum has provided an alternative to Dallas's image of itself as a staid and proper place modeled more after the great cities of the East and Midwest than those of Texas or elsewhere in the South or Southwest. Indeed, upon hearing that Fort Worth advertised itself as "where the West begins," humorist Will Rogers is said to have added, "And Dallas is where the East peters out." The reality of Dallas, of course, was quite different from the image it sought to portray.

[1] *The WPA Dallas Guide and History* (Denton: University of North Texas Press, 1992), 294. Hereinafter referred to as the *WPA Guide.*

[2] A. C. Greene, *Dallas U.S.A.* (Austin: Texas Monthly Press, Inc., 1984), 63.

[3] William L. McDonald, *Dallas Rediscovered: A Photographic Chronicle of Urban Expansion 1870–1925* (Dallas: Dallas Historical Society, 1978), 17.

[4] Darwin Payne, *Dallas, An Illustrated History* (Woodland Hills, California: Windsor Publications, 1982), 185.

[5] Larry Willoughby, *Texas Rhythm Texas Rhyme: A Pictorial History of Texas Music* (Austin: Texas Monthly Press, Inc., 1984), 60-62.

[6] Dave Oliphant, *Texas Jazz* (Austin: University of Texas Press, 1996), 43, 93.

[7] As quoted in *WPA Guide*, 294.

[8] *WPA Guide*, 294.

[9] J. Mason Brewer, ed., *Heralding Dawn: An Anthology of Verse* (Dallas: June Thompson Printing, 1936), 4.

[10] Louis Bedford, interview with Jay Brakefield, December 5, 1992.

[11] Sammy Price, interview with Alan Govenar, September 27, 1986.

[12] Rocky Goldstein, interview with Jay Brakefield, March 22, 1992.

[13] Ibid.

[14] Bill Neely, interview with Alan Govenar, August 29, 1984.

[15] Rocky Goldstein interview.

[16] Willard Watson, interview with Jay Brakefield, July 16, 1992.

[17] Robert Prince, interview with Jay Brakefield, January, 1993.

[18] Anna Mae Conley and Lucille Bosh McGaughey, interview with Jay Brakefield and Alan Govenar, October 3, 1992.

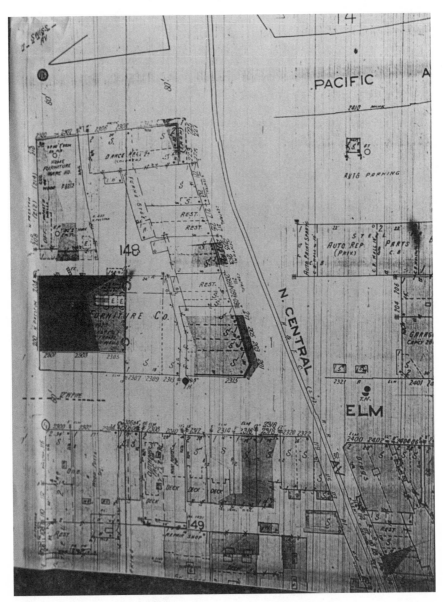

1920s Sanborn map of Dallas showing intersection of Elm Street and Central Track. At top and slightly left of center is the "Dance Hall (Colored)," which is the Tip Top dance hall. *Courtesy* Dallas Public Library.

Shotgun houses in Dallas, 1927. Baylor Hospital is in the background. *Courtesy* Dallas Public Library.

Central Track, 1926. From the *Dallas Morning News* Collection, DeGolyer Library, Southern Methodist University. #Ag84.294.3.123

Deep Ellum, ca. 1920s. *Courtesy* Texas/Dallas History and Archives Division, Dallas Public Library.

Ad from *The Dallas Express,* one of Dallas's African-American newspapers.

The Fair Store, owned by David Fair. Elm Street, 1905. *Courtesy* Jewish Community Center, Dallas, Texas.

1932 painting of Deep Ellum by Otis Dozier. *Courtesy* Dallas Museum of Art.

The Railroads Create Deep Ellum

Dallas was founded in 1841 by a Tennessee lawyer, John Neely Bryan, who settled on a bluff about where the former Texas School Book Depository now stands. At that time, long before the Trinity River was rechanneled for flood control, Bryan's bluff sloped down to a natural ford where travelers—first Indian, then white—often crossed. He knew that the Republic of Texas had selected the spot for the junction of two major thoroughfares, one of which survives as Preston Road. Bryan's earliest plan apparently was to found a trading post and to do business with the Indians.

Thus the Trinity River played a vital role in the establishment of Dallas. Despite attempts that continued into the twentieth century, however, it stubbornly resisted navigation. It became obvious that if Dallas was to become a business center, another means must be found. During the Civil War, Dallas served as a regional food distribution center, and the county's black population swelled from around 900 to 2,500 as slaves were imported to harvest crops. The city, relatively untouched by the conflict, had a population of about 2,000 at war's end. Its strong business leadership included men such as William Henry Gaston, a former Confederate army officer who became a banker and major landowner in Dallas. Sarah Cockrell, the widow of one of the city's early leaders, Alexander Cockrell, also wielded considerable power, but because of the male domination of the time, she worked quietly behind the scenes.

These leaders concluded that railroads were Dallas's route to commercial success. In this, of course, they had considerable competition; railroad fever was sweeping the nation. But they had an uncommon determination and were not above a bit of trickery—some would say ruthlessness.

After the war, the Houston & Texas Central Railroad resumed its northward progress. Its line was to have been built eight miles east of Dallas's courthouse, too far away to do the city much good. Here, Gaston's land holdings saved the day. His home was more than a mile east of the courthouse square—then considered so far from the city's life that he once attempted to recruit neighbors by offering free land to anyone who would build on it. Gaston offered the railroad right of way, and he and the other businessmen sweetened the pot with $5,000 in cash. The railroad accepted the offer. In anticipation of the laying of the track and construction of a station, the city cleared the wooded area and extended the major east-west streets: Elm, Main and Commerce. News of the railroad's coming triggered a boom. "Dallas is improving rapidly," lawyer John Milton McCoy, later Dallas's first city attorney, wrote to his brother in Indiana in December 1871. "The prospects are very flattering indeed. Everything points to the crossing of two great roads here. Property is at exorbitant prices. The people are crazy, talking about Dallas being the Indianapolis of Texas for a railroad center. Emigration pouring in and everybody talking about the town. . . . ."[1]

The first train steamed into town on July 16, 1872, and Dallas went crazy. As Robert Seay, a young lawyer recently arrived from

Tennessee, wrote: "Men whooped, women screamed, or even sobbed, and children yelped in fright and amazement. As to that, there were some grown folks there who had never seen a railway train before, and I think the chugging of the log-burning furnace and the hissing of the steam startled them, a little."[2] An estimated 5,000 to 10,000 people turned out to hear hours of self-congratulatory speeches by city leaders and railroad officials and to feast on free buffalo steaks.

The civic leaders also turned their sights on the Texas & Pacific Railroad, which had been chartered by Congress in 1871 to extend its line to San Diego. They planned the line along the 32nd Parallel, fifty miles south of Dallas. But a local legislator attached to the right of way bill a seemingly innocuous rider requiring the T&P to cross the H&TC within a mile of Browder Springs. It didn't mention, of course, that Browder Springs, south of town, was Dallas's water supply. (The site is now Old City Park.) When railroad officials learned this, they threatened to run the line south of the springs, so it would still miss Dallas. But Gaston kicked in 142 acres for right of way plus the ten for the station. The city came up with $200,000 in bonds and $5,000 in cash and offered to let the railroad run on Burleson Street, which would be renamed Pacific Avenue. The T&P reached Dallas in February 1873, just in time for a panic, or depression, that halted its growth for several years at the community of Eagle Ford, about six miles west of town.

A resident named Wood Ramsey wrote that when he came to Dallas in 1875, "The Union Depot building was a squatty, one-story structure. . . . The farmers, cowboys, Negroes, loafers and loungers who crowded the platform and opened a way for us to get from the train as it pulled up with a clanging bell, broke up into squads and leisurely gravitated back to the domino tables in the adjacent saloons from which the whistle of the locomotive had jerked them."[3]

Within a year of the H&TC's arrival, between 750 and 900 new buildings were erected in the city, including a $75,000 courthouse. Dallas was virtually starting over; the wooden buildings downtown had been destroyed in 1860 by a fire that was blamed (falsely, many believe) on a slave revolt. The post-railroad boom brought the terminus merchants, so-called because they had followed the H&TC north, setting up stores in the railhead towns: Bryan, Hearne, Calvert, Kosse, Bremond, Groesbeck, Corsicana. Because they had last stopped in Corsicana, many were called the "Corsicana Crowd" once they reached Dallas.

The new arrivals, many of whom were Eastern European Jews, erected portable buildings with amazing speed. As the young lawyer Robert Seay wrote:

> The merchants, professional men, gamblers and floaters who had followed the terminus all the way to the north moved from Corsicana to Dallas in a body. Up to that time the town had been confined to the courthouse square. The newcomers bought on the road now known as Elm Street, between Jefferson and Griffin, and began to set up their portable houses which in sections they had brought from Corsicana. Almost overnight they built a new town. It was all so sudden and amazing that the natives could liken it to nothing but the fiction they had read in *Arabian Nights.* But to most of them it was woefully lacking in the pleasures that went with the perusal of Aladdin's performances, for it looked very much as if the railroad and the people who had come with it were bent on killing the old town. . . . [T]he old town began to put up its dukes for a fight . . . but the town had started to wander from the square and there was no bringing it back — and by the time the towns had met at Jefferson and Market, everybody had become friendly, for it was plain that after all the two towns were only one."[4]

Some of the terminus merchants stayed to become major business and civic figures in Dallas. The Sanger brothers—Alex and

Philip Sanger—and E. M. Kahn established successful department stores downtown. The Sangers settled in the Cedars, a fashionable neighborhood south of downtown.

Dallas did not become another Indianapolis. It many ways, it was a typical frontier settlement. In the 1870s, cattle were driven through downtown Dallas to cross the Trinity at the ford below Bryan's cabin. Buffalo were shot in the nearby countryside, and the town became a center for the trade in their hides. Amusements included several red-light districts, dance halls, beer halls and gardens, boxing matches, cockfighting, rat killing and an occasional bear baiting. J. H. "Doc" Holliday practiced dentistry in Dallas for three years before he was asked to leave town following a saloon shooting. The outlaw Belle Starr also spent time around Dallas, living in the community of Scyene, which is now part of the eastern suburb of Mesquite.

People kept pouring in. Historian Philip Lindsley wrote of the city in 1875: "The flood tide of emigration was now on. Every train on the Texas and Pacific Railway was literally packed with emigrants from the older states. In addition there were regular emigrant trains with special rates, and these overflowed with men, women and children."[5]

In the 1870s, soon after the railroads came, the future Deep Ellum was a ragtag collection of pastures, cornfields, cattle and hog pens, restaurants, lodging houses and saloons. People went about armed, and gambling flourished at all hours. Cowboys whooped and fired their pistols as they rode up and down the unpaved streets—sometimes right into the saloons. Variety (vaudeville or burlesque) theaters featured scantily clad women, and alcohol and other drugs often heightened the patrons' fun.

Meanwhile, northeast of the city limits, another community was growing, one founded by freed slaves. It was referred to as "Freedmantown" in the city directories of the period; later, it became known as North Dallas. The intersection of Thomas Avenue and Hall Street became the heart of Freedmantown, whose growth, like that of the rest of the city, was fed by the railroads. The lines provided work for many black men and housed some of them and their families in narrow rent houses along the right of way south of Freedmantown. This strung-out community became known as Stringtown. The houses were called "shotgun houses" because, it was said, a shotgun shell fired through the front door would travel out the back without hitting anything (presuming, of course, that no one was unlucky enough to be standing in the way). South of downtown near the H&TC track was another black community, a sprawl of unpaved streets called the Prairie.

Black men also found jobs in the industrial area that grew up near the railroad junction, in planing mills, meatpacking plants, oil works, waste mills, and dairies. The black influx was fed, too, by the bollweevil that began devastating the Texas cotton crop in the early 1890s. Some African Americans continued to pick cotton after moving to Dallas, waiting near the railroad station to be hired. Farmers, first in wagons, later in trucks, hauled laborers to fields around Dallas or farther into East or West Texas, a practice which continued until after World War II.

Many black women worked in white homes. Some lived with their families in servants' quarters, others in houses purchased by their employers, who deducted the mortgage payments from their pay. Thus, segregated housing emerged, though the city would not codify it into an ordinance until the early twentieth century.

Gradually, black businesses were established along Central Track, replacing the shotgun houses of Stringtown and some of the white-owned businesses. By the turn of the century, the pattern was set: Central Track was predominantly black; Elm Street was mostly white-owned, but catering to customers of both races. For blacks and whites alike, Dallas was a city of opportunity, and Deep Ellum, near the railroad station and relatively far from the main business district, was a place to get started.

[1] From a letter from John Milton McCoy to his brother Addie in Indiana, December 19, 1871, published in *When Dallas Became a City: Letters of John Milton McCoy, 1870–1881,* edited by Elizabeth York Enstam (Dallas: Dallas Historical Society, 1982), 46–47.

[2] As quoted in John William Rogers, *The Lusty Texans of Dallas* (New York: E. P. Dutton, 1951), 117.

[3] Barrot Steven Sanders, *Dallas, Her Golden Years* (Dallas: Sanders Press, 1989), 83.

[4] As quoted in Rogers, 118–19.

[5] Philip Lindsley, *History of Greater Dallas and Vicinity,* Volume 1 (n.p.: Lewis Publishing Co., 1909), 108.

Union Station in Dallas, 1905. The tall building across the tracks, the railroad hotel, later housed the Tip Top dance hall.

North Dallas house with watermelon garden, near Thomas Avenue and Hall Street, ca. 1920s. *Courtesy* Nick Cammerata.

Cammerata family's grocery store near Central Track, ca. 1940s. In front of the car is one of the Cammerata brothers. *Courtesy* Nick Cammerata.

Issy Miller's cafe at Elm and Central Track, 1932. Issy is standing behind the cash register. *Courtesy* Jewish Community Center.

Looking north on Central Track, Dallas, 1947. Photograph by Alex Moore. *Courtesy* Documentary Arts.

2

....

The Architect of
Deep Ellum

William Sidney Pittman was one of those who took advantage of opportunity. He was a brilliant man who became a hero to his people, although he was apparently something of a monster to his family. Born in 1875 in Alabama to former slaves, he attended Booker T. Washington's Tuskegee Institute and, with Washington's backing, studied architecture at Drexel Institute in Philadelphia. He graduated in 1900 and returned to Tuskegee to teach. But after quarreling with an official, he departed to establish a successful architectural practice in Washington, D. C. In 1907 he returned to Alabama to marry Booker T. Washington's daughter Portia in a ceremony that was the height of the social season at Tuskegee.[1]

In 1913 the Pittmans and their children moved to Dallas. Pittman designed a comfortable two-story house in North Dallas on Germania Street, which was renamed Liberty Street during

World War I. Their neighbors were other African Americans and some Italian immigrants who operated a doll factory. For many years, Italian Americans operated a number of businesses, including bakeries and grocery and liquor stores, in North Dallas. Several cafes that served African Americans were owned by Greek immigrants.

Mrs. Pittman was a talented musician. She taught music at the black high school in Dallas, which was named for her father, and gave private lessons as well. Sammy Price, who later became a well-known jazz and blues pianist, did yardwork for the Pittmans and took lessons from Mrs. Pittman. "Sammy," she told him, "you will never play by music, but you have a wonderful ear."[2]

Pittman designed St. James African Methodist Episcopal (A.M.E.) Church in Dallas, Allen Chapel A.M.E. Church in Fort Worth, Joshua Chapel A.M.E. Church in Waxahachie, and an Odd Fellows Temple in Houston. His greatest Dallas achievement was designing the state headquarters of the Grand Lodge of the Colored Knights of Pythias[3] in the 2500 block of Elm, completed in 1916. It was, from an architectural standpoint, the most distinctive building in Deep Ellum. It was made of red brick and featured tall arched windows and a neo-classical facade. On the first floor were a barbershop and drugstore. The second and third floors included office space for many of Dallas's black professionals, including Dr. P. M. Sunday and agricultural agent Cedar Walton, father of the jazz musician of the same name. The Golden Chain of the World, an organization similar to the Pythians, also had offices there. It advertised in *The Dallas Express*: "Join to-day. Die to-day. Pay to-day!"[4]

The fourth-floor ballroom, complete with an elaborate chandelier, was used for dances, performances and other community events. In March 1919, the Fisk Jubilee Singers, who had done much to popularize black sacred music, performed "classics, songs and old plantation melodies" in the ballroom. General admission was a quarter; reserved seats, fifty cents.[5] That October, Sargeant Neadham Roberts, described in the *Express* as "Our First Colored Hero of the Worlds War" and "the Hell-Fighting Hero," lectured there, under the auspices of the NAACP. Admission was fifty cents.[6] In January 1923, George Washington Carver demonstrated sweet potato products at the Pythian Temple for an audience of 800.[7]

Despite the Pittmans' contributions to their community, their home life was troubled. She was, by all accounts, warm and caring. He was dictatorial, angry and abusive. His children, Booker, Sidney and Fannie, called him "Big Pitt." Booker Pittman later wrote that his father sometimes beat his children until he was exhausted and they were semiconscious.[8]

During the 1920s, Portia Pittman returned with her children to Washington. She lived there until 1978, having outlived her husband and all her children. Booker Pittman was a poor student who felt self-conscious about being known as Booker T. Washington's grandson. He became a jazz musician and lived much of his life in Brazil, where he died in 1969. His daughter, Eliana Pittman, a singer, says her father never discussed his father at all.[9]

After his wife left him, William Sidney Pittman became increasingly embittered and apparently abandoned architecture. In 1929 he founded a weekly paper, *The Brotherhood Eyes,* with offices in his home. Its masthead pronounced it "A Newspaper That Doesn't Cross the Color Line." Pittman called his anonymous contributors "The Eyes." Headlines from a surviving copy dated July 28, 1934, identify his targets: "Black (Rev) 'Dillinger' and Sis 'Rev' Healer Vie in Skinning Saps"; "Negro Murderers Hurt Dallas; Pulpit Wolves Not Having It Easy Any Longer." The slangy stories were really diatribes. A Waco-datelined story under the "Dillinger" headline on July 28, 1934, proclaimed:

> My friends, the Baptist 'so'sation [association] No. 2 is now on the screen here and we assure you that the fine change is coming in from all parts and old brer "rev" moderator "Dillinger" is one happy soul. He carries his "machine gun" in the Master's Holy Bible and when he cocks his machine gun of hypocrisy, and smiles, the saps drop their change. The

poor, starved church folks freely give up their last dime to 'so'sations and lodges, to insurance companies and undertakers and preachers (male and female) and then go home and choke their "chiterlins" slim because they roll over and growl and beg for food. Old paron "Dillinger" knows where they are hungry. He knows the white people can't use them. He knows they are blind to depression. And he knows they are weak in every way. Yet he and others take their little money from them because the poor saps want the moderator to see and love them best, and say great and good things about them after they are dead and can't even hear what "de pahsons" have to say about them. They know that's why the poor creatures go hungry to pay 'so'sation dues. Old brer "Dillinger" can sure look through a Negro, and he has kept him snoozing for lo, these many years. He had fleeced, and "skint" the Race dead poor until now he has plenty of money for his wife and boys and he himself is styled as one of our great men. In fact, he is too great to visit his sleepy bunch. Does this man love his Race? Or is it just their pocket he's after?[10]

In the 1940s, Pittman was charged with mail fraud. Testimony at his trial, heavily covered in the *Express* and other black papers, alleged that he had sometimes attempted to shake down business owners, offering positive coverage in return for advertising. He denied the charges but was convicted and spent two years in prison.

Upon his release, he returned to Dallas and campaigned for former Vice President Henry Wallace, a left-wing candidate for president, in 1948. Pittman often ate lunch in the Pride of Dallas Cafe on Allen Street, owned by longtime restauranteurs Quitman and Daisy McMillan. Their younger son Rudolph, who grew up working in the cafe, recalled Pittman years later: "He stepped on too many people's toes. When he came out [of prison], he was a very, very bitter man, but he was brilliant. Oh, he was brilliant. . . . He was a broken man. . . . He was very feeble."[11] Pittman died in 1958 and lies buried in a South Dallas cemetery. A street in that section of town once was named for him, but it is now called Bethurum Avenue.

Time was not good to the Pythian Temple, either. In 1939, a Robertson County woman sued the Pythians after the organization failed to pay her husband's death benefit. Under new leadership, the statewide group struggled to regain its financial health and resumed paying death benefits. But the building went into receivership and in 1946 was sold for $6,500 and back taxes to Ben Ackermann, a local Jewish businessman. In 1956, Ackermann sold it for $100,000 after a local lodge sued him. They were awarded $16,557 by state District Judge Sarah T. Hughes, who later became well-known for swearing in Lyndon Johnson as president after John F. Kennedy was assassinated. For a time, local Pythians maintained an office across the street, above a pawnshop owned by Rubin "Honest Joe" Goldstein.

Sargeant Roberts, the black World War I hero, also came to a sad end. He and his wife hanged themselves in their New Jersey home in 1949 after he was accused—falsely, it seems—of fondling a white girl in a movie theater.

For a number of years, the former temple housed Union Bankers Insurance Company. By the early 1980s, the red brick building had been redone in a dreary gray, as was the adjoining one, which housed various businesses, including Goodwill Industries and the Blue Cross/Blue Shield insurance company. In the early 1980s, Union Bankers began covering up the "Knights of Pythias" name lettered on the facade. Historic preservationists got a court order to preserve the lettering, in an effort indicative of the black community's initiative to reclaim an era when blacks, against great odds, achieved considerable success in business in Deep Ellum.

[1] Most of the information in this chapter on William Sidney Pittman came from newspapers and from Louis R. Harlan's *Booker T. Washington: The Wizard of Tuskegee, 1901–1915* (New York: Oxford University Press, 1983), 118–20.

[2] Sammy Price, interview with Jay Brakefield, June 7, 1991, Dallas, Texas.

[3] The lodge, founded in Galveston, Texas, in 1883, was a fraternal organization and burial society.

[4] October 2, 1920.

[5] *The Dallas Express*, March 14, 1919. Microfilm copies of *The Dallas Express* can be viewed at the J. Erik Jonsson Central Library (Dallas), in the Texas/Dallas Collection.

[6] *The Dallas Express*, October 18, 1919. Black troops were not unfamiliar to Dallas. They were deployed to the Texas-Mexico border in the years before World War I, and a photo shows a black regiment marching through downtown Dallas between 1911 and 1914.

[7] *The Dallas Express*, February 3, 1923.

[8] Ophelia Pittman, *Por Você, Por Mim, Por Nós* (n.p.: Editora Record, 1984), 17–18.

[9] Eliana Pittman, interview with Jay Brakefield, August 8, 1996.

[10] *Brotherhood Eyes*, July 28, 1934.

[11] Rudolph McMillan, interview with Jay Brakefield, April 9, 1993.

Architectural rendering of Phythian Temple, by William Sidney Pittman, 1916. *Courtesy* Louis Bedford.

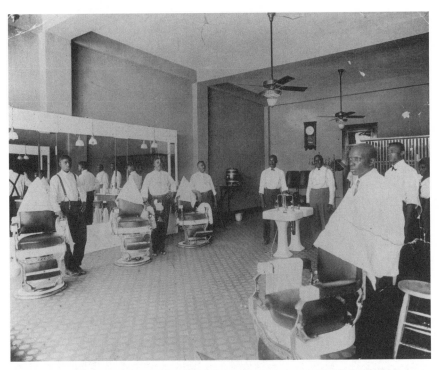

Barber shop in the Pythian Temple, ca. 1920s. *Courtesy* Louis Bedford.

Office in the Pythian Temple, ca. 1920s. *Courtesy* Louis Bedford.

3

································

Black Dallas

Within a few years after the turn of the century, African Americans in the area from Deep Ellum to North Dallas had created a community that was self-sufficient in many ways, despite institutionalized racism and limited access to capital. In 1899, educator John Paul Starks came to Dallas from Georgia and established a weekly newspaper called *The Bee*. Later renamed *The Dallas Express*, it survived into the 1960s. Other papers, such as William Sidney Pittman's *Brotherhood Eyes*, came and went. The black community seldom was covered in the mainstream white newspapers, the exception being news of a violent nature that seemed to back up racial stereotypes, as when *Express* editor W. E. King was slain in 1919 by a woman named Hattie Burleson.

Restaurants were established by entrepreneurs such as Quitman McMillan, born around 1880 in the East Texas town of Quitman. Never fond of farm work, McMillan moved to Dallas in 1907 and found work as a bartender. He went into partnership with a man named Watson in a cafe in the 100 block of North Central Avenue, between Main and Elm, but Watson couldn't stomach the back-room gambling that was essential for success and soon left the business. Within a few years, McMillan had established McMillan's Cafe in the 2400 block of Elm, a few doors from the black-owned Penny Bank, founded in 1909.

African Americans had their own "variety"—or vaudeville—theaters in Dallas by at least the 1890s. These included the Black Elephant, which occupied various locations around Central Track and was described as "notorious" in newspaper accounts. It appears that many such theaters, black and white, offered scantily clad women who entertained beer-swilling male patrons, so the Black Elephant's real distinction may have been simply that it was a black establishment. Some other similar (white) theaters at the time included: Thompson's Varieties, the White Elephant, the Palace Theatre, Hanlon's Varieties, Mascott (Varieties), the Gum Theatre, and the Camp Street Variety.

A July 1890 *Dallas Times Herald* article probably exemplified the white attitude toward such venues: "Two months ago, Robert Giles and Ed Watson, two *mokes* [a disparaging term for African Americans], were star performers at a Negro dive on Camp Street known to the public as the 'Palace Theatre.' Two Lang, a Chinaman in the vicinity, was robbed one night of $1.90 and identified Giles and Watson as the men who held him up and deprived him of one day's receipts of his 'washee-washee' house. . . ."[1] A few months later, the City Council passed an ordinance stiffening regulation of such theaters and drove several, including the Black Elephant, out of business.

Despite this setback, black show business flourished in Deep Ellum soon after the turn of the century, paralleling the growth of theaters offering films or high-class vaudeville entertainment, or both, in cities all over the country. In Dallas in 1908, John "Fat Jack" Harris opened the Grand Central Theater in the 400 block of North Central, near its intersection with Swiss Avenue. Everyone called the place "Fat Jack's." Harris often sat outside in overalls, smoking cigarettes, chatting with passersby and selling tickets at seventeen cents for adults, eleven cents for children. His leadership of the house band drew praise in *The Freeman*, a black-owned weekly paper in Indianapolis that devoted considerable coverage to black show business nationwide. In January 1910, Harris scored a coup by presenting a film of the great black heavyweight boxing champion Jack Johnson doing battle with a fighter named Ketchel.

Also by 1910, the Swiss Airdome Theater (described in an *Express* ad as "managed by colored people for colored people, and all the performers are colored") had been established on Swiss Avenue near Central. The Star opened in 1913 at 2407 Elm, and the Mammoth the following year in a building that had once been a white saloon. Another theater, the Circle, was replaced by the Palace, which started showing movies and added vaudeville in 1920. By the late teens, there was also a movie house in North Dallas—the High School Theatre at 3211 Cochran Street. The Park Theater in the 400 block of Central opened in March 1912. Two years later, its management was assumed by vaudevillians Chintz and Ella B. Moore, who came to Dallas from Charleston, South Carolina, where they had operated the Maceo Theater. Both had been popular performers. He was a comedian who hailed from Galveston, Texas; she, an actress described in *The Freeman* as a "character and novelty soubrette." Advertising in *The Dallas Express*, they said the Park offered "High class vaudeville and moving pictures. Visit the Park lawn, nicest place in town."[2] Mrs. Moore is generally described as warm and friendly, her husband as hot-headed. This is borne out by a 1920 *Freeman* article noting that he had been wounded by a theatrical company manager after taking five shots at the man.[3]

As more theaters were established, theater owners began organizing circuits, or "times." Fred Barrasso of Memphis founded the Tri-State Circuit, which was cut short by his unexpected death in 1911. The first successful black circuit is thought to have been the Dudley Circuit founded by Sherman H. Dudley, a comedian born in Texas—probably Austin—around 1880. Dudley became known for bringing a mule named Patrick onstage in his act. He bought a theater in Washington, D. C., in 1913, and by 1916 had almost thirty theaters in the South, East and Midwest, but none in Texas.

The Moores advertised that they booked their shows through another circuit, the Colored Consolidated Vaudeville Exchange. Chintz Moore also seems to have booked shows on his own in Paris and other Texas towns. Dallas theaters obtained national recognition, advertising in *The Freeman* and *The Chicago Defender*. Both these papers had contributing writers in Dallas and regularly published news from the city, as well as from elsewhere in Texas.

Vaudeville entertainment, with deep roots in nineteenth-century minstrel shows dating to slavery, took various forms, including the "tab" or "tabloid" show, a shortened version of a musical comedy, lasting about an hour and featuring a reduced cast. Overall, shows reflected the original name of the form, "variety," but appealed to a much higher-class, more family-oriented crowd than did the rowdy joints of a few years earlier. Dallas's black theater patrons enjoyed touring minstrel and stock companies; novelty acts, such as the 500-pound Cleo-Cleo, and Jack Rabbit, the hoop contortionist; comedians such as Little Jimmie Cox, a Charlie Chaplin imitator; beautiful, high-kicking dancers; duos such as Butterbeans and Susie; and musicians and singers.

With the national success of Mamie Smith's 1920 recording of "Crazy Blues" (which wasn't truly a blues at all), theaters in Dallas, as elsewhere, often featured her and other female "classic blues" singers, including Trixie and Clara Smith and the "Empress of the Blues," Bessie Smith (all of these Smiths being unrelated, as far as is known) and Ida Cox. Locally, singers such as Bobbie Cadillac, Lillian Glinn and others became so popular that they attracted the interest of record companies in Chicago and New York. Blues historian Paul Oliver speculates that many of the women blues singers of this period were "street-walkers, who sang with the brothel pianists before turning tricks."[4] There is little evidence to substantiate this, other than in the lyrics to the songs themselves, which recount the harshness of life on the street. Bobbie Cadillac, in her recording "Carbolic Acid Blues" (released in 1928 with an unidentified piano accompanist), reiterates the themes of betrayal and violence:

> I told her I loved her man,
> grave will be her resting place.
> (Repeat.)
> She looked at me with burning eyes,
> threw carbolic acid in my face.
> In my bed, my face burned to the bone.
> (Repeat.)
> If carbolic don't kill me,
> penitentiary gonna be my home.

Of all the women blues singers in Dallas during the 1920s, Lillian Glinn was certainly the most famous, performing first at the Park Theatre and later touring to theaters around the South. In an interview with Oliver in 1970, Glinn said that she didn't know her exact birth date, but that it may have been in 1902 in a small town about thirty miles east of Dallas. In her early twenties, she moved to Dallas, where she was heard singing at a local church by the respected though little-recorded Texas singer Hattie Burleson. (Whether this Burleson is the woman who shot King is unknown.) Through Burleson, Glinn was introduced to Ella B. Moore, and the two women persuaded her to sing blues and vaudeville songs.

Glinn's popularity at the Park Theatre in Dallas prompted R. T. Ashford, who owned a shine parlor and record stand at the corner of Elm and Central, to contact the Columbia label. As her manager, Ashford facilitated a recording contract. Ashford was a shrewd entrepreneur involved in establishing the Dallas Negro Chamber of Commerce. He had come to Dallas from Nacogdoches and worked at a succession of jobs, including doorman at Sanger Brothers' department store. Ashford was to play a pivotal role in the export of Dallas music.

In Lillian Glinn's first hit record, "Doggin' Me," she sang in a strong contralto voice and displayed originality in composition, though she used traditional blues themes. Although she rarely created her own blues verses, she was especially talented at restructuring them. She sang that "her daddy's love is like a hydrant, he turns it off and on," and that "men are like street-cars, runnin' all over town." In several of her songs, Glinn addresses other women, offering warnings about the unreliability of lovers, or advice on how to keep a man. In "Cravin' a Man Blues," she sings:

> There's one man I love, one man I crave,
> one man I'm wild about.
> (Repeat.)
> The one man I crave, he knows what it's all about.
> Someday, I'll get every man I love.
> (Repeat.)
> Just as sure as I kneel,
> and the stars shine up above
> Will there ever be a time
> when a woman won't need no man?
> (Repeat.)
> And when that day comes, I want to die if I can.
> I'm gonna tell you people something,
> as true as the stars above.
> (Repeat.)
> Now pretty ain't worth nothing,
> If you ain't got the man you love.
> (Repeat)

Glinn's singing was direct and her lyrics were easy to understand, underscored sometimes by half-spoken, half-sung passages in a preaching style, and sometimes, as in "Front Door Woman" and "All the Week," by a hummed stanza. Some of her songs are poignantly sexual with a yearning sound, such as "Wobble It Daddy," with its traditional door-key image, and "Packing House," which opens with the lines:

A bucket of blood,
a butcher's knife is all I crave. (Repeat.)
Let me work in your packing house, daddy,
while I am your slave.

One of Glinn's last recordings was "Atlanta Blues," which swings lightly and was apparently composed about her experiences in that city at the 81 Theater on Decatur Street, where she decided to give up professional blues singing and return to the church. In the late 1930s, she moved to California where she later married Rev. O. P. Smith in Oakland. During her relatively short career, Glinn had a national reputation as a singer. Although she had a distinctive Texas sound in her singing, her accompaniment often consisted of a New Orleans-style band with banjo, tuba and piano.

"Race records" was a catchall categorization for all styles of African-American music at this time, and it included blues, jazz, gospel, novelty tunes and popular songs. The term "race," however, was also commonly used in the black press as a means of distinguishing African Americans from others. Both female and male performers were also known as "race" musicians, and generally the male theatrical acts were as eclectic in nature as those of their female counterparts, catering to the demands of promoters and the ever-changing tastes of their audience. Typically, each half of a show featured an "olio," a short act performed outside the curtain, followed by a number of different musical acts and comedy routines. One of the most popular and influential male performers during the twenties was Lonnie Johnson, who had a crooner's voice and a light, jazzy touch on guitar.

This was a heady time for black show business in America, and the Moores' ads in The Express brimmed with racial pride: "Controlled and managed by colored people, catering to nothing but colored people. . . . Last year's books showed $50,000 paid to colored people," proclaimed an ad on March 13, 1920. Actually, however, the black theaters did cater to whites to some extent. Many offered a Friday night "Midnight Ramble," a late show for white patrons, who paid a bit more than black theatergoers did. White musician Bill Neely recalled: "They let white people in for the midnight shows, and it was rowdy. The girls took most of their clothing off. They had blues singers, hoochie-koochies, and the girls did whatever they were big enough to do." Black musician Sammy Price said the rowdiness has been exaggerated, that the Midnight Rambles were simply shows for whites and that the admission price was a bit higher.[5]

The regular admission price at the Park was thirty cents for adults, twenty cents for children. The theater opened at six in the evening and featured a Sunday matinee. On June 26, 1920, an *Express* ad touted "a seven-day colored street fair. Big brass band every day. Park Theatre Lawn, 424 Central." According to a May 8, 1915 *Freeman* article, "Mrs. Ella B. Moore has secured the whole first regiment K of P [Knights of Pythias] band to give concerts on the Parklawn every night, where great crowds of strollers can find ease and rest between acts." *The Freeman* and *The Defender* sometimes referred to "the Central Avenue Stroll," likening it to the Chicago black entertainment district called the Stroll.

In 1920, Chintz Moore and about thirty other black Southern and Midwestern theater owners established the premier black vaudeville circuit, the Theater Owners Booking Association (TOBA), which grew to more than eighty theaters. Performers joked that the acronym stood for "Tough on Black Acts" or "Tough on Black Asses," because contracts heavily favored management and conditions were often crude. A 1924 *Freeman* column called the Park "another barn, no toilets, water nor any other accommodations backstage."

Entertainment wasn't limited to theaters. In November 1919, *Express* publisher Starks's sons Clarence and F. E. opened the Green Parrot Jazzland at 2413 Elm. Admission was thirty-five cents, "including war tax." The owners advertised that their third-floor establishment had "the prettiest girls, the jazziest dancers." It was over the Buffalo Club and, at street level, the Royal Cafe. The Royal was replaced by Whittaker's Cafe, which advertised: "Call our rent cars, day and night." This spot, a few years later, became

McMillan's Cafe. Many of the traveling entertainers stayed at the Del Monico Hotel on Central, established in 1918.

The Tip Top dance hall on Central was a popular spot for music and dancing in the twenties. It was on the second floor of a former railroad hotel at Central Track and Pacific. The dance hall was also known by other names, including the Central Dance Hall and the Royal Social and Amusement Club. Its nickname of Tip Top apparently came from the Tip Top tailor shop downstairs. Bands often played outside on weekends for the shop's customers.[6] "Tip Top was tailors," recalled drummer Herbie Cowens, a Dallas native. "Tip Top was where I played every Saturday in front of that place, and they made clothes. . . . We played out in front, and people would come out to hear the music." Booker Pittman remembered the Tip Top from working nearby at a shoeshine stand and record store that he doesn't name but was probably Ashford's. T-Bone Walker recalled playing at the Tip Top. New Orleans trumpet player Don Albert praised the music, but described the hall as "shoddy."[7]

Asked about the musicians who played outside, Cowens referred to another New Orleans musician who frequented Dallas: "Most of the time it was Frenchy, who was a trumpet player. He had the band, and he had three or four different pieces on it. . . . He was kind of a heavyset fellow, and he could blow his horn; they say you could hear it from Elm Street to far North Dallas. His name was Christian Polite. I don't know how he spelled it, but he was from New Orleans."[8] Albert's assessment was similar but less charitable: "Frenchy wasn't a great trumpet player; but he was loud." In any event, Frenchy was well known and universally liked. The young Budd Johnson played drums with him, and clarinetist Jesse Hooker recorded with Frenchy's String Band in Dallas.

In October 1924, to national fanfare in the black press, the Moores opened a second theater, the Ella B. Moore, in the same block as the Park, with a performance by the Lafayette Players Stock Company. The theater was the showplace of the Southwest on the TOBA. It was described as:

modern in every particular. It has a ground floor which could accommodate 600 persons, a balcony that seated 500, loge seats for 100 and four boxes. It also had an office, an automatic entrance gate operated from the office, a reception room, and an office for the use of traveling managers. The structure was topped with a roof garden, and there were seven dressing rooms and an orchestra room. There was also a shower bath for the artists backstage.[9]

The year after opening the new theater, the Moores closed the Park.

Although black businessmen in Dallas were essentially self-sufficient and able to meet the needs of their community, they did, by necessity, interact with Jewish shopkeepers in Deep Ellum. Shopkeepers were generally sympathetic to the plight of African Americans, who, like them, were immigrants to Dallas and subjected to social discrimination and racism. Jewish businessmen in Deep Ellum encouraged blacks to patronize their shops, and offered not only credit and loans to their black customers, but the opportunity to "try on" clothing at a time when this was forbidden in stores in downtown Dallas.

---

[1] *Dallas Times Herald,* July 19, 1890, p. 2. Copy on microfilm at the *Dallas Morning News*; also available at J. Erik Jonsson Central Library, Dallas, Texas.

[2] *The Dallas Express,* June 5, 1920.

[3] *The Freeman* (Indianapolis), September 11, 1920.

[4] Paul Oliver, *Blues Off the Record* (New York: Da Capo Press, 1988), 162.

[5] Neely quote is from Brakefield interview, June 1989; Price quote from Brakefield interview, June 7, 1991.

[6] Don Albert, interview with Nathan Pearson and Howard Litwak, April 17, 1977. Official names of Tip Top are from Dallas city directories.

[7] Herbie Cowens, interview with Alan Govenar, January 20, 1992 and February 5, 1992.

[8] Ibid.

[9] Henry T. Sampson, *Blacks in Blackface: A Source Book on Early Black Musical Shows* (Metuchen, New Jersey: Scarecrow Press, 1980), 130.

Gypsy Tea Room, ca. 1930s. *Courtesy* Dallas Public Library.

Harlem Theatre, ca. 1940s. *Courtesy* Dallas Public Library.

Deep Ellum, 1922. *Courtesy* Texas/Dallas History and Archives Division, Dallas Public Library.

Tip Top Tailor Shop and dance hall, ca. early 1920s. Courtesy *Dallas Morning News.*

Herbert Cowens, Dallas, ca. 1926. *Courtesy* Rubye Cowens.

Restaurant owner Quitman McMillan, 1925. *Courtesy* Rudolph McMillan.

Woodmen of the World Brass Band, Dallas, ca. 1920s. *Courtesy* Texas African American Photography Archive.

"Negro Troops," corner of Elm and Arkard, ca. 1910–1915. *Courtesy* Luc Sante and Texas African American Photography Archive.

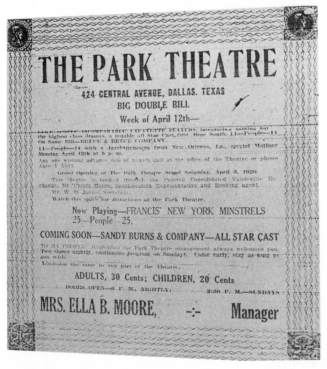

(above and opposite page) Ads and announcements from the African-American newspaper, *The Dallas Express,* during the 1920s.

Mrs. Ella B. Moore
OF THE PARK THEATRE, DALLAS, TEXAS
PRESENTS

Cleo-Cleo

The Fat Girl, weighing **500** Pounds, dancing the jelly role with a bevy of pretty girls and dancing boys, as a Colored Vaudeville Circus.

WANTED

A man piano player that can double stage as a straight man A few more good looking girls and boys. All managers looking for a box office attraction, write in today as the show opens some where in Texas or Oklahoma January 15, in route to N. Y. City. This show is backed by brains and capital. Nothing but first class talent wanted; everything done by contracts; we pay all after joining. We play theaters only. Write or wire at once-mail answered same day.

Mrs. Ella B. Moore, Prop
Chintz Moore, Manager

The Pretty Baby Show

Park Theatre, Dallas, Texas, 424 N Central Av.

THE FREEMAN AN ILLUSTRATED COLORED NEWSPAPER

BIG SPECIAL
Important Announcement!
CONCERNING THE

Southern Consolidated Vaudeville Circuit, Inc.
AND
Dudley, Klein and Reevin United Circuit

The Two Mammoth Circuits Have Become Affiliated for the Betterment of the Entire Show World.

THE FOLLOWING OFFICERS HAVE BEEN ELECTED:

E. L. Cummings,	S. H. Dudley,	Sam E. Reevin,	M. P. Cummings,
President	Vice President	Secretary	Treasurer
Chas. P. Bailey,	Martin Klein,	John T. Gibson,	Chintz Moore,	Tim Owsley
General Adjuster	Special Representative	Financial Adjuster	Southern Representative	Traveling Representative

THIS MEANS SHORTER JUMPS FOR PERFORMERS, MORE CONSECUTIVE WEEKLY WORK, AND ABSOLUTE SUCCESS FOR ALL THEATRE MANAGERS FOR INFORMATION OR BOOKING, ADDRESS ANY OF

E. L. Cummings	S. H. Dudley	Sam E. Reevin
91 NORTH DAYLEN ST., PENSACOLA, FLA.	903 ITH ST. N. W., WASHINGTON, D. C.	LIBERTY THEATRE BLDG., CHATTANOOGA, TENN.
John T. Gibson	Chintz Moore	Martin Klein
GIBSON'S NEW STANDARD THEATRE PHILADELPHIA, PA.	PARK THEATRE, DALLAS, TEXAS	... ST., CHICAGO, ILL.

The Rose Room, ca. 1940s. In North Dallas, at Ross and Hall Streets. *Courtesy* Texas African American Photography Archive.

Carden Cowens at Abe & Pappys, ca. late 1940s. *Courtesy* Rubye Cowens.

Abe & Pappy's club on Elm Street, ca. 1940s. *Courtesy* Texas African American Photography Archive.

Abe & Pappy's club on Elm Street, ca. 1940s. *Courtesy* Texas African American Photography Archive.

Juneteenth Parade, 1946. Behind float is the Pride of Dallas Cafe, owned by Quitman and Daisy McMillan. *Courtesy* Dallas Public Library.

Juneteenth Parade, 1947. Thomas Avenue and Hall Street. Photography by Alex Moore. *Courtesy* Documentary Arts.

Jewish Pawnbrokers
and Merchants
of Deep Ellum

Many of the pawnbrokers and merchants of Deep Ellum had migrated from Eastern Europe, fleeing oppression and seeking opportunity. Some landed at New York's Ellis Island before going south and west to cities such as Dallas. Others were among the 10,000 Jews who entered through the port of Galveston, Texas, between 1907 and 1914 under the Galveston Movement, or Galveston Plan, organized and funded by New York financier Jacob Schiff. A relocation agency helped them find work.

Among the Ellis Island immigrants was Volf Soltes, a native of Austria. In 1916, when he was about twenty-one, he moved to Dallas, where his sister Jenny lived. He later recalled arriving with "a black derby, red mustache and all that makes one look like a New Yorker."[1] Soltes also brought a toughness learned on the streets of New York, where he had learned to fight to protect his father from hoodlums who pulled his beard and called him a "Christ-killer" as he sold vegetables from a pushcart.

Among Volf Soltes's early employers in Dallas was Commercial Metals, which later grew into a giant company. In the early 1920s, he went into business with Sam Goldberg, operating Uncle Sam's Pawn Shop on Elm Street. Within a few years, Soltes, who had Americanized his first name to William, or Willie, bought out his partner, but he chose to keep the name of the shop. Uncle Sam's became a kind of training ground for most of the pawnbrokers who followed.

Willie and his wife, the former Sarah Rachovsky, lived on Caroline Street, in a Jewish neighborhood just north of downtown known as Short North Dallas or Frogtown, because it was inundated with frogs fleeing to higher ground whenever the nearby Trinity River flooded. By some accounts, the area had once been called "Little Jerusalem," or "Goosevalley" because many of its early residents raised geese. In 1925, the Soltes family bought a house on Park Row in South Dallas, which had become the city's primary Jewish community.

One of Willie's nephews, Dave Goldstein, came from New York for a visit and worked in the pawnshop. Dave was a tall, good-looking young man, and one day in 1923 he caught the eye of fifteen-year-old Dora Abramson as she was walking to school. Her friend Max Utay also worked in the store, and she asked him about Dave. The fact that Dave didn't have much money, that his widowed mother had sold goods from a pushcart and worked in a factory in New York, didn't deter Dora at all, but it enraged her father, Itzhak "Issie" Abramson, a Russian immigrant who had never had much success in America. His shoemaking trade brought him and his family to Dallas, where he started working in a Deep Ellum shop. The Abramsons initially stayed with the Utays, who lived in a run-down area south of downtown, then moved to a house on Cora Street on the edge of the black area of North Dallas. Issie disliked the confinement of working in the shoe shop and had a variety of other jobs. For a time, he drove an oversized taxi called a jitney between Dallas and Fort Worth, about thirty miles each way. He tried running his own store. And he worked with B. Schwartz, a wheeler-dealer who owned the Day and Night Pawn Shop in the 2400 block of Elm and invested in rental properties. Schwartz, a former New Yorker, also bought up quantities of goods for resale, and Issie accompanied him on buying trips to businesses that were failing or had overstocks.

Issie was determined that his eight children would do better than he had, and he had decided that Dora would marry one of B. Schwartz's sons, Hymie. So when Dora decided to marry Dave Goldstein, she told her mother, but not her father. Dave and Dora wed on New Year's Eve, 1924, at a friend's home in Fort Worth. The next day, when they returned to Dallas and stopped by to see Dora's parents, Issie threw them out. Dora returned the next week to help her mother, who had broken her leg and still had young children to care for. But Issie Abramson and Dave Goldstein never spoke again.

The first years of the marriage were hard. Dave and Dora worked at a dry-goods store in Deep Ellum. In 1930, Dave borrowed $2,000 from a bank and established a new dry goods store. With the Depression on, people kept asking about pawning things, so the couple added a small pawnshop operation. Eventually, they phased out dry goods altogether. Among their customers in the 1930s were Bonnie Parker and Clyde Barrow, who hadn't yet achieved notoriety. "They were just a couple of young kids in love," Dora Goldstein recalled. "He'd buy her a little gingham housedress for $1.98."[2]

Gradually, more of Dave's family moved to Dallas. When the stock market crashed, his brother Isaac was an eighteen-year-old law student in New York. Forced to discontinue his studies, he migrated to Dallas and went to work for his brother Dave. First he lived with his brother's family, then got a room in South Dallas. "I worked like a slave," Isaac "Rocky" Goldstein said years later. "Eight in the morning until ten at night; Thursdays and Saturdays until midnight. Half a day on Sunday—until 3:00 P.M."[3] Many of the pawnshops stayed open late, and hard work was common, but relations between the brothers were strained. "He mistreated me, pushed me around," Issac Goldstein said, "so I quit him and went to work for Klar and Winterman," an established, relatively upscale pawnshop at 2308 Elm. "I was supposed to get a commission, but there was no money, so I went to work for my uncle, William Soltes." He stayed with his uncle for ten years, then left when Soltes failed to deliver on his promise to give him part of the business.

Dave and Isaac's mother moved to Dallas, too, as did their sister Molly. In 1931, the third brother, Rubin, came for a Passover visit. He lived in New York, where he was in the scrap metal business with Leonard LaRosa. Rubin liked Dallas and soon returned to stay. He bought a stock of hardware from the old Starr Harness Company, which was going out of business, and opened a store at 2510 ½ Elm, next to a fish market. A few years later, he merged his store with Joe's Gun and Lock Shop, run by his sister Molly and her husband, Joe Doerner. When Doerner ran off with a woman from the produce market across the street, Rubin took over the business and helped his sister start another, Molly's Tool Shop. About 1936, Rubin moved to the location at 2524 Elm that he would occupy for the rest of his life as "Honest Joe," Deep Ellum's best-known pawnbroker. Honest Joe's son Eddie Goldstein said his father got his nickname in the thirties when a drunken house painter called Little Jimmy was waiting to hock his brushes for enough money to go over to Sigel's liquor store and get a bottle of cheap wine. When the woman ahead of him in line asked for a receipt, Little Jimmy reassured her, "Don't worry, lady, this is Honest Joe," and the name stuck.[4]

There are many stories about Honest Joe, a publicity genius whose name was always in the papers. He once saved a pickpocket called "Hook" from the penitentiary by testifying that the man's prosthetic hands were in hock when the crime was committed. Texas Utililties Company chairman John W. Carpenter loved his store and would come by to don a pair of overalls and browse through used tools. Retired Dallas police officer Joe Cody recalled that a captain once wanted Honest Joe arrested for something. Cody went to the shop and found Honest Joe in the back, playing dominos with Carpenter and Mayor Robert Thornton. "Arrest him yourself," Cody told the captain.[5]

The store was festooned with signs: "Honest Joe, Loan Ranger" and "YCMMSOYA," which stood for "You can't make money sitting on your afghanistan." There was even a sign proclaiming "Emmes Joe"—Honest Joe in Hebrew. A gaudy station wagon parked outside the store featured a nonfunctional machine gun. Joe Cody recalled that when things got slow, Honest Joe would drive the wagon downtown, park it illegally near the courthouse and stage a shouting match with whatever hapless officer showed up to ticket the vehicle. Anything for publicity.

Honest Joe's featured an amazing array of junk that extended to tables on the sidewalk in front. Max Wyll, who served for years as secretary-treasurer of the Dallas Pawnbrokers' Association, was always trying to get the papers interested in a picture of Klar and Winterman, the "nice clean store. But no, they wanted that slimy place."[6]

Color aside, pawnshops served a real need. For poor blacks and whites alike, the pawnshop operated as a bank, lending money and giving credit and selling merchandise at reasonable prices. Musician Marvin Montgomery, a longtime member of the Light Crust Doughboys, bought his first good banjo for $50 at Uncle Jake's Pawn Shop on Elm. His friend, guitar player Jim Boyd, said one of his band members once asked him for the time and he jokingly replied, "Well, I'll have to go by Uncle Jake's Pawn Shop and look at my watch."[7]

All the pawnshops were owned by Jews, and for years, virtually all were in Deep Ellum. Most made their money primarily on small loans at ten percent per month interest. People hocked, or "soaked," virtually everything: shoes, suits, guns, musical instruments, artificial limbs. Eddie Goldstein said his father regularly did business with a Hispanic man called Hot Tamale, who wore an overcoat even in the summer and made his living selling hot tamales from a pushcart. Hot Tamale regularly pawned his teeth for $5 with Honest Joe, then rented them back for a dime so he could eat lunch. "You got to meet a lot of funny people in the pawn business," Dora Goldstein recalled. "We knew Jack Ruby just like he was a brother, went to his nightclub. He was a real *schmoe* guy. Everybody liked him. His employees loved him. If my girls went to his club, he'd leave his business and take them home.

"I would say that ninety percent of our customers were black. Very few Mexicans. We had a few big-shot white customers. I would say that seventy-five percent of our black customers were in every week. They'd get it out on Friday and pawn it back on Monday. Suits, pants, jackets, wristwatches, rings, radios, TVs. One guy worked for a funeral parlor, and he'd pawn the ends on the caskets. One of them pawned his false teeth."[8]

Deep Ellum in some ways was a self-contained world. Shoe repairman Max Grabstahl had a deal with Klar and Winterman. He would pay one month's interest, ten percent, on unredeemed shoes, which he would then repair and sell.

The shops were required to keep items ninety days, though sometimes these rules were bent. Wyll recalled that one pawnbroker sold a suit to a black man moments after another had pawned it. "What will you do if the man wants his suit back?" Wyll asked. "I'll get him another one," the broker replied.

Sometimes exploitation was more overt. Businessman Sam Luterman was visiting a friend in his Deep Ellum pawnshop one day when a black man came in to pay on a loan. The clerk told the owner in Yiddish that she couldn't find a card on the customer. "*Schlep da gelt*," the owner replied, "get the money." After the black man left, Luterman told his friend, "Well, I guess you'll make sure the money gets to the right account."

"We're not in the habit of turning down money," his friend said.[9]

To some extent, this hard-nosed attitude may have come from the merchants' own hard-knocks background. Wyll's father Issie, an immigrant from Warsaw, couldn't afford to live in the Cedars, south of downtown, like the Sanger brothers and other rich merchants. They lived in Frogtown, north of downtown, near the area that became known as Little Mexico. Issie Wyll had a Schepps Bakery route and often woke his son at 4 A.M. to accompany him on his rounds. Max would hide under the bed, but his father would roust him, saying, "Come on, I know you're under there." Television producer Aaron Spelling, whose father was a tailor in Deep Ellum, recalled running from their South Dallas home to avoid a viciously anti-Semitic group of boys called the Purple Gang.

Still, although the Deep Ellum and Central Track area was generally thought of as rough and dangerous, robberies and muggings of business people were almost unheard of before the 1950s. Merchants walked to the bank with $1,000 or $2,000 in their pockets, right past the throngs of blacks around Central Track, with no fear at all. "It was respect," Eddie Goldstein said. Of course, a black person caught committing a crime against a white would have been in serious trouble.

Pawnbroking was not the only occupation open to Jewish immigrants. Sam Stillman's dad, Hyman, had come from a town near Kiev in 1908. Two years later his wife, Gertrude, and three-year-old Sam joined him in Dallas, where he had found work as a cabinet-maker. In 1920, the Stillmans joined the movement of Dallas's Jewish community to South Dallas, where Sam graduated from Forest Avenue High School. In 1926, Sam went to work for The Model Tailors, a prestigious clothing shop in Deep Ellum located in a space leased from Klar and Winterman.[10] "We were sort of the queen of the block," recalled Masha Porte, who worked at The Model Tailors from 1932–41, "because we were a two-story building with a little balcony (which is where our office was) on one side, and the cutting room on the other, and everything else was just pawnshops, and one-story, mostly, clothing stores and that sort of thing." She recalled walking to Oatis Drugstore at Elm and Central. "I used to walk down there all the time without any fear whatsoever, to buy cigarettes and what not. That's another thing I remember, never being afraid down there. And a lot of white gamblers and gangsters were there. In fact, Benny Binion was a customer. He used to have his clothes custom made at The Model Tailors."[11]

Willard Watson, who was a street hustler and pimp around Central Track in the early forties, recalled that he would buy a suit for $21 and have a friend sew a Model Tailors label in it. He'd wear it a few times, then pawn it for at least as much as he paid for it.[12] Sam Stillman, who worked at The Model Tailors until the early fifties, said they never charged more than $65 for a tailor-made suit.

Generally, the relations between Jews and blacks in Deep Ellum were more progressive than in other areas of Dallas, where blacks could not shop at all or were not allowed to try on clothes. "They were customers," said Joe Freed of Freed Furniture, which his father started in Deep Ellum. "And there was a certain warmth."[13] That warmth, though, seldom if ever led to socializing outside the workplace. And even the friendliest relations were often infused with the paternalism of the time.

"I got along with the blacks better than I did with the whites," Dora Goldstein said. "White people, even the cheapest ones, always want to be the big shots." But she admits that it was also rough at times dealing with blacks. "I wouldn't call it exactly fighting, but a lot of harsh words and dirty words and sometimes a slap or two. You had to be tough with blacks. You could not be soft with them. They respected you more if you were tough, if they couldn't get away with something. They had a relationship with us because we were good to them; we were kind to them."[14] She recalled using a long iron bar one time to ward off several large, angry, drunken black customers. But she also fondly remembered walking uptown for exercise and, on the way back, accepting rides from black cabbies who hollered out, "Mrs. Dave, you need a ride?"[15]

Label Feldman, one of the last of the old-time pawnbrokers, remained in business on Commerce Street west of Harwood until 1997, when he sold out to a chain operation. Some of Feldman's black customers had their checks mailed there for safekeeping and drew out money as they needed it.[16]

"The pawnshop was their bank," said Eddie Goldstein, owner of King Edward's Swap Shop on East Grand. "Credit grocery store, the credit clothiers, they were all in Deep Ellum. Deep Ellum in its heyday was pawnshop, pawnshop, pawnshop, dry goods store; pawnshop, pawnshop, pawnshop, grocery store; pawnshop, pawnshop, pawnshop, shoe store. There wasn't competition. Everybody complemented one another. Everyone worked together to get the customers there, then you cut the other guy's throat to get the customer away. It's just the exact same theory as they use today in the franchise locations."[17]

Some old-time Deep Ellumites believe there was a special relationship between blacks and Jews because of a shared heritage of suffering and discrimination. Sam Stillman said, "Jewish people having been persecuted for hundreds of years, when they came to this country and they were accepted, in general . . . they felt that after all, the black is a human being." Although the Jews, like others of the time, employed black maids or yard men, they treated them with more respect than many of their neighbors did. "We always invited them in and had them sit at our table and eat with us. . . . We never thought anything about it," Stillman said. Others, like Eddie Goldstein, see the relationship between the blacks and the Jews more in practical terms. "It wasn't because they were both minorities or anything like that; it was business," he said.[18]

But blacks and Jews both were victims of discrimination in an overtly racist era. The Ku Klux Klan wielded great political power in Dallas and the state in the 1920s. In the early twenties, Klan membership in the state may have reached 100,000, and the organization controlled the governments of both Dallas and Fort Worth. In 1921, Klansmen dragged black bellhop Alex Johnson from the Adolphus Hotel in downtown Dallas and branded the letters "KKK" on his forehead with acid. In 1922, a Klan candidate, Earle B. Mayfield, was elected to the U.S. Senate. Ku Klux Klan Day at the State Fair of Texas in October 1923 drew about 75,000 Klansmen and their families to Fair Park. Fort Worth Klansmen were believed responsible for the 1927 flogging of businessman Morris Strauss. A field near the South Dallas black community of Joppa was reportedly used for torture and hanging of African Americans who were deemed troublemakers.[19]

Though the political power of the Klan was essentially broken by the late 1920s, the ideology of white supremacy continued as a force in Dallas until the fifties and sixties when federal legislation began the process of desegregation and integration. However, by this time the housing and business patterns of blacks and Jews had changed, and so had Deep Ellum. The building of Central Expressway choked Central Track off from Deep Ellum proper, and both Jews and blacks dispersed into different parts of the city. South Dallas, which had been a Jewish area, became a residential and commercial district and neighborhood for African Americans. Many Jews resettled in the areas of the city north of Highland Park, building new homes, as well as synagogues and businesses.

---

[1] William Soltes, "A Little Story of My Life in America," unpublished manuscript written in 1967. Used courtesy of Zella Sobel.

[2] Dora Goldstein, interview with Jay Brakefield, February 28, 1992.

[3] Isaac Goldstein, interview with Jay Brakefield, March 22, 1992.

[4] Eddie Goldstein, interview with Jay Brakefield, April 3, 1992.

[5] Joe Cody, interview with Jay Brakefield, June 18, 1992.

[6] Max Wyll, interview with Jay Brakefield, March 25, 1992.

[7] Jim Boyd and Marvin Montgomery, interview with Alan Govenar and Jay Brakefield, January 29, 1992.

[8] Dora Goldstein interview.

[9] Sam Luterman, interview with Jay Brakefield, August 19, 1992.

[10] Sam Stillman, interview with Jay Brakefield, March 2, 1992.

[11] Masha Porte interview with Alan Govenar, March 4, 1992.

[12] Willard Watson, interview with Jay Brakefield, July 16, 1992.

[13] Joe Freed, interview with Jay Brakefield, May 6, 1992.

[14] Dora Goldstein interview.

[15] Ibid.

[16] Label Feldman, interview with Jay Brakefield, May 20, 1992.

[17] Eddie Goldstein interview.

[18] Sam Stillman interview and Eddie Goldstein interview.

[19] Bill Minutaglio, "The Buried Past," *Dallas Life Magazine, Dallas Morning News*, September 5, 1993.

The Goldstein family, 1930. *Courtesy* Eddie Goldstein.

Deep Ellum grocer Nathan Rosen, ca. 1930s. *Courtesy* Jewish Community Center.

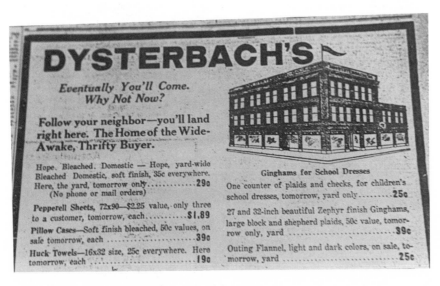

1920s *Dallas Express* ad for Dysterbach's store.

Klar & Winterman Pawn Shop, ca. 1920s. *Courtesy* Jewish Community Center.

Rocky Goldstein in his store in the 2200 block of Elm Street, ca. 1940s. *Courtesy* Jewish Community Center.

Sylvia and Label Feldman, Label's Pawn Shop, ca. 1940s. *Courtesy* Jewish Community Center.

Tommie Schwartz (left) and Morris Silverberg, Day and Night Pawn Shop, ca. 1940s. *Courtesy* Jewish Community Center.

Honest Joe's Pawn Shop, ca. 1950s. *Courtesy* Texas/Dallas History and Archives Division, Dallas Public Library.

5

Deep Ellum Blues: Song of the Street

The best-known song about Deep Ellum, "Deep Ellum Blues," is still performed more than sixty years after it was first recorded. Though the lyrics may not be factually accurate, they recall a past that is romanticized and distorted, but nonetheless evocative of a time and place where one had to be ready for anything.

> When you go down in Deep Ellum
> To have a little fun
> Have your fifteen dollars ready
> When that policeman comes.
> (Chorus) Oh, sweet Mama, Daddy's got them Deep
>   Ellum blues.
> Oh, sweet Mama, Daddy's got them Deep Ellum
>   blues.

Once I had a sweetheart
Who meant the world to me,
But she hung around Deep Ellum
Now she's not the girl for me
(Chorus)

When you go down on Deep Ellum,
Keep your money in your shoes
'Cause the women on Deep Ellum
Got them Deep Ellum blues.
(Chorus)

When you go down in Deep Ellum,
Keep your money in your pants
'Cause the redheads in Deep Ellum
Never give a man a chance.
(Chorus)

Once I knew a preacher
Preached the Bible through and through
But he went down in Deep Ellum
Now his preachin' days are through.
(Chorus)

When you go down in Deep Ellum,
Keep your money in your socks
'Cause the women in Deep Ellum
Will throw you on the rocks.
(Chorus)

Although Deep Ellum is usually associated with African Americans and their music, this song was first recorded in 1935 by a white string band, the Lone Star Cowboys, led by Joe and Bob Shelton (who also performed under the names Bob and Joe Attlesey), brothers from East Texas who had become radio celebrities in Dallas. The Sheltons claimed authorship, but "Deep Ellum Blues" appears to have been a true folk song, sung by whites and black alike. "Everybody who sang it added something to it," said Bill Neely, a white songster and guitarist from McKinney, Texas, who hitchhiked to Dallas in the 1930s and performed at the legendary Ma's Place on the fringe of Deep Ellum. This song, however, was not the first to use the phrase "Deep Ellum Blues." Apparently it first appeared in the song "Deep Elm (You Tell 'Em I'm Blue)," which was recorded by several dance bands in 1925, including Paul van Loan and his Orchestra, the American Dance Orchestra, Pete Massey's All-Black Band, Peck Mills and His Orchestra, and The Little Ramblers. Of these, The Little Ramblers, a small contingent from the famous California Ramblers, was probably the best-known. It featured Tommy Dorsey on trombone.

In 1926 "Deep Elm (You Tell 'Em I'm Blue)" was recorded by its composer, Willard Robison. Originally from Shelbina, Missouri, Robison was leading his own band by 1917, and his high, sweet singing voice was popular among the musicians of his day. While the 1925 recordings of "Deep Elm" had a jazz orchestration, Robison's arrangement was much simpler; he sang in a nostalgic style reminiscent of the popular songs of the period, and accompanied himself on piano. Robison had a deep interest in black music and culture and led a band he called the Deep River Orchestra. But whether he—or any of the other musicians who performed the song, for that matter—ever set foot in Deep Ellum is unknown. By the time he wrote the number, Robison may have passed through Dallas by train or met performers from Texas who, like him, had traveled around the country and gone to New York looking for commercial success. Clearly, Robison's composition, in addition to referencing Deep Ellum, focuses on the loneliness of traveling and the longing for home, although its overall mood is more reflective of the popular sentimentality of Tin Pan Alley:

You've heard 'em sing about Beale Street,
Way down in Memphis, Tennessee.

You've heard 'em say that Broadway
Was the only place to be.
I want to take exception
to tell you 'bout a place I've found.
Now just a street where they don't cheat
Down in Dallas town.
Deep Ellum, you tell 'em I'm blue
All the time that, that I'm away from you.
For I can see my 'used to be,
One sweet woman who cared for me
Waiting for the news,
Just any old thing to cure Deep Ellum Blues.
I've made up my mind that I'll go.
Back home in Dallas, I'll never roam no more.
I've been around more than I should.
I never done nothin' to do me no good, so
I'm catchin' a rattler today,
Hey, hey, hey, hey, hey,
To keep Deep Ellum Blues away.
I'm catching a rattler today
Back home in Dallas, I'm sure I'm headed that way.
Now I been around more than I should
And I've never done nothin' to do me no good, so
I'm catching a rattler today,
Hey, hey, hey, hey, hey, hey,
To keep Deep Ellum Blues away.

The line about "a street where they don't cheat" seems ironic used in reference to a street well-known for its wheeling and dealing. Whether the irony is intentional or simply the result of an easy rhyme is unknown. Unlike Robison's, the Sheltons' later record referred to the neighborhood as "Deep Elem." Why they chose this spelling over the generally accepted "Ellum" is unknown; perhaps it was a record company snafu, or perhaps they wanted to differentiate their version from others. Curiously, there appears to be no black recording of "Deep Ellum Blues," though it's known that at least one black musician performed it: Booker Pittman, grandson of educator Booker T. Washington and son of two key figures in the history of black Dallas. Hank Wackwitz, a Dutch-born musician and jazz collector living in retirement in North Texas, recalled playing in the 1950s in a cruise-ship band that included Pittman, a saxophonist and singer. When Pittman sang "Deep Ellum Blues," said Wackwitz, the other musicians, all Europeans, "hadn't the slightest idea what he was singing about."[1]

"Deep Ellum Blues" quickly spread beyond Dallas. Trumpeter Harry James, who had grown up in Beaumont, Texas, persuaded his boss, band leader Ben Pollack, to record it. Subsequently, it has been performed and recorded by a number of other bands, including the rock group, The Grateful Dead. In many ways, the song encapsulates a reality that has been distorted and embellished through the process of folklore and oral history. The extent to which the lyrics of "Deep Ellum Blues" project an accurate portrait of the neighborhood is certainly debatable. Nonetheless, this song, probably more than anything else, has made Deep Ellum one of the best-known and least-understood sections of Dallas. From its origins as a folk song to its popularity on radio and record, "Deep Ellum Blues" embodies the values of a city in transition. Certainly, within the lyrics there is a sense of irony and humor associated with the foibles of those who went there. The allusions to women, preachers and police cut across cultural boundaries and are reflective of a shared experience among the people of a particular time and place. "Deep Ellum Blues" is a window on music and life in Dallas, from its earliest years as a city through its heyday and its ultimate demise and redevelopment.

---

[1] Hank Wackwitz, letter to Alan Govenar, March 1992.

6

· ·

Blind Lemon Jefferson
and Downhome Blues

The Model Tailors was a Jewish-owned business in Deep Ellum where the black and white worlds converged. Its customers included underworld characters Benny Binion and his number two man, Harry Urban, George "Machine Gun" Kelly, and Joe Civello, a local Mafia boss. But plenty of legitimate people bought clothes there as well, including prominent blacks, such as civil rights leader A. Maceo Smith and blues musician Blind Lemon Jefferson. For many blacks, clothing from The Model Tailors was a status symbol. "They had to have a Model Tailors suit," Isaac Goldstein recalled. "Good slides [shoes], a good hat and a Model Tailors suit."[1]

For Blind Lemon Jefferson, a Model Tailors suit was a symbol of his newfound success in the mid-1920s. By then, Jefferson had become the most significant blues singer to perform in Deep Ellum. His life and career typify the downhome blues of his generation.

Lemon Jefferson was born September 24, 1893, to Alec and "Classy" Banks Jefferson on a farm in Couchman, a small community near Wortham, which was a stop on the Houston & Central Texas line seventy-five miles south of Dallas. Little is known about Jefferson's early life. He must have heard songsters and bluesmen, like Henry Thomas ("Ragtime Texas"),[2] and Alger "Texas" Alexander. Both Thomas and Alexander traveled around East Texas and performed a variety of blues and dance tunes. The cause of Jefferson's blindness isn't known, and he may not have been totally blind. (Why would a blind man wear glasses, as he does in one of the two known photographs of him?)

Jefferson came from a large family that included children from his mother's first marriage. He took up music at an early age and learned to get around the nearby small towns of Wortham, Kirvin, Streetman and Groesbeck. "Lemon started out playing his guitar on these streets, and I was on those same streets," said Quince Cox, born in 1903, who once served as caretaker in the Wortham cemetery, where Jefferson is buried. "I pitched quarters and nickels to him, and he'd play his guitar at any time of night. He used to play at Jake Lee's barbershop every Saturday, and people from all over came to hear him play. Then he'd get on this road at ten or eleven o'clock, and he'd walk to Kirvin, seven or eight miles. He'd play and keep walking, but he knew where he was going."[3]

Alec Jefferson, a cousin of Lemon (who had the same name as Lemon's father), told writer Sam Charters that his mother wouldn't let him go to the country suppers where Lemon was playing. "They were rough. Men was hustling women and selling bootleg, and Lemon was singing for them all night. They didn't even do proper kind of dancing, just stomping." Hobert Carter, another native of the Wortham area, said that Blind Lemon's family were members of the Shiloh Baptist Church in Kirvin and that the young Lemon was highly regarded for his ability as a singer of spirituals as well as blues.[4] Wortham postmaster Uel L. Davis, Jr., told a *Waco Tribune-Herald* reporter, "That was one thing about Lemon. He'd be singing in church one day, singing at a house of ill repute the next."[5]

The 1920 census shows Jefferson living in Freestone County with an older half-brother, Nit C. Banks, and his family. Jefferson's occupation is listed as "musician" and his employer as "general public." Sometime after 1920, Jefferson met Roberta Ransom, who was ten years his senior. They married in 1927, the year that Ransom's son by a previous marriage, Theaul Howard, died. Howard's son, also named Theaul, remained in the area, retiring in nearby Ferris, Texas. He recalled that when his father was laid out before the funeral, Blind Lemon held him up and told him to touch the body so he would never fear the dead.[6]

Theaul Howard and several long-time residents of Mexia said Jefferson and his wife lived in a house on West Hopkins Street and that Jefferson performed on "the Beat," a nearby strip of black businesses that included a movie theater, cafes and honky-tonks— apparently a small-town version of Deep Ellum. According to Charlie Hurd, who was 101 years old and living in a Mexia nursing home in 1993, Jefferson also played in a string band with the Phillips brothers: Wash, Tim and Doc. This Wash Phillips may have been Washington Phillips, who recorded in Dallas in the late 1920s, singing religious songs and accompanying himself on a small, autoharp-like instrument called the dulceola.[7]

At least by his teens, Jefferson also began spending time in Dallas. In the Deep Ellum area, apparently about 1912, he met Huddie Ledbetter, better known as Leadbelly, one of the most legendary musical figures to travel and live in Texas. Ledbetter was born in 1889 on the Louisiana side of Caddo Lake, which spans the Texas-Louisiana border. His wild and reckless youth in that frontier country foreshadowed the trouble that would keep him in prison for much of his life. His musical talent was evident early, too. Leadbelly first played a small, accordion-like instrument called a windjammer. He soon learned other instruments, including guitar, and played for country dances, or "sukey jumps."[8]

Leadbelly married in Kaufman County, Texas, east of Dallas, in 1908, and it's believed that he and his wife, Lethe, moved to Dallas about two years later. They alternated between doing farm work in outlying areas and living in the city, where Leadbelly worked as a musician. He said later that in Dallas he heard his first jazz band, and that may also be where he discovered the instrument that became his favorite: the twelve-string guitar, at that time associated mostly with Mexican musicians.

In the extensive interviews he gave later, Leadbelly gave various dates for his initial meeting with Jefferson, sometimes placing it as early as 1904. But he mentioned 1912 most consistently, and that seems plausible. Jefferson would then have been eighteen or nineteen years old.[9] The two became musical partners in Dallas and the outlying area. Leadbelly learned much about the blues from Blind Lemon, and he had plenty to contribute as a musician and a showman. Leadbelly was a dancer, too, and he'd often break into a "buck and wing," a kind of flat-footed shuffle, as the two performed on the street and around Union Depot near Central and Elm.

Leadbelly said they were so popular that "the women would come running, Lord have mercy. They'd hug and kiss us so much we could hardly play. He was a blind man, and I used to lead him around. When him and I go in the depot, we'd sit down and talk to one another."[10] Sometimes the two strolled through white neighborhoods "serenading" for tips. They also performed on the Interurban, the electric railroad that ran from Dallas north to McKinney and south though Corsicana to Waco. "I'd get Blind Lemon right on," Leadbelly recalled. "We get out two guitars; we just ride . . . anything. We wouldn't have to pay no money in them times. We get on the train, the driver takes us anywhere we want to go. Well, we just get on, and the conductor say, 'Boys, sit down. You goin' to play music?' We tell him, 'Yes.'"[11]

Another favorite haunt was Silver City, a wide-open place where Leadbelly said they went by bus. There were several Texas towns named Silver City, and it's not known which one the duo frequented, but the one in Navarro County, not far from Wortham, seems a likely candidate. The partnership broke up in 1915 when Leadbelly left Dallas. In 1918, he was sentenced to prison for murder. The two apparently never saw each other again, though Leadbelly often talked about Blind Lemon after he was released from his second prison term in 1935 and went on to become internationally famous as a folk singer, recording such classics as "Irene" before he died in 1949.

It's unclear how much time Jefferson spent in Dallas and whether his wife moved there with him. Musician Sam Price said Jefferson would play and sing daily around Central and Elm until about ten at night, then walk back to his home in the Prairie, in South Dallas. Price added:

> He was a bootlegger and when he'd get back home he had such a sensitive ear. He didn't want his wife to drink. Well, when he'd go away she'd take two or three drinks out of the bottle and she'd think he wouldn't know it. But he'd take the bottle when he came home and say, "How you doin' baby? How'd we do today?"
>
> "Nobody bought no whiskey," she'd answer.
>
> Well, he'd take the bottle and shake it, and he could hear that there were two or three drinks missing. And what he'd do, he'd beat the hell out of her for that.[12]

It may be that Jefferson traveled back and forth from Dallas to Mexia. His name does not appear in Dallas city directories, although in 1929 and 1930 there's a listing for an Alex Jefferson, farmer, and his wife Classie on Beal Street in South Dallas. Blind Lemon played up and down Central Track outside and in the honky-tonks and cafes. By most reports, he was often seen around the intersection of Elm and the track. Willard Watson, who later became well-known as the folk artist the "Texas Kid," recalled seeing him playing at the Tip Top dance hall. But Sam Stillman, who worked for years at The Model Tailors in Deep Ellum and said Jefferson bought his clothes there, says Blind Lemon seldom if ever performed on Elm Street.[13]

Bluesman Sam "Lightnin'" Hopkins first encountered Blind Lemon at a Baptist church picnic in Buffalo, Texas, in 1920. Hopkins, then eight years old, watched Jefferson intently all day, then attempted to play along. Hopkins recalled that Jefferson, displeased, shouted, "Boy, you've got to play it right!"[14]

Navasota songster Mance Lipscomb told biographer Glen Myers, "When we got to Dallas, we hung around where we could hear Blind Lemon sing and play. . . . [T]here were hundreds of people up and down that [Central] Track. So, that's where I got acquainted with him, 1917. He hung out 'round the track, Deep Ellum. And people started coming in there, from 9:30 until 6:00 that evening, then he would go home because it was getting dark and someone carried him home."[15] Lipscomb's description of Jefferson is similar to that of others who saw him: "a big, loud songster . . . a big, stout fella . . . and he played dance songs and never did much church songs. He had a tin cup wired on the neck of his guitar. And when you pass to give him something, why he'd thank you. But he would never take no pennies. You could drop a penny in there, and he'd know the sound. He'd take it and throw it away."[16]

Others recall Jefferson's putting his hat down in the street for contributions, rather than using a cup. There are several accounts that attest to his skill in identifying the money given him. Singer Victoria Spivey, who knew him in Texas, said Jefferson often used the expression "Don't play me cheap," and that he meant what he said.[17] When Blind Lemon was in Atlanta for a recording session, he asked producer Tom Rockwell for a $5 advance. As a joke, Rockwell handed him a dollar bill, but Blind Lemon seemed to recognize it and complained. "You could hand him a dozen bills," bluesman Tom Shaw commented. "He'd tell you just that fast whether it's a five- or a one-dollar bill."[18]

Accounts of Blind Lemon's ability to get around are somewhat contradictory. Any number of other musicians claim to have led him through the streets when they were young. But others who knew him were astounded by his sense of direction. In an interview with Sam Charters, Lightnin' Hopkins said, "He didn't allow no one to lead him. He say then you call him blind. No, don't call him blind. He never did feel like that. He was born like that."[19] Researcher Mack McCormick said Blind Lemon's sister talked of his independence and said that when she'd visit him in Dallas he'd show off how well he could get around unaided.[20]

Bluesman T-Bone Walker claimed, "I used to lead him around, playing and passing the cup, take him from one beer joint to another. I liked hearing him play. He would sing like nobody's business. He was a friend of my father's. People used to crowd around him so you couldn't see him."[21] Josh White, a singer who spent much of his childhood as a lead boy for blind beggars, told writer Paul Oliver that he took Blind Lemon into the streets around noon when the crowds were thickest and that sometimes he accompanied him with a tambourine, tapping a loud rhythm on his knee to draw a good crowd. Then he would turn the tambourine over and cry, "Help the blind, help the blind."[22] James Thibodeaux, a Dallas photographer and painter, substantiates this and rem embers seeing Jefferson and White walking together on Thomas Avenue in North Dallas. Perhaps Blind Lemon used a lead boy at some times—particularly when he was in unfamiliar surroundings—and not at others. Some of those who claim to have led him may be embellishing their own stories. Or perhaps the stories are true, and Blind Lemon simply liked the company or enjoyed serving as a mentor to younger musicians.

Jefferson's ramblings often took him by Ashford's shine parlor and record shop on Central near Elm Street. Sam Price said that he worked there and told his boss the singer should be recorded; others doubt that claim. At any rate, Ashford talked to Paramount Records about the singer, and the Wisconsin-based company invited Jefferson to make race records in Chicago. Ashford accompanied him on his first trip, in 1925.

When commercial recording scouts came to Texas, they discovered that field recordings usually posed a variety of technical problems. Portable equipment of the time was large and unwieldy, making sound engineering and acoustics hard to control. In some areas in the South, carbon microphones, introduced in 1925, had to be kept on ice because hot weather and humidity made them crackle. In addition to technical problems, there were difficulties in finding suitable locations. According to historian Samuel Charters, "during one company's trip to Dallas, they first tried to rent a room in a hotel but were refused: The management would not allow blacks on the premises. Next they tried setting up in a church, but that led to a near riot when the congregation found out what kind of music they were performing and the gear had to be scrambled out the back door. The next day they tried their luck in a roller-skating rink. It was the noisiest damn place in the world, and when drunken skaters started brawling with the musicians and forcing the engineers up against the wall at knife point it was clearly time to move on again. They eventually used a banquet hall."[23]

In the 1920s, after Blind Lemon's initial success, there were numerous commercial blues recording sessions for other artists in Dallas, in various locations around downtown. The exact locations, however, remain unknown. Jefferson, who was the most successful blues performer to come from Dallas, apparently never recorded there, though there's an unverified story of an early session in the rug department of a furniture store.[24] Jefferson was taken instead to studio facilities in Chicago.

His first recordings, though not the first released, were the spiritual songs "I Want To Be Like Jesus in My Heart" and "All I Want Is That Pure Religion." These were later released under the pseudonym Deacon L. J. Bates. In early January, 1926, Jefferson recorded four songs, including "Long Lonesome Blues," which became his first national hit.

Blind Lemon's guitar style and singing were distinctive. He made extensive use of single-note runs, often apparently picked with his thumb. He played in a variety of keys and tunings, but favored the key of C for the blues. He held the guitar almost perpendicular to his chest, which some have attributed to his girth. Musicologist David Evans, however, thinks it had to do more with Jefferson's style of playing, noting that the position was favored by two electric guitarists much influenced by Jefferson: T-Bone Walker and Charlie Christian. Also, as Evans points out, Jefferson, in his singing, uses not only the flatted third and seventh tones of the chord common to the blues but also flats the fifth and sometimes even the sixth tones.

Jefferson, like other blues players, relied on a stock of musical figures, or "licks," but also could improvise—brilliantly at times. And his rhythmic sense was fluid, even quirky, making him difficult to emulate. As Evans says, "He knew how to 'whip' the guitar, push the beat, and accelerate the tempo. At times the underlying pulse is implied but not stated on the guitar or is kept by Lemon's foot patting." Jefferson often trilled notes on the guitar, which Evans suggests may indicate that he also played mandolin.[25]

His vocal range was unusual, too, comfortably spanning two octaves. Jefferson knew how to play slide guitar, but did so on only one record, "Jack O'Diamond Blues." During his career, he recorded seventy-one blues songs, five spirituals and two ragtime pieces.[26]

Many of the songs that Blind Lemon recorded were personalized versions of traditional folk blues from East Texas that utilized proverbs and other elements of African-American folk speech. These songs included "Jack O'Diamond Blues," about the perils of gambling; a rendition of "Two Horses Standing in a Line" that he renamed "See That My Grave Is Kept Clean"; "See, See Rider," which he transformed into "Corina Blues"; and "Boll Weevil Blues," a legendary song about the creature that devastated the cotton fields of his homeland. In his songs, Blind Lemon identified himself with the experiences of his audience's suffering and hope, economic anxiety and failure, the breakup of the family and the desire to escape through wandering, love and sex. In "Shuckin' Sugar Blues," he sang:

> I've got your picture, and I'm goin' to put it in a
> frame.
> I've got your picture and put it in a frame, shuckin'
> sugar,

Then if you leave town I can find you just the same.

In "Sunshine Special," though, his attitude toward travel was less optimistic:

> Gonna leave on the Sunshine Special,
> gonna leave on the Santa Fe.
> Leave on the Sunshine Special,
> goin' in on the Santa Fe.
> Don't say nothin' about that Katy
> because it's taken my brown from me.

In Blind Lemon's songs, travel was a means of achieving freedom and escape from the burdens of day-to-day life, but wandering also led to separation from loved ones and to loneliness. This ambivalence toward "leaving" and "settling down" was a common theme in his music, reinforced in one of his best-known songs, "Matchbox Blues":

> I'm sitting here wonderin' will a matchbox hold my
>   clothes.
> I'm sitting here wonderin' will a matchbox hold my
>   clothes.
> I ain't got so many matches, but I got so far to go.

Here again, the advantages of traveling outweighed the pleasures of "settling down," though the message was not completely despairing. Jefferson's music expressed the emotions many African Americans of his generation must have felt, leaving rural towns of East Texas and moving to the city of Dallas looking for work and a place to live.

Humor was also a very important element in Blind Lemon's blues, expounded with a wry irony and an almost blustery exuberance about sexuality and sexual relations. In "Baker Shop Blues," he declared,

I'm crazy about my light bread and my pigmeat on
the side.
I say I'm crazy about my light bread with my pigmeat
on the side.
But if I taste your jellyroll, I'll be satisfied.
I want to know if your jellyroll is fresh.
I want to know if your jellyroll's stale.
I want to know if your jellyroll is fresh.
I want to know if your jellyroll's stale.
I'm gonna haul off and buy me some if I have to
break it loose in jail.

Overt sexual references were often combined with humorous
metaphors and analogies. In "Oil Well Blues," he underscored his
own sexuality with an almost self-mocking tone:

Ain't nothin' to hurt you, sugar, ain't nothin' bad.
Ain't nothin' to hurt you, honey, ain't nothin' bad.
It's the first oil well that your little boy ever had.

In "That Black Snake Moan" series of songs, Blind Lemon was
even more obvious about his sexual allusions and accentuated his
lascivious sense of humor:

Mmmm-m, black snake crawlin' in my room.
Mmmm-m, black snake crawlin' in my room.
Some pretty mama better come and get this black
snake soon.

In "That Black Snake Moan, No. 2," he reiterated his desires with
greater emphasis:

I woke up this morning, black snake was makin' such
a ruckus in my room.
Black snake is evil, black snake is all I see.

Black snake is evil, black snake is all I see.
I woke up this morning, black snake was moved in
    on me.

In contrast to this scurrilous sexual humor was Blind Lemon's ambivalent attitude toward women. In some of his songs they were called "good gal," "sugar," "baby," "honey," and "high brown," but in others they were scorned as "wild," "dirty mistreaters" and "deceitful." In "Elder Green," Blind Lemon expressed his attraction for his woman with enthusiasm:

I've got a high brown, and she's long and tall.
Lord, Lord, Lord, she'll make a panther squall.

But in "Got the Blues," he was both intrigued and repulsed by his "good gal":

You can't ever tell what a woman's got on her mind.
Man, you can't ever tell what a women's got on her
    mind.
You might think she's crazy about you; she's leaving
    you all the time.

In "Piney Woods Money Mama," his antagonism was directed toward a woman's scheming mother:

Lord, heavy-hip mama, she's done moved to this
    piney wood.
Heavy-hip mama, she done moved to this piney
    wood.
She's a high-steppin' woman, she don't mean no
    man no good.
She got ways like the devil and hair like an Indian
    squaw.

> She got ways like the devil and hair like an Indian
> squaw.
> She's been tryin' two years to get me to be her son-
> in-law.

In general, the women in Blind Lemon's songs were revered for their sexuality and allure but condemned for manipulative personalities and fickleness in matters of love. In "Pneumonia Blues," he held his women responsible for his illness; in "Deceitful Brownskin Blues," for robbing him; and in "Peach Orchard Mama," for cheating on him. The details of Blind Lemon's actual relationships with women and his family life are sketchy. Sam Price said he and Roberta had a child soon after they married in the twenties. The reference book *Blues Who's Who,* citing a 1970 booklet called "Blind Lemon Jefferson" by Bob Groom, says Blind Lemon and Roberta had a son named Miles who was a musician. But Theaul Howard, Hobert Carter and others who knew Jefferson say he had no children.

By casting women into such a wide range of roles in his songs, Blind Lemon was able to more fully identify with the experiences of his audience, an identification that carried over into other areas of life and suffering. In "Mosquito Moan," he recounted the displeasures caused by a common insect, but retained his sense of humor:

> Now I'm sittin' in my kitchen, mosquitoes all around
> my screen.
> Now I'm sittin' in my kitchen, mosquitoes all around
> my screen.
> If I don't arrange to get a mosquito bomb,
> I'll be seldom seen.

Blind Lemon's songs also talked of other pests and animals found in East Texas farming communities, including mules, cows, horses, snakes and rabbits. These references conveyed a sense of time and place, but animals also served as references to travel, sexuality and despair. In "One Dime Blues," "Broke and Hungry" and "Tin Cup Blues," Blind Lemon commented poignantly on the poverty and oppression rampant among African Americans. In "Tin Cup Blues," he lamented:

> I stood on the corner and almost bust my head.
> I stood on the corner, almost bust my head.
> I couldn't earn enough to buy me a loaf of bread.
> My gal's a housemaid, and she earns a dollar a week.
> I'm so hungry on payday, I can hardly speak.
> Now gather 'round me people, let me tell you a true fact.
> I said gather 'round me people, let me tell you a true fact.
> That tough luck has struck me, and the rats is sleepin' in my hat.

In addition to the personal hardships of his audience, Blind Lemon sang about the ravages of natural disaster in "Rising High Water Blues," and about the injustices of the criminal justice system in his songs about prison life, though there's no record that he actually spent time in jail. In "Hangman's Blues," Blind Lemon demonstrated his ability to project himself into another man's fear and anxiety:

> Well, mean old hangman is waitin' to tighten up that noose.
> I have a mean old hangman waitin' to tighten up that noose.
> Lord, I'm so scared I am tremblin' in my shoes.
> Jury heard my case and said my hands was red.
> Jury heard my case and said my hands was red.
> And judge he sentenced me to be hangin' till I'm dead.

The crowd is around the courthouse, and time is
    goin' fast.
And the crowd is around the courthouse and time
    is goin' fast.
Soon a good for nothin' killer is goin' to breathe
    his last.

Blind Lemon recorded two versions of this song. The first was
more dramatic, with a fast, pulsating guitar accompaniment designed to simulate the rapid heartbeat of the convicted man. In
"Hangman's Blues," as well as in "Prison Cell Blues," "Lectric Chair
Blues," "Lockstep Blues" and "Blind Lemon's Penitentiary Blues,"
he depicted jail life as grim and cruel and criticized the unfairness
of the court system. The bluesman's songs about prison and the
longing for freedom were not his most popular, but they nonetheless reflected the social conditions of the times and represented
themes that were vital to the country blues tradition.

During the zenith of his brief recording career, between 1926
and 1928, Blind Lemon often commuted between Dallas and Chicago, where he had a South Side kitchenette at 37th and Rhodes.
But he continued to travel around Texas and to other states including Oklahoma, Georgia and Mississippi. Mississippi Delta
bluesman Houston Stackhouse remembered seeing Jefferson in
his hometown. "He came to Crystal Springs and was playin' in some
little show for a doctor. . . . They had it in Freetown, there at the
colored school. There was plenty of people there. It was a big school
and crowded all indoors, people couldn't get to see him. They
had to bring him out to the front, on the porch."[27]

Blind Lemon's producer for Paramount, Mayo Williams, who
was African American himself, marveled at the appeal of his songs.
In appreciation of Blind Lemon's earning power, Williams bought
him a $725 Ford, and the singer hired a chauffeur to drive it for
him. Blind Lemon also owned a 1923 or '24 Dodge, often mentioned in his performances. According to Williams, Blind Lemon's
royalties accumulated so quickly that he was encouraged to open

a savings account, which reached a balance of $1,500. For a black performer to receive royalties at all was extraordinary for the time. In an interview with Stephen Calt, Williams called Jefferson "a soul singer, naturally," but he doubted that Blind Lemon could have originated all his song themes. "He was just as cool and calm and collected as any artist I've ever seen," Williams said.[28]

By 1929, interest in Blind Lemon's music began to decline. His instrumental arrangements became more derivative of his earlier work, and he no longer brought his old enthusiasm to the recording studio. Some see a decline in his vocal range, though Evans disagrees. Jefferson could have been running out of material, or it's possible that the stories about his raucous, whiskey-fueled lifestyle are true and that it was beginning to take its toll. Of course, 1929 also marked the beginning of the Great Depression, which devastated the recording industry.

No one knows what would have happened to Blind Lemon Jefferson's career if he had lived. But late that year, he died in Chicago. The circumstances and even the date of his death are unclear. No official record has been found, and the oral accounts are contradictory. Arthur Laibly, who had succeeded Williams as Blind Lemon's producer, said the singer died of a heart attack, based on a report from Laibly's office assistant. Laibly heard that Blind Lemon died during a blizzard, information later substantiated by Williams, who added that the singer had collapsed in his car and was abandoned by his chauffeur. According to other accounts, someone failed to pick Blind Lemon up at the train station, and he tried to walk to his hotel and froze after losing his way in the snow, which disoriented him by muffling sounds. When asked about the funeral, Quince Cox, then working as the Wortham cemetery caretaker, was quick to reply. "Anyone over the age of sixty remembers that day well," he said in a hoarse voice. "They brought his body back to Texas by train. People said he died in the snow after a recording session in Chicago, that he was lost, couldn't find his way. Some thought it was foul play. Two or three hundred people came to the funeral, black and white, to watch his coffin lowered into the ground."[29]

Six months after Blind Lemon's death, Paramount attempted to capitalize on his tragic misfortune by issuing six posthumous records. The last was a sermon by the Reverend Emmet Dickenson called "The Death of Blind Lemon," which compared the singer to Jesus Christ. The sermon did little to explain the reality of Blind Lemon's life and death, but it was testimony to the magnitude of his career and its importance in African American culture.[30]

Blind Lemon Jefferson's death marked the end of the riotous 1920s, a time when the commercial possibilities of African-American popular music were first explored, but his art also looked forward. As an early recording artist, he was an influence on other performers and writers. He taught Leadbelly much about the blues and apparently introduced him to slide guitar. The line "I walked all the way from Dallas to Wichita Falls," from Jefferson's "Long Lonesome Blues," has appeared in the repertoire of countless blues singers. A verse of "Black Horse Blues" turned up in slightly altered form in Mississippi singer Charley Patton's "Pony Blues": *Got to get on my black horse and saddle up my gray mare.* His line *Well, the train I ride is eighteen coaches long* became the basis for Little Junior Parker's "Mystery Train," later recorded by Elvis Presley. And there's another Elvis connection, a line from Jefferson's "Teddy Bear Blues": *Say, fair brown, let me be your teddy bear/Tie a string on my neck, I'll follow you everywhere.* Robert Johnson apparently borrowed from Jefferson's "Change My Luck Blues" in his "Walking Blues": *She got Elgin movements from her head down to her toes/And she can break in on a dollar anywhere she goes.* Jefferson's "Jack O'Diamond Blues" became a hit for Lonnie Donnegan during the 1950s skiffle craze in England. And of course "Matchbox Blues" was the basis of hits for both rockabilly pioneer Carl Perkins and the Beatles. Blind Lemon's phrasing, the "suspended time" of his guitar playing, was a harbinger of the swinging Texas style of guitar playing that T-Bone Walker and others would make popular on a much wider scale. They would electrify that sound, put it in front of a full orchestra and take it to California. His use of flatted fifths may even be seen as a harbinger of bebop, which made extensive use of them.

Today, more than a century after his birth, Blind Lemon Jefferson lies buried in the black section of the small Wortham cemetery. A state historical plaque erected in 1965 marks the burial place, which is flat and wind-swept, an eerie fulfillment of his plea, "See that my grave is kept clean." The town began a blues festival named for the singer in 1997 and erected a new headstone. In his adopted city, Dallas, he's little known. A caricature of him appears each month, however, on the inside back cover of a Swedish blues magazine called *Jefferson*. The singer is in the same characteristic pose as his publicity photo but instead of wearing a suit and tie, he is depicted in a Hawaiian-style shirt. In each issue, editor Tommy Löfgren puts new words in Swedish in the singer's mouth: "Can I change my shirt now? Is the world ready for me yet?"

[1] Sam Stillman, interview with Jay Brakefield, March 22, 1992.

[2] Mack McCormick, "Biography of Henry Thomas: Our Deepest Look at Roots," liner notes to the album, *Henry Thomas: Ragtime Texas.*

[3] Quince Cox, interview with Alan Govenar, March 18, 1987. For more information, see Richard U. Steinberg, "See That My Grave is Kept Clean," *Living Blues* 83 (1982): 24–25.

[4] Samuel Charters, *The Country Blues* (New York: Rinehart, 1959), 178.

[5] Laura Lippman, "Blind Lemon Sang the Blues: Wortham Man Recalls His Memories of Musician," *Waco Tribune-Herald* (June 2, 1983) 11A. For more information, see Robert L. Uzzel, "Music Rooted in Texas Soil," *Living Blues* 83 (1982): 22–23.

[6] Theaul Howard, interviews with Jay Brakefield, October and November, 1993.

[7] Charlie Hurd, interview with Jay Brakefield, November, 1993.

[8] Kip Lornell and Charles Wolfe, *The Life and Legend of Leadbelly* (New York: HarperCollins, 1992), 42–43.

[9] Paul Oliver, *Blues Off the Record* (New York: Da Capo Press, 1988), 64–65.

[10] Giles Oakley, *The Devil's Music* (London: Ariel Books, 1976), 67. For more information on Blind Lemon Jefferson and Huddie "Leadbelly" Ledbetter, see William Barlow, *Looking Up at Down: The Emergence of Blues Culture* (Philadelphia: Temple University Press, 1989).

[11] Lornell and Wolfe, 45.

[12] Alan Govenar, *Meeting the Blues* (Dallas: Taylor Publishing, 1988), 16.

[13] Willard Watson, interview with Jay Brakefield, July 16, 1992 and Sam Stillman, interview with Jay Brakefield, March 2, 1992.

[14] Samuel Charters, *The Bluesmen* (New York: Oak Publications, 1968), 178.

[15] Mance Lipscomb, interview with Glen Myers, Center for American History Center Collection, Austin, Texas.

[16] Victoria Spivey, "Blind Lemon Jefferson and I Had a Ball," *Record Research* 78 (May 1966): 9.

[17] Roger S. Brown, "Recording Pioneer Polk Brockman," *Living Blues* 23 (1975): 31.

[18] Spivey, 9.

[19] Charters, 179.

[20] Mack McCormick, interview with Jay Brakefield, July 29, 1989.

[21] "T-Bone Walker in His Own Words," *Record Changer* (October 1947), 5.

[22] Oliver, 65.

[23] Samuel B. Charters, *The Country Blues* (New York: Da Capo Press, 1975), 87–88.

[24] Sammy Price, interview with Jay Brakefield, June 7, 1991.

[25] David Evans, "Ramblin'," *Blues Revue Quarterly* 9 (Summer 1933): 16–18.

[26] Stephen Calt, liner notes to *Blind Lemon Jefferson, King of the Country Blues*, Yazoo 1069.

[27] "Interview with Houston Stackhouse," *Living Blues* 17 (1974), 20–21.

[28] Calt, Yazoo 1069.

[29] Cox interview.

[30] Oliver, *Blues Off the Record*, 69–70 and Paramount 12945-B, *The Death of Blind Lemon*, 1930.

Blind Lemon Jefferson, ca. 1927. *Courtesy* Documentary Arts.

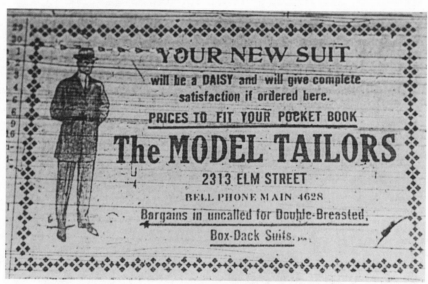

A 1920s *Dallas Express* ad for The Model Tailors, where Blind Lemon Jefferson bought his clothing.

The Contemporaries of Blind Lemon

As a result of the success of Blind Lemon Jefferson, blues guitarists from around Texas and elsewhere in the South came to Dallas in the late 1920s and early 1930s looking for work. Undoubtedly, these musicians were influenced by Jefferson, but given the transient nature of many blues singers of this generation, it is difficult to assess the extent of any direct parallels in the music of those who recorded after him. Clearly, Jefferson was most influential in the way he established the commercial viability of downhome blues, and it was the potential for financial success that attracted other musicians to Dallas.

Jesse and Willard "Ramblin'" Thomas, Alger "Texas" Alexander, J. T. "Funny Paper" Smith, Gene Campbell, Carl Davis, Bo Jones, Willie Reed, Coley Jones, and Dennis "Little Hat" Jones, all played in the areas of Central Track, Deep Ellum, Freedmantown and South Dallas. Jesse Thomas came to Dallas in 1928, following his brother, Willard "Ramblin'" Thomas, from Logansport, Louisiana, where they both were born (Jesse in 1911 and Willard, 1902). In an interview with Bruce Nixon, Jesse recalled that when he was young he didn't sing blues because he was "raised where the blues was all around. People were singing in the fields, day and night. I thought it was something lonesome and sad, not really something I liked. But when I came to Dallas, I saw that people enjoyed them, and then I liked them better. I saw that there was more to them than just a sad story."[1]

In Dallas, Jesse lived with his brother on Flora Street off Hall Street and eked out a living playing on the street and at house parties. On summer evenings he sometimes put together a small string band and went from house to house in the Highland Park suburb of the city playing the popular songs of the day (such as "Shine on Harvest Moon" and "Meet Me in Dreamland") to entertain the wealthy white families who sat on their front porches as the sun went down. At house parties, Jesse said, "We'd get paid a small salary to play. I carried that little wooden box [the guitar] everywhere I went. If you weren't hired, you'd just go visiting, take up a collection. People would tip you to play a certain tune. But the cost of living was so low, you could get by. A house was a dollar-and-a-half a week to rent, and if you were playing, you'd get meals and drinks practically for free everywhere you went."[2]

Willard Thomas was considered a more accomplished blues performer than his brother. Willard had met Blind Lemon in Deep Ellum and, reportedly, they played together. Evidence of this association, historian Bob Groom points out, can be heard in Thomas's "No Baby Blues" which incorporates a Jefferson-like guitar line.[3] Moreover, it was probably through Jefferson and R. T. Ashford that Thomas was able to get a recording contract from the Paramount label, which sent him to Chicago in February, 1928, to record eight sides. Later that year, in November, Thomas was invited back to Chicago to record six more sides, including his song "Hard Dallas Blues," in which he warns his listeners:

> Man, don't never make Dallas your home,
> When you look for your friends, they will all be gone.

He was recorded in Dallas by the Victor Company in February, 1932, and four songs were released, two of which were versions of his "Ground Hog Blues." After these sessions, Ramblin' Thomas moved on and Jesse heard little of him until he died in Memphis of tuberculosis in 1935.

Through Ashford, Jesse Thomas was given an audition by Paramount around 1928, but he wasn't recorded until the following year, when he was offered a contract from Victor. On these four recordings and as an accompanist on two Bessie Tucker titles—"Better Boot That Thing" and "Katy Blues"—he was identified as Jesse "Babyface" Thomas.

Gene Campbell was a blues guitarist and singer who was a contemporary of the Thomas brothers, but the biographical details of his life are not as well documented as theirs.[4] In his song "Western Plain Blues," he says that he was "born and raised in Texas" although he never explains where. It is likely, however, that he lived in or near Dallas during the years 1929 and 1930 because he recorded in field sessions there. It is also possible that he was an itinerant who happened to travel through Dallas during the time that the recording engineers had already set up their equipment.

In October, 1929, an obscure group, Jake Jones and the Gold Front Boys (of unknown origins), recorded two "blues stomps" dance tunes for the Brunswick label in a Dallas session: "Monkeyin' Around" and "Southern Sea Blues."[5] That same month Sam Price also recorded two sides for Brunswick, "Blue Rhythm Stomp" and "Nasty But Nice," with a band he called his "Four Quarters," featuring "Kid Lips" on trumpet, Bert Johnson on trombone, Percy Darensbourg (from New Orleans) on banjo and Price himself on piano.[6]

It is clear from existing discographies that the recording activity in Dallas during this period was intense, and that the major companies came to the city on an annual basis, frequently during the fall months when the weather was temperate. In November 1929 Gene Campbell made two sides for the Brunswick label (which had recorded Sam Price a month earlier), and in December Coley Jones, "Oak Cliff T-Bone" Walker and Willie Reed recorded for Columbia, and "Bo" Jones, for Vocalion.

Coley Jones lived in Dallas and performed as a solo guitarist and vocalist, as well as with his own string band. His repertoire consisted of blues, dance tunes and popular songs, but also vaude-ville and tent show numbers such as "Army Mule in No Man's Land" (which is an ironic depiction of blacks in the armed forces) and "The Elder He's My Man" (which parodies the relations between the minister and his church).[7] His song "Drunkard's Special" was based on a British ballad called "Our Goodman"; "Chasin' Rain-bows" and "I Used to Call Her Baby" were turn-of-the-century popu-lar songs; and "Dallas Rag" was a ragtime tune.

Coley Jones's Dallas String Band was well known around the city, playing at community picnics, dances and shows for white and black audiences, and serenading on the streets in front of Ella B. Moore's theaters. The band had varying personnel and configura-tions that sometimes included one or two violins, two guitars, man-dolin, string bass, clarinet, and trumpet. The bass player for Coley Jones was Marco Washington, who had himself run a string band that included his stepson, Aaron "T-Bone" Walker, as a child gui-tarist and dancer. The nickname T-Bone derived from his mother's pet name for him: "T-Bow," short for Thibeaux.[8] Walker was born in Linden, Texas, in 1910. He moved with his mother to Dallas at age two and lived there and in Fort Worth until 1933, when he moved to California. In Walker's early recordings (as Oak Cliff T-Bone), "Trinity River Blues" and "Wichita Falls Blues," the influ-ence of Blind Lemon Jefferson's guitar style is evident. In these recordings Walker was accompanied by Doug Finnell on piano and Carl Davis on guitar.

Many talented musicians, such as Ailus Patterson, never re-corded. Patterson was born just after the turn of the century near Brenham, in Central Texas. He showed musical talent early and had a mentor in Tom Shaw, a friend of Blind Lemon Jefferson's. Patterson performed at times at the Big House, a night spot between Temple and Waco for which Jefferson named a song. Patterson was a versatile musician who could play both four- and six-string guitars, mandolin and bass. Around 1929, he met Coley Jones and his band on the streets of Deep Ellum and performed with them. He was scheduled to record with the band but became ill with smallpox and missed the session. Patterson remained active as a musician, playing around Central Texas with his band the Five Black Aces through the early 1960s.[9]

Recording activity in Texas continued into the early 1930s, when field sessions were scaled back because of the Great Depression. Gene Campbell recorded four sides for Brunswick in Dallas in November 1930, including "Don't Leave Me Blues," which has references to Waco, Fort Worth and San Antonio and seems to allude to his travels around the state. Kip Lornell suggests that his "expressive, though easy drawl" is reminiscent of Willard and Jesse Thomas, although his "vocal inflections are restricted in range, almost always less than an octave" and "his penchant for descending vocal phrases calls Denis 'Little Hat' Jones to mind."[10]

Like Campbell, Jones was known to perform around Dallas, but he never recorded in the city.[11] Jones was from the San Antonio area and he recorded twelve songs there in 1929. He had an idiosyncratic approach to the guitar that is especially evident in his solos in "Cross the Water Blues" and "Hurry Blues." However, some of his repertoire was traditional; his song "Kentucky Blues," for example, is a version of W. C. Handy and Chris Smith's "Long Gone" (1920). Jones is also credited with backing the blues singer Alger "Texas" Alexander on eight songs in a San Antonio session in June 1929. Jesse Thomas remembered Alexander from his days in Dallas and told interviewer Bruce Nixon that he was "always singing with some guitarist or piano player in the black joints around Deep Ellum and South Dallas."[12] Alexander, however, traveled often and recorded regularly, mostly in New York, where he was backed by Lonnie Johnson or guitarist Eddie Lang or both.

J. T. Smith was another blues guitarist who reportedly played in Dallas during the 1920s and 1930s, but did not record there. Smith called himself "Funny Papa" (though it was misspelled on his records as "Funny Paper") or "Howling Wolf" after the success of his "Howling Wolf Blues." Between September 1930 and April 1935 Smith recorded forty-one songs, only twenty of which were issued at the time.

Very little is known about Smith's birthplace or life, although bluesman Thomas Shaw (who was discovered in 1970 and died in 1977)[13] said that Smith was overseer "at the plantation where he worked" and that he allegedly killed a man in an argument over a woman.[14] Shaw met Smith in late 1930 in Wickoffs, Oklahoma, a small town in the southwest corner of the state, and thereafter they played regularly together for weekend dances until Smith was arrested for murder.

Musically, Shaw said that "Wolf wasn't too great of a guitar player"[15] because his guitar seemed to always be out of tune, even on his recordings. Yet, his stylistic approach was similar to that of many of the Texas guitarists of his generation, and in some ways, he was more sophisticated. "While he often used the same steady, non-alternating thumb basic to Texas blues," record producers Stephen Calt, Woody Mann and Nick Perls indicate in their notes to one of Smith's reissue albums, "he also used alternating thumb picking. The various thumb rolls, rapid thumb runs (as on 'Hungry Wolf') and double-timed notes produced by the thumb gave his work much rhythmic variation. When using a regular thumb bass, he had the unusual tendency to accentuate the first beat of each measure rather than play the more standard four or five basically equal beats per measure."[16] Smith's lyrics were often unconventional and reflected upon his travel and personal experience. His song "Seven Sisters Blues," like "Howling Wolf Blues," is divided into two parts; the first recounts an anticipated visit to a conjurer in New Orleans, and the second looks at the visit in retrospect.

Part One: They tell me Seven Sisters in New Orleans,
    that can really fix a man up right,
    And I'm headed for New Orleans, Louisiana,
    I'm travelin' both day and night.
Part Two: I went to New Orleans, Louisiana,
    just on account of something I heard
    The Seven Sisters told me everything I
      wanted to know,
    and they wouldn't let me speak a word.

In "Fool's Blues" he begins by admitting his weakness—"You know, I'm a single-handed fool, and getting old too"—but later he assumes a more bitter tone:

This musta been the devil I'm serving,
 it can't be Jesus Christ,
Cause I asked him to save me
 and look like he tryin' to take my life.

Overall, Smith's life and career typified the blues guitarists of his generation who traveled in and around the Dallas area. Although these performers were influenced to varying degrees by the guitar style of Blind Lemon Jefferson, they nonetheless displayed their own idiosyncrasies combined with other regional variations. Babe Kyro Lemon Turner, nicknamed "The Black Ace," and Oscar "Buddy" Woods, for example, liked to tune their guitars to an open chord (often a D major), placing the instruments in their laps and then using a bottleneck or slide to fret them.[17] This style of playing was used as early as the late 1800s, but gained widespread popularity due to the influence of Hawaiian music during the 'teens.

Turner was born in 1907 in Hughes Springs in East Texas; in the early 1930s he moved to Shreveport, where he met and later teamed up with Woods. By 1936 they both had moved to Fort Worth, where they worked as musicians in local night spots and were featured in live broadcasts over KFJZ from 1936 to 1941 (when Turner appeared in the all black film *The Blood of Jesus*).[18]

Woods and Turner, however, never recorded together. Woods had recorded first in Memphis in1930 in a band that featured him and Ed Schaffer on twin slide guitars, accompanied by kazoo with Schaffer and the white singer Jimmie Davis on vocals. Two years later, Davis arranged another session at the Jefferson Hotel in Dallas, and Schaffer and Woods accompanied him on four sides. Davis, at that time, was a struggling hillbilly singer who favored the yodeling of Jimmie Rodgers and the blues he had heard among blacks when he was growing up in Louisiana. Later in life, Davis claimed authorship of "You Are My Sunshine" and was twice elected governor of Louisiana.

Turner's early efforts at recording were not as successful as were Woods's. His first sides, made in an ARC field studio in April 1936, were never issued, although he was invited to record six sides for the Decca label in Dallas in February 1937. On these recordings, including "Trifling Woman," "You Gonna Need My Help Some Day," and "Christmas Time Blues" Turner was accompanied by guitarist Smokey Hogg.

The recording scouts of the day searched for virtuosity in performance and attempted to record as many different styles of blues as possible in their search for commercial success in the "Race" market.[19] Consequently, there is little homogeneity in the recordings made during this period. Some guitarists, like the obscure Sammy Hill, Otis Harris and Bo Jones, were given the opportunity to record two sides each, but were never invited back; others, such as Willie Reed and Carl Davis, were recorded as solo performers and then as accompanists for musicians as varied as Texas Alexander and the Dallas Jamboree Jug Band, which featured a washtub bassist named Shorty and a washboard player named Charles "Chicken" Jackson.

The blues musicians who followed Blind Lemon Jefferson, with the possible exception of T-Bone Walker, never achieved the success that he did. Still, they were afforded recording opportunities which may have been precluded had Jefferson not been discovered. Despite their limited audience, they brought to Dallas a rich array of musical talent. It is evident that they represented a variety of musical styles, most of which were rooted in East Texas and elsewhere in the south, but nonetheless became emblematic of the character of Deep Ellum during in its heyday.

[1] Bruce Nixon, "The Sounds of Deep Ellum," *Dallas Times Herald* (September 23, 1983), C2.

[2] Nixon, C3. Also see Keith Briggs, liner notes to *Jesse Thomas, 1948–1958,* (1993), Document BDCD-6044.

[3] Bob Groom, liner notes to *"Ramblin" Thomas & The Dallas Blues Singers: Complete Recorded Works 1928–1932* (1992), Document DOCD-5107.

[4] Kip Lornell, liner notes to *Gene Campbell: Complete Recorded Works 1929–1931* (1993), Document DOCD-5151.

[5] Kip Lornell, liner notes to *Texas Black Country Dance Music, 1927–1935* (1993), Document DOCD-5162.

[6] Sammy Price, *What Do They Want? A Jazz Autobiography* (Urbana: University of Illinois Press, 1990), 25, 28, 86.

[7] Paul Garon, liner notes to *Texas Blues: The Complete Recorded Works of Coley Jones, "Bo" Jones, Little Hat Jones, Willie Reed, Oak Cliff T-Bone Walker 1927–1935* (1993), Document DOCD-5161. Also, Lornell, liner notes to *Texas Black Country Dance Music.*

[8] Garon. For more information on the career of Aaron "T-Bone" Walker, see Helen O. Dance, *Stormy Monday: The T-Bone Walker Story* (New York: Da Capo, 1990).

[9] Danny Williams, letter to Alan Govenar, September 30, 1996.

[10] Lornell.

[11] Garon.

[12] Nixon, C3.

[13] It is not known whether this Thomas Shaw is the same man as Tom Shaw, mentioned on p. 90 in connection with Blind Lemon Jefferson.

[14] Stephen Calt, Woody Mann, and Nick Perls, liner notes to *Funny Papa Smith: The Original Howling Wolf,* Yazoo L-1031. Also, see Teddy Doering, *J. T. "Funny Paper" Smith, 1930–1931* (1991), Document BDCD-6016.

[15] Calt, Mann and Perls.

[16] Ibid.

[17] Kip Lornell, liner notes to *Texas Slide Guitars: Complete Recorded Works 1930–1938, Oscar Woods and Black Ace,* Document DOCD-5143.

[18] For more information on the film *Blood of Jesus*, see George William Jones, *Black Cinema Treasures: Lost and Found* (Denton: University of North Texas Press, 1991).

[19] For additional information, see Paul Oliver, *Blues Off the Record* (New York: Da Capo Press, 1988) and Robert Dixon and John Godrich, *Recording the Blues, 1902–1940* (New York: Stein & Day, 1970).

Elm Street theaters at night, 1925. Photography by Frank Rogers. *Courtesy* Texas/Dallas History and Archives Division, Dallas Public Library.

Race records ad for songs by "Little Hat" Jones, ca. 1920. *Courtesy* Alan Govenar.

Race records ad for Henry "Ragtime Texas" Thomas. *Courtesy* Alan Govenar.

Ailus Patterson, ca. 1940. *Courtesy* Danny Williams.

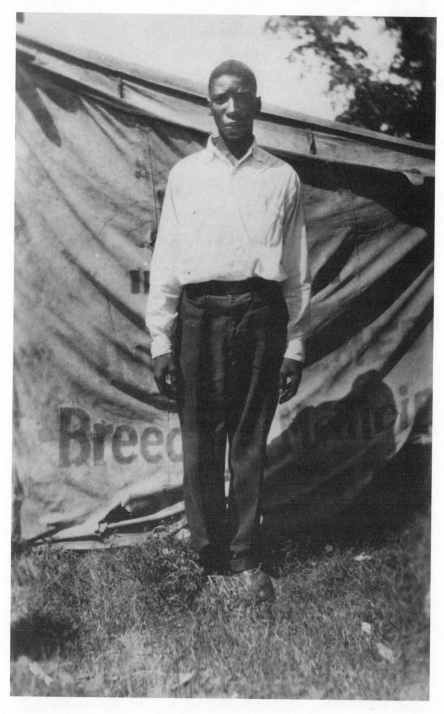

Aaron "T-Bone" Walker, assistant to Dr. Breeding's Medicine Show, mid-1920s.
Courtesy Helen Oakley Dance.

Blind Willie Johnson and Arizona Dranes: The "Holy Blues" of Deep Ellum

While blues singers and string bands vied for the attention of passersby on the sidewalks of Deep Ellum, street preachers and religious singers prayed to the Lord and proselytized anyone who might stop to listen. Recording scouts who came to Dallas may have looked hard for musical heirs to Blind Lemon, but they were attracted to African-American religious music as well. Contrary to popular belief, there was considerable interplay between blues musicians and religious singers. Moreover, the blues and religious songs drew from similar musical forms, especially evidenced in the use of twelve- and sixteen bar structures, flatted or "blue" notes, slide guitar and barrelhouse piano styles.

Deep Ellum's greatest exponent of what has been called "holy blues" was Blind Willie Johnson, who made thirty recordings for the Columbia label between 1927 and 1930. He was born in 1902 or 1903 near Temple, Texas, but as a baby moved with his family to

Marlin, a small town about 100 miles south of Dallas. Johnson's widow, Angeline, told music historian Sam Charters that Willie was blinded at age seven by his stepmother, who threw lye in his face after his father found her with another man.[1] Bluesman Tom Shaw, however, said that Johnson informed him that he had gone blind from wearing a pair of discarded eyeglasses. Another unidentified source, folklorist David Evans wrote, stated that Johnson went blind by watching an eclipse through a piece of glass.[2] Johnson's interest in music began at the age of five when he told his father he wanted to be a preacher and made his first guitar out of a cigar box. His father nurtured his interest in being a performer and took him to Marlin, Hearne and other nearby towns to play on the streets for tips.

Adam Booker, a minister living in Brenham, Texas, remembered that on Saturday afternoons in Marlin, the farm people came to town, and Johnson sang religious songs on one corner while Blind Lemon Jefferson sang blues on another. About Johnson, Booker said, "He was there, you know, he came to see his daddy, and while being there, that being good cotton country, people were all there picking cotton, and they would come on the street every Saturday, and he'd get on the street and sing and pick the guitar, and they would listen and would give him money . . . every Saturday, he wouldn't hardly miss."[3]

Johnson made his first recordings for Columbia on December 3, 1927, in a field session in Dallas, where he was already known as a street singer of religious songs with a tin cup on a wire loop around his neck. During this first session, he recorded six songs, including some of his greatest performances: "I Know His Blood Can Make Me Whole," "Jesus Make Up My Dying Bed," "It's Nobody's Fault But Mine," "Mother's Children Have a Hard Time," "Dark Was the Night—Cold Was the Ground," and "If I Had My Way I'd Tear This Building Down."

Washington Phillips, a religious singer from East Texas, was recorded by Columbia on December 2, 1927, and then invited back on December 5th. Phillips was older than Johnson; he was born in 1891 in Freestone County, not far from where Blind Lemon Jefferson was born. As Mexia resident Charlie Hurd indicated, Jefferson and Phillips may have played together. Other older residents around Mexia recall Phillips singing religious songs and playing his dulceola, though they didn't know what it was called. Frank Walker, who directed the field recording unit that recorded both Phillips and Johnson, remarked: "He had no name for it; it was something he made himself. Nobody on earth could use it except him. Nobody would want to, I don't think."[4]

From Phillips's promotional photograph, the instrument looks like a zither with a few dozen strings and a few frets, which he may have gotten from some of the German immigrants in Central Texas. He plucked and strummed it, accompanying himself much as guitarists did and achieving a similar sound. The instrument may not in fact have been Phillips's creation. According to the liner notes of a compilation of his recordings, the dulceola was invented around 1902 by a piano tuner named David Boyd. According to the notes, Boyd and his brother produced the instrument at a small factory called the Toledo Symphony Company, and Boyd and his wife sold them out of their car throughout the country. After his death, production ceased. The notes describe the dulceola as consisting of a walnut and cherrywood zither frame and a keyboard that plays the strings. A photograph shows Phillips with two instruments without keyboards. These may have been dulceolas that he had modified; the keyboards were easy to remove.

Phillips recorded eighteen sides in three sessions in Dallas, in December of 1927, 1928 and 1929. About half his recorded songs were traditional, half original. His most powerful recording, made in the 1927 sessions, was "Denomination Blues," which takes up both sides of a record. A holy blues, as the title suggests, it lambasts dogmatic Christians and predatory preachers: "Lot of preachers is preaching and think they're doin' well/And all they want is your money, and you can go to hell." Apparently he soon thereafter was placed in the state mental hospital in Austin, where he died in 1938. He is largely forgotten, though roots-rock musician Ry

Cooder recorded a version of his song "You Can't Stop a Tattler" in the 1970s.

Blind Willie Johnson was more extensively recorded. With the success of his first records in the popular Columbia 14000 Race series, he was invited back for sessions in Dallas in 1928, in New Orleans in 1929 and in Atlanta in 1930.

Despite conflicting accounts about Johnson's early life and the date he married Angeline, it is likely that his first marriage was to another woman named Willie B. Harris, who was found by researcher Dan Williams in Marlin, Texas. Harris had vivid memories of Johnson, whom she said she had married in 1926 or 1927. She recalled that Johnson wasn't a preacher, but "just a songster," and that he was a member of the Church of God in Christ on Commerce Street in Marlin, where he played both piano and guitar for services and revival meetings.

Harris recalled that her husband's travels to his recording sessions often took longer than the actual days spent in the recording studio. "They come and got him and carried him," she told Williams, "and when they would come and get him it didn't cost nothing to ride. . . . He'd be gone sometime thirty days, something like that, but he wouldn't be over there doing all that much work. He would, you know, just go, and then after he'd go he just stay over there and then play on the streets. He loved to play on the streets."[5]

It is likely Johnson was accompanied by Harris's vocals in his Dallas session of December 5, 1928, when he recorded four songs: "I'm Gonna Run to the City of Refuge," "Jesus is Coming Soon," "Lord I Can't Just Keep from Crying," and "Keep Your Lamp Trimmed and Burning."

Johnson often used open tunings, especially open D, and played his guitar with a slide; according to bluesman Blind Willie McTell, Johnson used a steel ring as a slide. When playing slide, he often hammered at the bass strings with his thumb, yielding "an insistent, chugging bass sound" similar to that employed by Blind Lemon Jefferson, Leadbelly and other blues musicians and songsters. He often sang in a rough bass voice with which his wife harmonized beautifully. Johnson's recordings sold well and were released as late as 1935, though he made his last records at the April 1930 Atlanta session.

After the Depression ended his recording career, Johnson moved with his wife to Beaumont, Texas, where he continued playing on the streets and in churches, sometimes venturing about sixty miles west to Houston to play for larger religious gatherings. He died in 1949 after contracting pneumonia while sleeping on a wet mattress after a fire that damaged the Johnsons' home.

Religious music continued to be a presence on the streets of Deep Ellum after the recording stopped. Taxi driver and dispatcher Julius Walker, who came to Dallas from East Texas in the 1920s, remembered the music made by the followers of a Reverend Stevenson. The minister, Walker said, "stayed out there long enough and got enough money. He built him a church. He'd have six or seven singing (accompanied by a tambourine and a drum) and boy, I'm telling you, they'd have themselves a time. They were out there every day and every night."[6]

In addition to the street preachers and religious singers, there is evidence that advocates of some of the back-to-Africa movements of the 1920s proselytized on the streets of Deep Ellum.

Like his fellow pawnbroker, Rocky Goldstein, Label Feldman recalled the "holy roller women." Feldman said:

> Saturday, or sometimes in the middle of the week, some black preacher would come and get right in the middle of the track and start preaching. And you could hear them from pretty far away. Everybody would come running. All the blacks would come and listen to the preacher, you see. And on some days, those holy roller women would join in and start singing.[7]

The most well-known of these women was probably Arizona Dranes, who performed not only in the Dallas and Fort Worth area, but traveled to Oklahoma City and Chicago, where she ultimately built a reputation for herself through her recordings for the Okeh Phonograph Company. Arizona Juanita Dranes was born in Dallas, reportedly between 1904 and 1906, of mixed black and Mexican descent.[8] She was blind from birth and learned the piano as a teenager, playing for religious services and singing on the street with the followers of the Church of God in Christ in the Dallas and Fort Worth areas. The Church of God in Christ was one of many small storefront sanctified and Pentacostal churches which flourished in Texas and elsewhere across the South around the turn of the century. These small churches nurtured the personal and emotional involvement of their members and welcomed the use of musical instruments, like piano, guitar and tambourines, which were considered "too worldly" by other Christian denominations.

Reverend Samuel Crouch of Fort Worth recommended Dranes to Okeh, which sent talent scout Richard M. Jones to audition her. She was then invited to Chicago for a recording session. Once there, "Dranes signed a basic recording contract which gave her twenty-five dollars per issued side and twenty-five percent of royalties collected on any of her compositions recorded by other artists."[9] Dranes's first session, on June 17, 1926, led to the release of four songs: "In That Day," "It's All Right Now," "John Said He Saw a Number," and "My Soul is a Witness for the Lord." This session was followed by another on November 15, 1926, which included Dranes as vocalist on piano with Reverend F. W. (Ford Washington) McGhee and the Jubilee Singers.

McGhee was born in 1890 while his mother was visiting Winchester, Tennessee. When he was five, his family moved to Hillsboro, Texas, between Dallas and Austin, where his "performing abilities were first noted during his involvement in school plays."[10] Around 1912, McGhee moved to Oklahoma with his wife to accept a position teaching school, and in 1918 he converted to the Church of

God in Christ. While pastoring in Oklahoma City, McGhee met Dranes, who helped him to build his congregation.

Dranes, however, only made two recordings with McGhee on the Okeh label, and did not record again until 1928, when she was invited to a session in Dallas. In these recordings, she was accompanied by a choir and possibly also by Coley Jones. Later that year, she was apparently again recorded by Okeh in Dallas, this time accompanying the Texas Jubilee Singers; the songs released were "He's the Lily of the Valley" and "He's Coming Soon." Little is known about the Texas Jubilee Singers, though it is likely they were itinerant musicians who were members of the Church of God in Christ.

Her recording career, like so many others, ended with the onset of the Depression, and Arizona Dranes's whereabouts are unknown after that. She apparently left Texas. According to the notes for a Document collection of her work, "It would seem she returned to the network of sanctified churches where a number of later gospel celebrities recalled her impact. Alex Bradford remembered her performing in Bessemer, Alabama, at the "America Back to God Day" presented at the local white ball park, Legion Field. "And there was Arizona Dranes, the blind Sanctified lady. She'd sing 'Thy Servant's Prayer,' and crackers and niggers be shouting everywhere."[11] Rosetta Tharpe heard her sing "The Storm is Passing Over" in St. Louis.[12] Ray Funk, in the liner notes to Columbia Legacy CK 46779, mentions a last intriguing item: an August 1974 advertisement for a gospel concert with an "all star program, the greatest ever presented in Cleveland, including nat'l known Blind Pianist Arizona Dranes from Chicago, Ill."[13]

The record company seems to have been somewhat mystified by Dranes and her piano style. With some perspective, we can see that she was playing a sanctified version of the piano style variously known as "fast Western," "fast Texas," boogie woogie or barrelhouse. In its more secular incarnation, it had people shouting in places Arizona Dranes probably would never have entered.

[1] Sam Charters, liner notes to *The Complete Blind Willie Johnson*, Columbia 52835.

[2] David Evans, liner notes to Blind Willie Johnson, *Sweeter As the Years Go By*, Yazoo 1078.

[3] Charters.

[4] Ronald Clifford Foreman, "Jazz and Race Records, 1920–32," PhD dissertation, University of Illinois, 1968.

[5] Charters.

[6] Julius Walker, interview with Jay Brakefield, August 1, 1992.

[7] Label Feldman, interview with Jay Brakefield, May 20, 1992.

[8] Ken Romanowski, liner notes to *Arizona Dranes: Complete Recorded Works in Chronological Order 1926–1929*, (1993), Document DOCD-5186.

[9] Romanowski.

[10] Ken Romanowski, liner notes to *The Complete Recorded Works of Reverend F. W. McGhee in Chronological Order 1927–1929*, (1992), Document BDCD-6031.

[11] Malcolm Shaw, liner notes for *Arizona Dranes, 1926–1928*, Herwin Records, 210.

[12] Tony Heilbut, *The Gospel Sound: Good News and Bad Times*, New York, Simon and Schuster, 1971.

[13] Ray Funk, liner notes, *Preachin' the Gospel: Holy Blues*, Columbia Legacy, CK 46779.

9

··

Alex Moore and Dallas Piano Blues

The wide success and influence of Texas blues guitar styles has tended to obscure the importance of the piano. Yet blues historian Paul Oliver writes that Dallas produced a very distinctive style of piano blues, featuring lyrics full of allusions to the city and the trains that constantly passed through it:

> No other blues school, with the possible exception of Chicago, gives us such a picture of the urban life which inspired it. It could, of course, be coldly descriptive, sensational, or even sentimental, but the special quality of the Dallas tradition is its poetry. Here the piano is used as a complementary poetic instrument, setting off the words and the mood of the blues instead of challenging it with pyrotechnic displays.[1]

Oliver's thesis is backed up by discographies of the twenties and thirties, which suggest that there probably were as many blues pianists as guitarists in Dallas. Like their guitarist counterparts, blues pianists were usually solo performers, whose virtuosity and idiosyncratic styles made it difficult for other musicians to work with them. Blues piano, however, proved to be much less viable in the "Race" marketplace than down-home guitar blues, and no pianist attained the fame of a Lemon Jefferson. Consequently, there is less documentation of blues pianists. Much of what is known is anecdotal and is preserved to the greatest extent in the performance style of Alex Moore, whose career in Dallas spanned nearly seven decades.

Moore was born in North Dallas in 1899 and lived in the city until his death in 1989. He may not have been the best of the local piano men, but he certainly had the greatest longevity and was the best-documented. In his youth, he was one of many who played at Saturday night suppers and house-rent parties and in chock houses and cafes. As Moore said, in the 1920s "there was a piano in every shack in Deep Ellum, Elm Thicket [a black neighborhood near Love Field airport] and Froggy Bottom [near downtown Dallas and the Trinity River]."[2]

The settings in which Moore played parallel the origins of the music he performed. In the sawmill and turpentine camps of the late nineteenth and early twentieth centuries, black laborers lived apart from women in crude quarters and had little in the way of recreation. But the companies did provide entertainment by setting up "barrelhouses," shacks where liquor was served over a bar that typically consisted of a plank set on barrels. Here the workers could listen to music played on battered upright pianos by traveling musicians who developed a style sometimes called "fast Texas" or "fast Western" piano. However, within this general approach— which came to be known as "barrelhouse music"—there were distinct regional variations, even within the state of Texas. And as we have seen in the case of Arizona Dranes, it could be used in a spiritual as well as a secular setting.

Blues historians distinguish between the performance styles found in different areas of the state: the "Santa Fe group" who worked in Fort Bend County, the Thomas family from Houston, the pianists centered around Galveston, and those in Dallas and North Texas. Within those areas, the blues pianists demonstrated certain similarities in style and approach that reflected the environments in which they worked, their friendships and associations with other pianists and, in some instances, their isolation.[3]

Dallas pianists of the twenties included Neal Roberts, Willie Tyson, Lovey Bookman and Frank Ridge. Some of these musicians never recorded, and their names were kept alive only in the memory of survivors such as Moore, who passed them along to interviewers. Those who did record often sang the blues or provided accompaniment for women blues singers of the "classic" variety, the slow or medium-tempo music interacting in call and response with the vocal. Other instruments were seldom involved in these recordings, though Coley Jones did play guitar on some of Bill Day's sessions.

In "Frisco Blues," Roberts used gently rolling bass figures to evoke the distant train rhythms of the St. Louis-San Francisco line without resorting to mimicry. Similarly, Tyson in "Sun Beam" recreated the sounds of the "Sunshine Special" that ran during the day on the Texas-Pacific line. On this and other train songs, such as "Interurban Blues" about the electric line that brought country people to the city, Billiken Johnson whistled and added other effects that helped shape the mood of the song.

Johnson, who was considered a "clown" by his musician friends, frequently employed his "vocalizing" to accompany their piano playing and singing. On Bill Day's "Wild Jack Blues," Johnson provided a braying noise, while on his "Elm Street Blues," Johnson made vocal effects through what sounds like cupped hands—rather than using a kazoo or comb-and-paper—as a kind of bluesy response to the lyrics. In "Elm Street Blues," Day compared Elm Street to Main and commented on the women of ill repute:

Main Street's paved in gold.
Main Street's paved in gold.
I've got a good girl lives on East Commerce,
I wouldn't mistreat her to save nobody's soul.

The verse was followed by Johnson's vocal effects, to which Day in turn replied:

Oh, Billiken, Elm Street women
don't mean you no good.
(Repeat.)
When you turn your back
they're with every man in the neighborhood.

Ida May Mack, in her version of "Elm Street Blues," which was released a year earlier, used Elm Street as a metaphor for her unrequited love. She began the song by pleading, "Lord, have mercy," and then sang:

I woke up after midnight,
I took to walking my floor.
(Repeat)
Trying to find my daddy
and some place to go.
I walked up Elm
And then I went back up Main,
And the way that I cried,
Lord, was a dirty shame.

In the song, Mack was accompanied by pianist K. D. Johnson, whom she called "Forty-Nine," a name that appears to imply where she may have met him, since "Forty-Nine" was a slang term sometimes used for tent shows. Johnson's style of performance bears similarities to those of Day and others from Dallas, but it is also somewhat idiosyncratic in its emphasis and is perhaps reflective of the music performed in tent shows.

In 1928, Johnson was an accompanist not only for Ida May Mack, but also for Bessie Tucker on her recordings "Penitentiary" and "The Dummy." According to Moore, Tucker had in fact served time at a prison farm and sang about her personal experiences. In her songs, she also made reference to the railroads, especially the Fort Worth and Denver, the Santa Fe and "The Dummy," which was a traditional name for a logging company train.

The origins of these piano players and their musical training are largely unknown. Here again, we have Alex Moore, who recalled that he first heard pianos played in the white homes along Ross Avenue where he delivered groceries as a boy. "Every time I'd walk by, I'd pluck one note," he said, "and every day it would be a different note. That's the way I learned the piano."[4] During the 1920s, Moore, nicknamed "Papa Chitlins," was much in demand, going from his day job to playing till all hours in joints around town. He said that once, he didn't pull his clothes off for a week.[5]

Highly regarded among his contemporaries, Moore was one of the first to record. In 1929 he was recruited by Columbia and traveled to Chicago, where he recorded six sides, including "Blue Bloomer Blues," "Ice Pick Blues" and "West Texas Woman." But these recordings did not sell well, and he was unable to get his music issued on record again until 1937, when he recorded four sides for Decca and was accompanied by guitarist Blind Norris McHenry on two others.

On these records, Moore sang original compositions and accompanied himself by whistling, somewhat like Billiken Johnson, and got the nickname "Whistling" Alex Moore. His distinctive piano style included elements of ragtime, barrelhouse, boogie and blues and showed the influence of musicians he had heard on record, including Pete Johnson, Albert Ammons, Pinetop Smith and Meade Lux Lewis as well as local players.

In 1947, Moore was recorded at KLIF studios in Dallas, but only two sides were issued, "Miss No Good Weed" and "Dishwasher's

Blues." The latter selection may have been autobiographical, for Moore was never able to support himself through his music and worked at a variety of jobs, including dishwashing, driving mules to haul gravel and serving as a custodian and hotel porter. A photo shows him playing for dancers while still clad in the coat he wore to wash dishes. In the background is his boss, Walter E. Wilden, dancing with Mrs. Wilden. On the photo Moore inscribed his name, followed by the address where he was performing: "3817 Lem[m]on Avenue, playing at the Southern House, White Patrons Only." When asked about this particular occasion, Moore laughed, "He liked my playing so much he took me down to KLIF on that very day to record eight songs."[6]

In 1951, Moore made four sides for RPM Records. In 1960, blues researchers Paul Oliver and Chris Strachwitz found him on the screened porch of a small North Dallas bar and recorded him for Strachwitz's Arhoolie label. About these recordings, Oliver wrote:

> Alexander Moore had boundless ideas. Betraying hardly a hint of any influence from other singers, he played with great variety and sang in a throaty, husky voice. A man rich in worldly wisdom he was yet a man curiously limited in his knowledge of the world. Only once in his life had he left Texas; most of his life had been spent in a small section of Dallas. So, his blues reflected a very personal, singular view of life, and because he is an eccentric man his words are often unexpected and manifestly original. The immediate circumstances of his environment are reflected in "Going Back to Froggy Bottom" or "From North Dallas to the East Side," but his sharp eye and neat wit led to such highly unconventional blues lines as "Sack dress is all right but I'd rather see you in a pair of pants."
>
> Interspersed with his playing were reminiscences of playing at "Minnie's Tea Room" or of police raids

in district chock-houses; memories that would lead
him to new blues improvisations. He talked of the
years he had driven his horse and cart through the
streets of Dallas; years when life was wild and cheap
and money scarce—and broke into "Black-eyed Peas
and Hog Jowls." Such blues as "Rubber Tired Hack"
or "Miss No Good Weed" were spur of the moment
creations played and sung with feeling and pleasure
in his own music. His bass figures were varied and
intensely interesting and he took an off-beat pride
in sudden flashes of inventiveness and flurries of
right-hand creations. Then he doubled back his lip
and shrieked a piercing whistled blues by which he
had gained his name of Whistling Alex Moore but
which had in the past, as now, presented problems
in recording.[7]

In the mid-1960s, as a result of the Arhoolie recordings, Moore
was invited to perform at festivals in the United States and abroad.
In 1969, during a tour with the American Folk Blues Festival, he
did a session in Stuttgart, Germany, that resulted in the Arhoolie
album *Alex Moore in Europe.*

Moore never considered himself a full-time professional musician and kept working at his various trades until he retired in 1965.
From the sixties until his death, he played for a predominantly
white audience. In his later years, Alex Moore's style changed. His
performances became more autobiographical, his ramblings at the
piano more freestyle. He interspersed details from his life with
piano sounds that changed tempo with his mood. Short vocal passages were followed by long piano interludes in which the bass was
soft and steady and the right hand wandered unpredictably on
the keys. The tone was sometimes contemplative, sometimes thun-
derous and fast. Heartfelt blues gave way to ragtime, barrelhouse,
boogie and stride. Moore's approach was intuitive and took shape
in performance. He said he never knew exactly what he was going

to play until he played it. Throughout his career of more than six decades, he never owned a piano and said he never practiced or rehearsed.

His other passion was dominoes, which he played in his later years daily at the Martin Luther King Recreation Center in South Dallas. "I love to play dominoes," he said. "The music is always here when I get ready. I just go sit down at that piano and play it. That piano kind of plays itself. That's what I'm talking about. That's why nobody can play with me. They can write that stuff, blues, boogie, ragtime, that's me. I've always said that if I don't improve every night, then you don't owe me nothing, but they always paid me."[8]

Alex Moore's life spanned much of the history of blues and jazz, and his music represented a synthesis of a wide variety of styles. But Moore also was atypical in having a certain sensitivity. His lyrics could be bawdy, but as folklorist Mack McCormick said, "Unlike any other bluesman I've ever encountered, he had a romantic sense—that kind of gentleness, sense of romance. He was focused in the human condition—I think that's what made him unique."[9]

Moore was also a visual artist whose letters became keepsakes. Even the envelopes were artworks, embellished with colorful curliques and asides such as "Music, Maestro, Please." His humanity is embodied in the lyrics of his "Heart Wrecked Blues":

> Hatred is self-punishing.
> Forgiveness is better than revenge.
> There's no heart in buying love
> Or to lose and not to win.

Oliver described Moore as a "true original, a folk blues singer of the city who can sit at the piano and improvise endless piano themes and blues verses that are sometimes startling, sometimes comic, sometimes grim, and very often pure poetry."[10]

Near the end of his life, Moore received numerous accolades. In 1983, the mayor of Dallas declared June 17 "Alex 'Blues Artist'

Moore Day." His fellow senior citizens at the Martin Luther King Center voted him Senior Citizen of the Month, noting that "he was very easy to get along with, always cooperative in every way and everybody loves him. He sings, plays a whole lot of piano and sometimes he whistles."[11] In 1987, Moore was awarded the prestigious National Heritage Fellowship from the National Endowment for the Arts, and in December, 1988, one month before he died of a heart attack on a city bus, Moore received another mayoral proclamation in Dallas, recognizing his achievement in a concert honoring him at the Majestic Theatre, just across Harwood Street from historic Deep Ellum.[12]

Throughout his career, Moore lived in poverty. Over the course of his life, he moved from one low-income housing apartment to another, first in old North Dallas, which came to be known as the State-Thomas area, then in South Dallas and Oak Cliff. Shortly before his death, Moore, laughing, said that he couldn't afford apartments that cost more than $50 a month. When he died, he didn't have enough resources to cover the cost of his own funeral and burial. Nevertheless, he was laid to rest in style, wearing a suit with lapel pins proclaiming him a blues artist.

Moore was an exemplar of his generation who attributed his longevity to "clean living." In many ways, he typified the music of Deep Ellum and Dallas's black community in the 1920s and 1930s. Although his piano playing was essentially traditional, his performance style was idiosyncratic. He was a solo performer who defied accompanists and whose enduring legacy is in the limited recordings he made. The extent to which Moore exemplified a Dallas piano style was defined mostly by his associations with other pianists in his youth and by his isolation as an adult, having outlived his contemporaries by two or three decades. Ironically, Deep Ellum was the place where Moore began and ended his career. In the last few years of his life, like a few others of his generation, he was performing in newly renovated clubs in places he recalled from years before.

[1] Paul Oliver, *Blues Off the Record* (New York: Da Capo Press, Inc., 1988).

[2] Alex Moore, interview with Alan Govenar, April 9, 1982.

[3] Oliver.

[4] Alan Govenar, *Meeting the Blues* (Dallas: Taylor Publishing 1988), 31.

[5] Alex Moore, interview with Alan Govenar, November 5, 1988.

[6] Alex Moore, interview with Alan Govenar, November 8, 1988.

[7] Paul Oliver, notes to *Alex Moore: From North Dallas to the East Side,* Arhoolie CD 408, 1994.

[8] Govenar, *Meeting the Blues,* 32.

[9] Mack McCormick, interview with Jay Brakefield, July 1989.

[10] Oliver, *Blues Off the Record,* 217; Alex Moore, interview with Alan Govenar, November 5, 1988.

[11] Footage from this tribute became part of the documentary film, *Black on White/White and Black,* Documentary Arts, 1989. Documentary Arts also released the audio cassette *Alex Moore: Then and Now,* DA 105, which includes his 1947 KLIF recordings and those made by Alan Govenar in 1988 at El Centro College in Dallas. The KLIF recordings were re-mastered by Chris Strachwitz and released on the CD *Whistlin' Alex Moore: From North Dallas to the East Side* with the 1960 recordings made by Strachwitz and Paul Oliver.

[12] Oliver, *Meeting the Blues,* 32.

Alex Moore in Dallas, 1938. *Courtesy* Documentary Arts.

Alex Moore playing at the Southern House, a "White Patrons Only" club, 1947. Moore is still wearing his dishwasher's coat. The club's owner, Walter E. Wilden, is dancing with his wife in the background. *Courtesy* Documentary Arts.

Alex Moore, 1981. Photograph by Alan Govenar. *Courtesy* Alex Moore.

10

Buster Smith: Dallas Jazz Goes to Kansas City and New York

Dallas did not play as clear or dramatic a part in the development of jazz as it did in the blues. There is no single towering figure who was the obvious Dallas jazz counterpart to Blind Lemon Jefferson, yet in the mid- to late-1920s, in the words of jazz historian Ross Russell, Dallas was "the most important band town in Texas."[1] The city and the surrounding area produced a number of musicians who went on to play vital roles in swing and bebop: saxophonists Budd Johnson, Herschel Evans, Buddy Tate and Henry "Buster" Smith; trombonist Jack Teagarden; and electric guitar pioneer Charlie Christian, who was born in Bonham, in East Texas, and grew up in Oklahoma, but spent a great deal of time in Dallas.

Buster Smith, though he recorded little under his own name and never achieved national recognition, was the most significant of these. Russell called him "a Dallas man with roots in the urban blues, pioneer of the early barrelhouse bands in the city, self-taught musician unblooded in musical schools, master of an empirical method on alto saxophone, and major saxophone stylist."[2]

Smith was born in 1904 on a cotton farm in Ellis County, south of Dallas. This was Texas's blues country, the east-central area that produced Blind Lemon Jefferson and Blind Willie Johnson and, a bit later, Lightnin' Hopkins, Albert Collins and Johnny Copeland. As Smith said later, "The blues was all around when I was growing up." As a child, Smith played an old organ at home, but his first serious musical experience came when he was about eighteen, after his family had moved to Collin County, north of Dallas. He saw a $3.50 clarinet in a store in town and got permission from his mother to buy it if he picked 400 pounds of cotton daily for several days. A few months later, when the family moved to Dallas, he had become fairly proficient on the instrument.[3]

In Dallas, Smith found a vital music scene. "On Central Track, you could at times hear four different interpretations of the blues," Booker Pittman wrote of his boyhood. "They would drift from some of these fellows from Memphis, Georgia, Alabama, with their banjos and guitars, each telling a different story." A similar account came from Margaret Wright, a white woman, who recalled a childhood trip to Deep Ellum with her mother in 1924:

> I was born in Dallas, and as a small child, I can remember an occasion when my mother took me walking down Elm Street, across Central Tracks, and on to wherever an errand carried her. My mother was a tall, stately woman and was always treated with the utmost respect, no matter what the surroundings. On this day, I remember holding tightly to her hand. I was really frightened. There was certainly no need to be, but I was out of familiar surroundings. As we walked down the street near the Central Tracks, loud music could be heard up and down the streets. Black musicians seemed to be in every store and "joint."

Blues and jazz players were everywhere. At that time, I had never seen so many black people. One thing I distinctly remember, every black man who was on the sidewalk, stepped back, took off his hat, and bowed slightly when my mother passed.[4]

In addition to street singers such as Jefferson, who performed alone, there were groups such as Coley Jones's Dallas String Band, which included Marco Washington, a versatile musician whose stepson was Aaron "T-Bone" Walker, born in 1910. The whole family, including Walker's mother, was musical, and they organized a band that played for money on the streets on weekends. The instrumentation included bass, guitars, fiddles, mandolins and homemade instruments. Sometimes Jesse Hooker joined in on sax and clarinet. Like other street bands, they played both blues and popular tunes to satisfy a diverse audience, white and black. "I couldn't play good then, but I had learned to dance," Walker said later. "I learned splits and spins. That's what put change in the kitty most times. When I got older, maybe twelve, I could play the ukulele, and I worked up an act. I would sing anything they asked. I entertained at church picnics and at Riverside Park."[5]

Jazz was being played in Dallas as well, indoors and out. Brass bands played in parks and in "colored carnivals." They were even used in funerals to some extent. A 1925 *Dallas Morning News* article recalled a black funeral procession with a brass band coming up South Lamar Street. In these and other ways the music reflected the influence of New Orleans, whose jazz was a marching music, collectively improvised into a dense tapestry of intertwining melodies—in musical terms, it used polyphony, or counterpoint. A number of New Orleans musicians played in Dallas, too, as they fanned out across the country following the closing of the Storyville red light district in 1917. Booker Pittman recalled being inspired to take up clarinet by hearing Kid Ory in Dallas. He bought his first instrument from a bearded Jewish pawnbroker in Deep Ellum for $3.

Despite the New Orleans presence, Dallas had its own musical identity. Don Albert put it this way:

> The rhythm was especially the thing that was different from New Orleans. The drums used a silent beat . . . and the sustained beat which was different with the big bands in Texas. The drummers would read in parts and consequently they got off of the rhythm a little bit and came back to it, which the New Orleans drummers didn't do.[6]

As Buster Smith said:

> We didn't hear as much about New Orleans in those days as we did a little later on. We called that kind of music gutbucket or barrelhouse. The trumpet players and clarinet players concentrated on that. I'll tell you, a lot of it started around here on these medicine shows. We used to have them all over town, and that's where it started. A medicine show used to have four or five pieces: trombone, clarinet, trumpet and a drummer, and every man blowing for himself as loud as he could blow to attract a crowd for the "doctor." Then there would be a couple of comedians clowning a little bit, then the doc would have the boys blow again to attract another crowd after he'd sold the first crowd. He'd sell them this patent medicine—good for anything—at a dollar or a dollar-fifty a bottle, and the comedians would go through the crowd selling it. Then the boys would get up and blow again to attract another bunch of suckers. That's how all that jazz started down in these parts. They tried to get me on one of those things in 1922, but I didn't go.[7]

T-Bone Walker, did, though; he spent a summer during his youth working for Dr. Breeding's medicine show.

Smith found steady work in Dallas: "I got playing around with a little three-piece band—Voddie White. Voddie played piano. I played clarinet, and [we had] a drummer—I forget his name. We played around town at a few places and at Saturday night suppers and that sort of thing. That was around 1923 and 1924." Around this time, too, Smith became acquainted with the alto sax. That nameless drummer gave him an old horn he'd given up on playing. "It was so old it was turning green," Smith recalled. "Anyway, I cleaned it up and learned it in three days."[8]

Of the Dallas scene, Smith said:

> T-Bone Walker was around; he used to dance where I played down on the Central Track. He wasn't singing much then, just dancing. Sammy Price was down there, too. He was a dancer too, at first. Of course there were a lot of bands around here, too. Alphonso Trent, Jap Allen, T. (Terrence) Holder, George E. Lee. They all made a circuit around here from Kansas City, Oklahoma City, Houston, Dallas, San Antonio and a lot of the smaller towns, too. We had two bands here as good as you could find anywhere: Troy Floyd and Alphonso Trent. In 1928, Trent was playing at the Adolphus Hotel. Another band was Fred Cooper's. And then there was Carl Murphy's little seven-piece band. They called themselves the Satisfied Five or something like that when they first started out. They played at the Adolphus Hotel evenings, and Trent played there later in the night. Then there were any number of four- and five-piece bands playing around the roadhouses and after-hours spots. Trent and Floyd were the big bands and did most of the traveling."[9]

Smith's words are echoed by Ross Russell, who wrote that Trent's band had "the greatest success ever achieved by any band, black or white, in the city."[10] And Budd Johnson said, "Let me tell you about Trent; that was the greatest band I'd ever heard! They used to thrill me. They were gods back in the twenties, just like Basie was later, only many years ahead of him. Nobody else had gold instruments in those days; his whole band had them! They made $150 a week a man. Imagine! They worked nothing but the biggest and finest hotels in the South."[11] Trent's band may not be remembered because its only recording sessions were done while on the road in 1928 and 1933, and apparently fell far short of what it played for live audiences.

Though some black musicians played for white audiences in the big hotels, many played exclusively for black audiences in areas such as Deep Ellum. "Man, Deep Ellum was wide open," Buster Smith said. "You could see everybody you knew in Deep Ellum; they'd hang out by the railroad tracks and listen at the medicine shows, and then go to the Tip Top. It was the most popular place down there. . . . There were other places, but the Tip Top was the most popular because they used the biggest bands."[12] That was where Smith heard Hooker, whom he called "an awful good clarinet player. . . . He couldn't read [music] either. I'd go down there and listen to him till he moved on. This was in 1922."[13]

In 1925, apparently while playing at the Tip Top, Buster Smith was hired by the Blue Devils, a highly regarded territory band headquartered in Oklahoma City. The leader was Walter "Big 'Un" Page, a versatile musician who played tuba, string bass and baritone sax. The Blue Devils, formed in 1923, included at one time or another many of the top musicians of the time, including a number of Texans: Dallas trumpet player and vocalist Oran "Hot Lips" Page (no relation to Walter Page); trombonist Dan Minor of Dallas; singer Jimmy Rushing of Oklahoma City; trombonist, guitarist and arranger Eddie Durham, originally from San Marcos, Texas, near San Antonio; pianist Bill (later Count) Basie; and, late in the Devils's career, alto sax player Don Byas and Mississippi-born tenor player Lester Young.

Basie opens his autobiography with a description of his first encounter with the Blue Devils, in Tulsa in 1927. The band, playing outside ("ballyhooing") to advertise a dance that night, awakened him after a rough night: "I forgot all about my hangover and about catching up on my sleep. I just wanted to hear those guys play some more. . . . Everything about them got to me, and as things worked out, hearing them that day was probably the most important turning point in my musical career so far as notions about what kind of music I really wanted to play was concerned." The Blue Devils was the first big band he had heard, Basie said, "and it was the greatest thing I had ever heard. I had never heard the blues played like that. . . . Not that the Blue Devils were just playing the blues. They were not really playing all that much blues that night. But they were still bluesy. But the main thing about that band was that they had their own special way of playing everything."[14] Basie was determined to join the band, and he did, a bit later in Oklahoma City.

He didn't stay long; in fact, he had moved to Bennie Moten's band by the time the Devils made their only recording, in November 1929. One side of that record is "Blue Devil Blues," a fairly conventional blues with a Rushing vocal. As Basie says, even in his early days, the Oklahoma-born singer had a very distinctive style. The other side, the instrumental "Squabblin'," is more interesting from a musical standpoint. It marks an interesting transition between early New Orleans jazz and swing. The piece is in march time, 2/4, but it definitely swings, looking forward to the looser, more flexible Kansas City 4/4. Smith's alto work is light and flowing; as Budd Johnson said, Smith was already playing in his "lope-along style."[15] The banjo and tuba, hallmarks of New Orleans music, were gone. Walter Page had switched to string bass.

By the time they made their record, the Blue Devils were facing the end of their road. Moten had begun raiding the band at the urging of Basie and Durham. Even Walter Page finally made the move, though he was nominally the Devils's leader. The group was a "commonwealth" band in which all the money was split equally and everyone had an equal vote. This may have contributed to the camaraderie Basie found so appealing; but as Smith noted, it also figured in bad decisions such as turning down a radio date with Fats Waller because a slim majority of the musicians thought he wasn't offering enough money. When Walter Page left, Smith took over leadership of the Blue Devils, which continued to attract good musicians.

But the country was in the depths of the Great Depression, and times were tough for bands. The Blue Devils broke up in 1933 after being stiffed by a promoter and stranded in Binkley, West Virginia. The musicians couldn't pay their bills, so the sheriff impounded their instruments and locked them in the jail. Some of the band members "hoboed back home," as Smith said, but he and others joined Moten, who sent a car to pick them up. Moten was based in Kansas City, where the musicians found a scene that Smith characterized as "like Dallas used to be, only more so."[16] Fueled by money from the corrupt Tom Pendergrass regime, the city jumped twenty-four hours a day, with clubs that offered jazz and earthier pleasures, including live sex shows in some cases. Big Joe Turner held forth as a singing bartender in Piney Brown's Sunset Club on Vine, sometimes wandering into the street in full cry, often improvising lyrics on the spot.

Moten's band came to an end with his death in 1935 following surgery. He was just thirty-four years old. His brother Ira "Buster" Moten tried to keep the band together, but proved too hotheaded. Smith and Basie formed a band called the Barons of Rhythm that included Hot Lips Page and Durham. By this time, Smith had taught himself to read music and had become a skillful arranger. Because of his scholarly appearance and total immersion in his music, he became known as "Prof" to his fellow musicians. "He'd be up there on the bandstand blowing for all he was worth," Kansas City pianist and band leader Jay McShann recalled. "He'd get into the number so much, you know, totally involved, and his eyeglasses would slip down to the end of his nose. The guys used to look at him and say, 'Hey, don't he look like some absent-minded professor standing up there?' And then somebody piped up and yelled 'Prof' at Buster. From that time on we called him Prof."[17]

According to several accounts, Basie's theme song, "One O'Clock Jump," resulted from a session involving Smith, "Lips" Page, Durham and Basie. Smith set the riff, the recurring musical figure on which the tune is based, then wrote the arrangement that Basie made famous. Unfortunately for Smith, he failed to copyright it. The song was retitled after the original name, "Blue Ball," was deemed too racy for a radio broadcast. Basie's band, of course, went on to world fame—but without Buster Smith, who left just before the group was discovered—moved to New York and was given national radio airplay by John Hammond of Columbia Records. The Basie band sound, which came to embody hot swingband music, fused the influences of the Blue Devils and Moten. As Basie's longtime drummer Jo Jones said, "When Bennie Moten's two-beat, one-and-three rhythm [that is, the stress on the first and third beats] and the two-and-four of Walter Page's Blue Devils came together in the Basie band, there was an even flow, one, two, three, four. . . ."[18]

Smith started his own band, which included a teenage alto player named Charlie Parker. "Well, he used to tell me he wanted to play like me," Smith said. "He used to call me his dad, and I called him my boy. I couldn't get rid of him. He was always up under me. . . . He did play like me quite a bit, I guess. But after awhile, anything I could make on my horn, he could make too, and make something better out of it. We used to do that double-time stuff all the time. I used to do a lot of that on clarinet. Then I started doing it on alto, and Charlie heard me doing it, and he started playing it. . . ."[19]

In the early forties, Smith tired of life on the road and returned to Dallas, where he continued to lead bands that played in Texas and neighboring states. He made a living from music while enjoying a home life and finding time for his hobbies, fishing and working on cars. Though he disappeared from the national scene, he remained a vital musical force. He played the 1942 opening engagement at the Rose Room, a prime nightspot in North Dallas, and played there regularly for years. T-Bone Walker and other noted figures sometimes sat in with his bands. Smith made his only recording under his own name in 1959, when musicologist and composer Gunther Schuller came to Dallas and tracked down the leader and his musicians for an album on Atlantic. The album is long out of print. Listeners who secure one of the taped copies circulated among aficionados hear what Ray Charles called "some of the filthiest alto around,"[20] a loping, fluid, imaginative style.

It's not hard to see why Charlie Parker regarded Buster Smith as his musical father. As writer Nathan W. Pearson said, Smith "strongly influenced Charlie Parker by stretching the harmonic dimensions of the alto saxophone and using a lightning-fast 'dancing' style that anticipated and influenced Parker's."[21] An interesting perspective comes from Jay McShann, who said, "I don't think anybody ever knew just how much alto Buster could play. I don't think Buster ever found out, himself, how far he could go."[22]

Basie and other old friends visited Smith when they played Dallas, but he never saw Parker again. "Bird" died in 1955, thirty-four years old, ravaged by alcoholism and heroin addiction and other personal demons. "Charlie came down, too, one time, but I missed him," Smith said. "He was here for a couple of days with Stan Kenton. . . . It was just a little while before Charlie died. I didn't even hear about them being here till they were already gone. They told me Charlie was looking for me up on Hall Street. I went on up there, but he was gone."[23]

Smith's early influence, Jesse Hooker, recorded in Dallas in the late 1920s. He played clarinet on blues singer and harmonica player William McCoy's "Out of Doors Blues." And he is listed as vocalist on Frenchy's String Band's recording of "Sunshine Special" a blues about a fast daytime Texas & Pacific train:

> That mean TP Railroad sure have done me wrong.
> That mean TP Railway sure have done me wrong.
> It let that Sunshine Special carry my good gal from
> home.

The blues come down like showers of rain.
I can see nothing but smoke from that train.
Every time I hear that Sunshine Special blow,
Every time I hear that Sunshine Special blow,
It makes me want to pack up all my clothes and go.

Hooker's life illustrated the overlapping of blues and jazz. He moved to Fort Worth about 1930 and lived there until he died around 1950. He played for a time in a street band led by Jesse Thomas, brother of blues singer Willard Ramblin' Thomas. Apparently Hooker quit performing in his later years, perhaps influenced by his wife, Birdie, a churchgoer who didn't want him playing the "devil's music." A former neighbor remembers him as a medium-sized, medium-complexioned, round-shouldered man who would sometimes sit on the back steps and play one of his horns or a tambourine.

Sammy Price, too, left Dallas in the twenties. Bert Goldberg, manager of Alphonso Trent's orchestra, accompanied Trent to a dance in the black community and saw Price dancing the Charleston, surrounded by an attentive crowd. They asked him to join the band as a dancer, and Price "jumped at the chance." He toured and recorded widely and lived the remainder of his life in New York. In his later years, he returned to Dallas several times, playing and reminiscing for local audiences. Herbie Cowens, who became known as "Kat," left town with Cleo Mitchell's Shake Your Feet vaudeville company and performed with such stars as Buck and Bubbles, "Stuff" Smith, Eubie Blake and Fletcher Henderson. After a number of years playing UFO shows, Cowens retired and returned to Dallas.

Booker Pittman made records with bands led by Lucky Millinder and Cab Calloway's sister Blanche Calloway. Pittman played alto sax and sang in a raspy voice somewhat similar to Louis Armstrong's. He spent the last twenty years of his life in Brazil, where he became very popular and often performed on television with his daughter Eliana, a well-known singer in her own right. He died in 1969.

Budd Johnson remained musically active almost until his death in 1984. His importance as a jazz figure is often overlooked, possibly because he seldom led his own bands. He was a common thread linking the large bands of the early and mid-1940s that were involved in the transition from swing to bebop: those of Earl Hines, Boyd Raeburn, Billy Eckstine, Woody Herman and Dizzy Gillespie. Johnson wrote music for all these bands and played tenor sax in live performance or on records with all but Raeburn's. Johnson organized the first bop record date, a 1944 Coleman Hawkins session featuring Gillespie. That same year, he played in the first small bop combo, with Gillespie and Oscar Pettiford, at the Onyx Club on 52nd Street. Jazz historian Dave Oliphant said Johnson played tenor like Lester Young and alto like Charlie Parker before he had met or heard either.

Eddie Durham became an important arranger for Basie and other bandleaders. According to one story, he received $5 from Glenn Miller for his arrangement of "In the Mood," which became a huge hit for Miller.[24] Durham was also a mentor to Charlie Christian, who became one of the first black musicians with a major white band when Benny Goodman hired him at the urging of his brother-in-law, John Hammond. Christian, probably the first electric jazz guitarist, took part in late night jam sessions in the early 1940s that were the leading edge of bebop. Had he not died of pneumonia at age twenty-four in 1942, Christian would have taken part in the postwar jazz revolution with Johnson, Miles Davis, Dizzy Gillespie, Charlie Parker and others.

Buster Smith quit playing sax after extensive dental work in 1959, not long after his Atlantic session. He taught himself electric bass, but by the early 1970s he had stopped playing professionally and was roofing houses with his brother, pianist Boston Smith. Smith remained well-known among Dallas musicians, however, and became a mentor to such figures as David "Fathead" Newman, who played tenor sax with Ray Charles for a number of years. Rediscovered by Alan Govenar in the 1980s, Smith organized a band named after one of his earlier outfits, the Heat Waves of Swing. It included

Boston Smith, Cowens and trumpet player Benny "Chops" Arredando. They played at several of Govenar's Dallas Folklife Festivals, and some of these performances were recorded and released by Documentary Arts. Smith was also featured, along with Basie, Budd Johnson and others, in the 1977 documentary film *The Last of the Blue Devils.*

By the last phase of Smith's career, the Deep Ellum of his youth was long gone. The building that had housed the Tip Top was torn down in 1968. An article in *The Dallas Morning News* reviewed the building's days as a hotel, but said nothing of its more recent history as a dance hall. In a sense, though, Smith must have felt that he had come full circle.

---

[1] Ross Russell, *Jazz Style in Kansas City and the Southwest* (Berkeley: University of California Press, 1971), 59.

[2] Russell, 74.

[3] For more information, see Alan Govenar, "Buster Smith: Dallas Jazz Patriarch," *Parkway* (April 1983): 28–31, and Alan Govenar, *Meeting the Blues* (Dallas: Taylor Publishing, 1988), 38–41.

[4] Margaret Wright of Greenville, Texas, letter to Alan Govenar, March 20, 1992.

[5] Helen Oakley Dance, *Stormy Monday: The T-Bone Walker Story* (New York: Da Capo Press, 1990), 12.

[6] Nathan W. Pearson, Jr., *Goin' to Kansas City* (Urbana: University of Illinois Press, 1987), 29.

[7] Don Gazzaway, "Conversations with Buster Smith," *Jazz Review* (December 1959), 20.

[8] Gazzaway, 20.

[9] Ibid.

[10] Russell, 61.

[11] Frank Driggs, "Budd Johnson, Ageless Jazzman," *Jazz Review* (November 1960).

[12] Tim Schuller, "The Buster Smith Story," CODA (December–January 1987–88), 4–5.

[13] Gazzaway, 20.

[14] Count Basie as told to Albert Murray, *Good Morning Blues* (New York: Random House, 1985), 3–8.

[15] Driggs, 4.

[16] Don Gazzaway, "Conversations with Buster Smith," Part 2, *Jazz Review* (January 1960), 11.

[17] Mary Lee Hester, "Texas Jazz Heritage," *Texas Jazz* (June 1979), 3.

[18] Count Basie, 170.

[19] Gazzaway, Part 2, 14.

[20] Ray Charles and David Ritz, *Brother Ray: Ray Charles' Own Story* (New York: The Dial Press, 1978), 147.

[21] Pearson, 197.

[22] Hester, 4.

[23] Don Gazzaway, "Conversations with Buster Smith," Part 3, *Jazz Review* (February 1960), 16.

[24] Gunther Schuller, *The Swing Era: The Development of Jazz, 1930–1945* (New York: Oxford University Press, 1989), 675.

Henry "Buster" Smith with an unidentified band in Dallas, ca. 1940s. *Courtesy* Texas African American Photography Archive.

Henry "Buster" Smith in South Dallas, ca. 1981. Photograph by Alan Govenar.

Ad for Herbert Cowens's band, date unknown. *Courtesy* Documentary Arts.

L–R, Herbert Cowens, Sam Price, and an unidentified friend at the Dallas Folk Festival, 1991. Photograph by Alan Govenar.

Marvin Montgomery: Country Crossover

While Blind Lemon Jefferson and Buster Smith are generally acknowleged as seminal figures, Marvin "Smokey" Montgomery is not. The standard works on the history of country music fail to acknowledge Montgomery's importance as a musician and his contribution to the Dallas/Fort Worth area.[1] This is due in part to the style of banjo that he performed. Clearly, the five-stringed Appalachian banjo has been studied far more than the four-stringed tenor that Montgomery and some of his contemporaries played. As an instrument, the tenor banjo has not been recognized for its importance in the crossover of white and black musical styles. Tenor banjo was used in the rhythm sections of early country, classic blues and New Orleans-style jazz.

As a musician, Montgomery touches on all the musical diversity that Deep Ellum has come to represent. He performed in professional tent and vaudeville shows and western swing bands, as well as in numerous Dixieland jazz groups over the years. Stylistically, Montgomery is completely eclectic, integrating elements of black and white minstrelsy, popular songs, and show tunes with strains of traditional country, jazz, and blues.

Montgomery came to Dallas in December 1934 on his way home to Rinard, Iowa. He had been earning $11 a week with the J. Doug Morgan-Neale Helvey tent show and had managed to save $30 over a year and a half—but when he got to Union Station he realized he didn't have enough cash to make it all the way back home. "It was three or four in the morning," he recalled, "and I stayed there at the station. I curled up on one of those benches until about six o'clock. And then I went looking for the Adolphus Hotel, where I knew that Blackie Simmons and his Blue Jackets had a radio show on KRLD." He continued:

> When I got there the band was rehearsing, and I introduced myself as a musician. So, they let me listen, and then after a while one of them handed me one of their guitars and I strummed aound on it. That's when Blackie said, "You lookin' for a job?" And I answered "Yes," and he told me that Mrs. Davis, the manager of KRLD, was looking for a guitarist to play with the piano player that night. Well, I went and talked to Mrs. Davis and she said the job paid $3 which I thought was great, but I needed it in advance to get my guitar, banjo and suitcase out of the baggage check at Union Station and find a hotel room.[2]

Mrs. Davis was sympathetic, and Montgomery set off to get ready for his first job in Dallas. He found a hotel room on Elm Street near the Majestic Theatre and on the edge of Deep Ellum. Thinking back, Montgomery said, "The hotel must have been a house of ill repute—when I'd practice my banjo, I'd sit on the edge of the bed and these gals would stick their head in the door and listen, but they were wearing these fancy, black see-through type things and I eventually caught on."[3]

But on that first night in Dallas, Montgomery didn't know exactly what to think. The piano player picked him up in front of the hotel and took him to the Dallas Country Club to play at a stag party, where a "gal took off everything" and he thought, "Boy, this is the wildest town I've ever seen."[4]

As it turned out, the pianist—whose name Montgomery has since forgotten—told him that the Wanderers, a hot fiddle band which performed on WFAA radio in the Baker Hotel across from the Adolphus, was looking for a banjo player. "Well," Montgomery said, "I went to talk to the Wanderers and got the job. They tried me out on a dance they were doing in Kilgore, Texas, and paid me $12 for the night. And I had only made $11 a week on the tent show."[5]

The Helvey-Morgan tent show which Montgomery had previously been involved with was based in Jacksonville, Texas, and toured into the Midwest during the summer months, traveling through Iowa, Illinois and Missouri before returning. At the time he joined the tent show, Montgomery, whose real name is Marvin Dooley Wetter, had just finished the spring semester of his sophomore year at Iowa State College, where he was majoring in industrial arts with the hope of becoming a school teacher. His mother, Mabel Wetter, had wanted him to become a Methodist preacher, but he said he got side-tracked: "I entered a talent show at the tent show and you only played one song, 'The World is Waiting for the Sunrise.' I imitated two banjos at once. I played the lead on the A string and the rhythm part on the other three strings, and I won second prize. Three dollars. Well, they took down my name and in about three weeks they wired me a telegram and asked me to join them."

It was during the Great Depression; jobs were scarce, and Montgomery seized the opportunity.

The tent show usually had a three-act play like "My Wild Irish Rose"—they had maybe seven people in the crew and about ten actors and actresses. And I'd play as part of the vaudeville orchestra twenty or thirty minutes before the show and during intermission. They had a five- to seven-piece band: saxophone, trumpet, piano, drums and two banjos. Sometimes I'd play solos; other times I'd follow the midget King Rector, who played the xylophone and tap-danced.

Neale Helvey, who was co-owner of the show, played piano in the vaudeville orchestra and was a real showman. And he didn't like my real name: "Wetter." He'd say to me, "One day your name will be in lights and we have to give you a better name than that." And I said, "Well, I liked the name Robert Montgomery," and he said "Okay, we'll call you Marvin Montgomery" and that's the name I've kept ever since.[6]

In the tent show, Montgomery was able to expand his repertoire but also had the chance to play a lot of the popular tunes he already knew. Born in 1913, he had started playing the banjo ukulele at age nine. His mother played the piano, and whenever she went to Fort Dodge, said Montgomery:

she'd bring back two or three new songs and the sheet music would have ukulele chords. Then she bought a $10 banjo for my younger brother and he didn't do anything with it. So, I picked it up and tuned it like a ukulele and played it in that style.

Then one night outside a dance I saw this banjo player from St. Paul playing and he was doing different fingering than what I knew. And when he came out to smoke a cigarette during his break, I asked him and he said it was called tenor banjo style. Next day, I ordered a chord book from Sears and Roebuck and I learned that style and have been playing ever since.[7]

When he was a teenager, Montgomery and his mother played together in a small dance band called the Iowa Orioles. His father, Charlie Wetter, was an alcoholic gambler. His parents divorced when he was thirteen, and Montgomery had to help support the family.

My mother played piano and I played banjo and sometimes drums and sometimes both. And we had a guy named Dick Danson who played drums and sang a lot with a megaphone. Farlow Matice was the sax player, and we'd play two round dances, then maybe a waltz and then we'd have to have a square dance. For the square dance we'd need a fiddler and that fiddler was Charlie Hogan, who was the foreman of a section gang on the railroad during the day. Charlie Hogan was a good fiddler. He was the head cat on the breakdowns and waltzes.

We played all the popular songs of the twenties. "That's My Weakness Now," "The Waltz You Saved for Me," "Five-Foot Two," "Ain't She Sweet" and others. That's the way we did it, round and round, all night long, no curfew. You played till two or three o'clock in the morning sometimes. I'd get back just in time to go to school.[8]

Given the experience with his family dance band and the rigors of the tent show, Montgomery was able to easily adapt to the busy schedule of dances and radio broadcasts that he played in Dallas and East Texas with the Wanderers. Dick Reinhart, the guitar player for the Wanderers, became his close friend. After a week of staying in a hotel on Elm Street, Montgomery moved to a room in South Dallas, on Holmes Street, where Reinhart and his wife had an apartment. In the spring of 1935, Montgomery returned to Iowa and moved his mother and sister to Dallas. "I got my old Model A and drove it to Texas. My grandfather had taken care of it when I was gone on the tent show. He jacked it up and stored it in an old corn crib." In Dallas, Montgomery rented an additional bedroom and kitchen in the house where he lived, to accommodate his mother and sister. Later, they moved to a duplex in Trinity Heights, south of Oak Cliff, and he rode the streetcar back and forth to the Baker Hotel for the daily broadcasts of the Wanderers.

During this period, Montgomery remembers going to Deep Ellum after hours with Reinhart. In fact, it was in Deep Ellum that Montgomery was introduced to African-American downhome blues.

> Dick would say, "Come on, let's go down Elm Street." He'd name a place. I don't remember what the names were. But he'd take his guitar, and I'd listen and watch them play. We'd be the only white people in there . . . on Elm Street on down past the Majestic Theatre. . . . It was on ground level, and you'd just walk in. These guys knew Dick, and when he'd come in they'd wave him over and he'd take his guitar.
>
> Mostly, it was a drinking place. . . . I don't remember any food; they probably had it. Some of them would get out there and kinda dance. Seems like there always was a little square where they could do a little dancing. They didn't have a stage. They'd be sitting on the floor in a corner of the building or at one end of it. Usually, there were just one or two guys, a guitar player, maybe a mouth organ.
>
> One of them might pick up a bottle or something. They all do that now, but that's the thing that

amazed me. I was seeing things I'd never seen before . . . it was a kind of slide. They'd lay the guitar
down flat in their lap and take that slide up and
down [the neck]. They'd have an old six-string guitar all beat up and scratched up. I never did see a
real good instrument.[9]

Montgomery remembers that some of the songs Reinhart
played in Deep Ellum were also tunes that he brought back to the
Wanderers. "Dick was the only one I knew who really picked up
their songs and learned them. If he had made a record by himself
on guitar, you'd probably think he was a black guy. He'd do 'Matchbox Blues,' and 'Gulf Coast Blues.' Others, we'd play at dances—
'Trouble in Mind,' 'Sitting on Top of the World.'"

In characterizing the sound of the Wanderers, Montgomery
said the group was mainly a "hot fiddle band. . . . We'd turn it
loose on the first chorus. . . . That's the reason we played so many
blues. The blues format, you know, the three-chord thing, it's easy
to follow, and there's always a hot chorus or two." He explained
further:

The hokum is when you play the hot chorus. You're
playing your own thing against the chords that are
laid down by the tune. That's hokum. Uncle Art
[Satherly] used to call it "noodle"; he'd say "noodle
on the bridge" or something. We'd improvise on
the melody and the chords, follow the chord pro-
gression. You'd lose the melody a lot of times. A lot
of these guys had about three or four licks, as they
called them, and after that they played one or two
choruses, they'd play every lick that they knew and
they had to use them over on all the tunes. And on
a lot of these tunes, if you didn't hear the first chorus, you didn't know what they were playing.[10]

In October of 1935, Montgomery, Reinhart and Bert Dodson left the Wanderers to work for the Light Crust Doughboys, which played less "dance music" and more "listening music." Said Montgomery, "We had a strong dance beat with the Wanderers, but with the Doughboys, we played two or three hymns a week, cowboy songs and the slow waltzes: 'Home on the Range,' 'Red River Valley' and a lot of tunes written by the Sons of the Pioneers."[11]

When Montgomery joined the Doughboys, his banjo playing changed somewhat. With the Wanderers, he had played primarily rhythm, while with the Doughboys, he started to play solo. In describing his approach to the banjo, Montgomery said, "I tuned my banjo like a viola and fingered it the same as a violin, only it was pitched a fifth lower. This came out so vaudeville musicians could switch from violin to banjo. When Dixieland jazz got popular in the 1920s and earlier, a lot of fiddle players began to lose their jobs and they started playing the banjo."

In assessing the differences between black and white tenor banjo players, Montgomery said,

> they played the rhythm the same way as I do. I probably copied them by listening to records I heard growing up. We had one of them hand-crank 78 players in Iowa; it was a portable that I took along on the tent show in my suitcase. As far as I can remember, the black banjo players didn't really solo for more than four bars, nothing like Eddie Peabody or Harry Reser, who played in the vaudeville show. Harry Reser was the guy I really tried to copy playing solo. "The World is Waiting for the Sunrise" I learned from Eddie Peabody. Harry Reser had a radio show band called the Kliko Club Eskimos.
>
> When I solo with the tenor banjo, I use a combination of single strings and chords: "Bells of St. Mary," "Tiger Rag," "Sweet Georgia Brown." A lot of the songs the old Dixieland bands played adapted

themselves well to banjo solos. I'm credited for introducing Dixieland banjo to western swing.[12]

In addition to the Dixieland style evident in Montgomery's banjo playing, the Doughboys had other musicians who were also influenced by African-American music, most notably guitarist Reinhart, fiddlers Gross and Dodson, and pianist John "Knocky" Parker. Gross and Dodson, though proficient musicians themselves, essentially followed the swing style of Bob Wills, while Knocky Parker was more of an innovator. Montgomery recalled meeting Parker in 1934. "He played with Blackie Simmons, and I knew he was good. He was running across the street from the Adolphus Hotel to the Baker, where the Doughboys broadcast, and got struck by a car. Didn't hurt him very bad. I was there. That's where I got acquainted with him, and I'm responsible for him playing with the Doughboys."[13]

Parker started playing piano when he was four, while growing up near Palmer, Texas, south of Dallas, but never really learned to read music very well. He said his first teachers were the black musicians he met when he accompanied his father to Dallas between 1925 and 1928.

> Daddy would go there searching for musicians to come work in the cotton fields. . . . We'd go over there in Deep Ellum. . . . He'd go to all kinds of places. Sometimes the place he'd go to would have a piano, and I'd start playing. . . . They'd call up all of the people around at these Negro [places] . . . all kinds of, sometimes disreputable places, in degree at least, and people would come with their homemade instruments. A lot of guitarists, especially. . . . I remember they would come there and we'd play together. The pianists, too, would sit down, would play four hands on the piano, and shift your hand, so there'd be my left hand, his left hand, my right

hand, his right; and move all over the piano, playing all kinds of ways and variations. I'd try to copy everything they did, you see, and they liked this very much. They would laugh and show me everything they played. This is how, then, I learned from them. They were my first teachers. Terrific musicians, really. . . . They got to where they would look forward to my coming up there. Blind Lemon I met one time up there. . . . They saw that I liked them, and there was never any feeling of black and white at all. Never involved, which is kind of strange. Sometimes I stayed behind the bar in the back room, or somewhere, and go to sleep. Daddy would go off, doing some kind of business. . . . One time when there was some kind of a fight, some of the people would hustle me out of there. They sort of took care of me.[14]

Parker described the pianists' music as "very much like the later Chicago barrelhouse idiom. . . . Close to fundamental boogie woogie. Not in the complicated forms of Pine Top [Smith]. But earlier, like the Cow Cow [Davenport] school. . . . A lot of times, they would get on one note and repeat it for a long time, up high or low. . . . A whole lot of that." He described the music as "kind of stripped . . . bare."[15]

Montgomery said that by the time they met, Parker "was a very good piano player. He liked the blues. When we were with the Doughboys, he'd get those old Bob Crosby records and Dixieland things and bring them in. I'd transcribe them and we'd do them with the Doughboys. Two fiddles and guitar playing the lead—songs like 'South Rampart Street Parade' and all those 'Bourbon Street Blues.'" He further described the band's playing style:

Knocky played things like "Honky Tonk Train," which is on the blues, and all those things the black piano players were doing. Knocky could play them just as good as they could, and we played them on the air. We recorded them. All the boogie-woogie and blues things. Knocky could play stride and a variety of other styles. We did "Dallas Blues," "Beale Street Mama," "Memphis Blues," of course, "St. Louis Blues." All the fiddle bands played the "St. Louis Blues," and some of them made up words kind of on the risqué side: "There was an old woman who lived in a shoe. She didn't have any children cause she knew what to do." Things like that. These came from the blacks. These were words that we'd hear those guys singing and we'd pick up on them.[16]

The musicians in the Doughboys thought of Deep Ellum as a place to hear black music and also to buy used instruments in the pawnshops. Montgomery bought himself what he calls his "first good banjo" for $50 in a pawnshop there. In October 1935, when the broadcasts of the Doughboys relocated from the third floor studios of WFAA at the Baker Hotel in Dallas to WBAP on the top floor of the Blackstone Hotel in Fort Worth, most of the musicians moved as well.

Although Fort Worth is generally associated with the origins of western swing, Montgomery didn't really see a substantial difference in the music played in the two cities during the 1930s. Blues, in addition to the hot fiddle bands of the period, may have also been as common in Fort Worth as it was in the Deep Ellum area of Dallas. In fact, Montgomery recalled seeing Leadbelly in Fort Worth in the 1930s, though he didn't realize who it was until later when he heard records of the singer with a twelve-string guitar. "I'd hear blues singers, maybe a blind guy with a cup out there with a guitar. I never saw any bands. And there was a black hotel [the Jim Hotel] right off downtown Fort Worth where all the white musicians would go when they got off playing a dance around two o'clock in the morning. They'd go play with these black musicians in this hotel in a kind of jam session."[17]

Montgomery believed that stylistically, the fiddle bands of the mid-1930s were evolving in a manner parallel to the jazz groups of the period.

> All the musicians listened to the swing bands—black and white on radio and on record. Fred Calhoun, the piano player for Milton Brown, for example, tried to imitate Earl "Fatha" Hines, a black musician who broadcast from Chicago. Instead of calling him "Fatha" though, they named him "Papa." Knocky Parker was the same way when we auditioned. He played that boogie-woogie piano. Cecil Brower would listen to a hot clarinet chorus by Benny Goodman and he would copy it almost note for note on the fiddle.[18]

The 1930s were transition years in the development of both country music and jazz and this was especially evident in the Dallas and Fort Worth area. When the Shelton Brothers made "Deep Elem Blues" a hit in 1935, that song in particular articulated the way in which Deep Ellum was a metaphor for the interplay between black and white musicians of the period.

Clearly, the influence of African-American blues and jazz trumpet (Louis Armstrong), clarinet (Sidney Bechet), piano (Earl Hines), violin (Stuff Smith), and guitar (Charlie Christian), is apparent in the performance styles of a diverse array of white musicians. "Even if they didn't show it all the time in their radio broadcasts and recordings," Montgomery maintained, "this is what they played when they were jamming. We did it in the Wanderers and the Light Crust Doughboys, and I heard it in the playing of Milton Brown and the Brownies, Bob Wills and the Texas Playboys, as in the Shelton Brothers, Bill Boyd and the Cowboy Ramblers, Jim Boyd and the Men of the West, and Roy Newman and his Boys. Swing jazz was new and that made us all want to try it."[19]

Knocky Parker recalled that the Doughboys had, in effect, three repertoires: "We had much more Dixieland, and more blues, in our radio programs." About this, Montgomery concurred, "Pappy O'Daniel never let us play dances in public. . . . [H]e insisted upon at least one religious song, or hymn . . . but on the radio we incorporated more of that jazzy sound."[20]

In addition to the crossover to white country, black jazz also affected its white counterpart. "I wanted to play jazz on the side, and so did others," Montgomery maintained. "Cecil Brower went with Ted Parrino in the Ted Fio Rito band. Parrino was with WRR and KRLD and was a Dallas-based jazz musician who had a number of different groups. Parrino and his contemporaries played at the country clubs and in hotels, such as the Century Ballroom of the Adolphus Hotel."[21]

Montgomery also played jazz himself. After World War II, he had his own band, called the Marvin Montgomery Orchestra, which played the swing and Dixieland standards of the day. When the Doughboys reorganized after the war, Montgomery recalled, they had Walker Kirkes, of Roy Newman's band, playing banjo with them for about three months.

> While this was going on, I was playing jazz. I was the drummer and I had piano, bass fiddle, trumpet and three saxophones. The trumpet also played sax. We played at a place called the Midway Inn about halfway between Dallas and Fort Worth on Highway 80. It was an old gambling and bootleg place with a lot of secret rooms. We got to see all of them, but they were already closed down for that—dice tables, roulette wheels, the whole thing. When I played there it was a dinner and dance kind of place. And we played a lot of Dixieland jazz—"When the Saints Go Marchin' In," "A Closer Walk With Thee," "Sweet Georgia Brown," "Rosetta," and Irving Berlin's "Blue Skies."[22]

Even after Montgomery went back to the Doughboys, he continued to have some kind of Dixieland band on the side. He

150

changed the names of the groups to meet what he thought might have the most popular appeal—the Mississippi Ramblers and "anything that related to New Orleans: riverboats, ramblers, anything like that." In 1962, he started Smokey and the Bearkats ("Smokey the bear was in back then") and that group became his most successful. "So, I kept the name Bearkats. . . . I think we must have opened every shopping center in Dallas in the 1960s."[23]

Aside from Montgomery and a few others such as the Shelton Brothers, only a few white musicians have cited the Deep Ellum neighborhood as a direct influence. Neither Bob Wills nor Milton Brown, the prime figures in western swing, seems to have spent much time in Deep Ellum. The area's influence is more peripheral and indirect. Like the Beat, the Mexia neighborhood where Blind Lemon Jefferson sometimes played; like Deep Second in Oklahoma City; like Shreveport's Fannin Street, immortalized in a Leadbelly song; like similar neighborhoods in other Southern and Southwestern cities, Deep Ellum was an incubator for the black music that fed into the popular music of the wider society. It was in a sense a microcosm of Texas's overall diversity and the resulting cultural cross-fertilization.

The live radio broadcasts of Roy Newman, the Shelton Brothers, the Cowboy Ramblers, Bob Wills and others on WRR, WFAA, and KRLD are fondly remembered by many of the merchants in Deep Ellum. The daily broadcast of Roy Newman and his Boys on WRR, for example, was sponsored in part by the Ben Morris Jewelry Company, located at 1924 Elm Street. Certainly, the country styles broadcast on Dallas radio reflected the popular music of the day, including cowboys songs, country fiddling, novelty music and the western swing most commonly associated with Bob Wills and Milton Brown.

Western swing developed in the Dallas-Fort Worth area in the 1930s. The term had been used by black musicians. A 1937 record by the Carolina Cotton Pickers is called "Western Swing," and Buster Smith told an interviewer later, referring to his days in New York in the 1930s: "Several cats wanted me to do some arrangements for them. Out of all them great arrangers, they thought I had somethin' special—that western swing."[24] By that time, however, western swing was already being challenged by the harder, more guitar-driven sound of artists such as Hank Williams and Texans Ernest Tubb and Lefty Frizzell. An incredibly broad and rich variety of music fell under the general category of "fiddle bands," "hillbilly" or "country" from the 1920s at least through the 1950s: Anglo-Saxon ballads that evolved in the South and then were transplanted to Texas and other Southwestern states; blues and other African-American music; pop songs; novelty and nonsense material, some with the distinct imprint of the medicine show; and cowboy songs and the cowboy image, both the real and the Hollywood varieties. It is true that these forms coalesced into what came to be called western swing, but that was hardly the be-all and end-all. This music continued to evolve while coexisting with other forms, often within the same band. As banjo player Walker Kirkes said, "These bands played the popular music of the day."[25] In this way, it hardly seemed foreign to a white "country" musician of the 1930s to perform both "Shine on Harvest Moon" and "Black and Blue," making ironic its lament, "My only sin is in my skin." It was all just good music that people liked to dance and listen to.

Country music in Dallas underwent an evolution somewhat like that of jazz, becoming increasingly complex and varied—a development that speeded up when records and radio became widely available. This process started with the transformation of the country fiddling tradition brought from the Appalachian mountains of the southeastern United States to the plains of Texas by its first white settlers. The early fiddlers who were part of this migration were exposed not only to African-American music but to the traditions of Germans, Bohemians and other Central Europeans who brought polkas, schottisches, and waltzes. Moreover, in southeast Texas, the influences of Cajun French and Creole cultures were prominent.

It is known from oral accounts that the tradition of fiddling was fairly widespread among rural African Americans in Texas during the nineteenth century.[26] A white fiddler who requested anonymity when interviewed at a fiddle contest in Hallettsville in 1984 explained that "in the 1800s the fiddle was considered the devil's instrument, and only blacks could play the instrument because it was believed they didn't have any soul."[27] The string and fiddle band traditions were, to some extent, carried on by African-American musicians such as Coley Jones in Dallas and John T. Samples in Sweetwater, in West Texas.[28] Clearly, many Christian groups disparaged the performance of blues and early country music as the "devil's music." Nonetheless, fiddling was widespread as a form of musical entertainment. The fathers of jazz guitarist Eddie Durham, country bluesman Mance Lipscomb, western swing steel guitar innovator Bob Dunn and rhythm and blues singer Gatemouth Brown were all fiddlers, and Brown continues to play the fiddle as well as the guitar.[29]

The distinctive style attributed to Texas contest fiddling,[30] and for that matter fiddling in western swing, shows a distinct African-American influence. Texas style fiddling is characterized by intricately fingered and rhythmically varied interpretations of traditional tunes, which sometimes include the slurring of notes to produce a bluesy or swing sound. About this, Bob Wills said, "I slurred my fiddle in order to play the blues," and, referring to his vocal style with his band, commented, "I have always been a blues singer."[31]

In the 1920s, however, the variations in the so-called "Texas style" of fiddling had not become so pronounced, in performance or on recordings. M. J. Bonner, for example, was a contemporary of Eck Robertson. He was recorded by Victor in 1925 as Captain M. J. Bonner (The Texas Fiddler), probably as a result of the renown he achieved as the host of the initial broadcast of the WBAP "Barn Dance" on January 4, 1923. In this broadcast Bonner was backed by Fred Wagner's Hilo Five Orchestra, and over the course of an hour and a half, played an array of old-time fiddle tunes, interspersed with Hawaiian music. Like Robertson, Bonner's repertoire was composed mainly of hoe-downs, and consequently, his recording career was relatively short-lived.

In addition to Robertson and Bonner, other Texas fiddlers from the Dallas and Fort Worth areas were also recorded during the late 1920s. These included Ervin Solomon and Joe Hughes, as well as Steeley and Graham. Solomon on fiddle and Hughes on second fiddle were later accompanied by the guitar playing of Jim Solomon, Ervin's younger brother. Their only recording consisted of two traditional tunes: "Ragtime Annie" and "Sally Johnson." Similarly, A. L. Steeley and J. W. Graham also had a traditional repertoire. In fact, Steeley and Graham recorded "Ragtime Annie" for Brunswick at the same that Solomon and Hughes were recording it for Victor. However, Graham, somewhat atypical of the Texas tradition, played the five-string banjo.

Prince Albert Hunt, who lived in the black section of Terrell, Texas, east of Dallas, was another fiddler who achieved some acclaim in the late 1920s. Hunt was a showman and a legendary performer at house parties and country dances. In his repertoire, he combined elements of traditional Anglo fiddling with African-American blues, especially apparent in his recording of "Blues in the Bottle." Hunt's career was abruptly ended and his legend enhanced in 1931, when he was slain on a Dallas street. The story goes that the killer was the jealous husband of Hunt's companion. In his recording session for the Okeh label, Hunt was accompanied by Oscar Harper and his nephew, Doc. Oscar, a fiddler himself, was well-known in the rural areas of East Texas and was recorded by John Lomax for the Library of Congress in 1942.

The Harpers were one of several string bands in East Texas during this period, but they were not as commercially successful as the East Texas Serenaders, who recorded for Brunswick, Columbia and Decca from 1927 to 1934. Led by a left-handed fiddler, D. H. Williams, whose parents had moved to Texas from Tennessee, the East Texas Serenaders included Claude Hammonds on guitar, John Munnerlin on tenor banjo, and Henry Bogan on a string bass that was actually a three-string cello. Together, they played traditional tunes such as "Sally Goodin'" and "Old Joe Clark," but also performed rags, including "Mineola Rag" and

"Combination Rag," which extend beyond the repertoire of most fiddle bands. Moreover, they introduced elements of swing jazz and in many respects were transitional figures in the development of western swing.[32]

Unlike traditional string or fiddle music, western swing employed a band sound that featured a much more extensive and varied instrumentation, utilizing acoustic, electric, and pedal steel guitars as well as piano, bass, fiddles, horns, and drums. Dallas may not have been as important a center of early country music as was Fort Worth, but the music was performed and recorded there in the 1920s and 1930s, and was also broadcast on its radio stations.

Like the blues and jazz of this period, however, country music was essentially rural-based and regionally defined. Many musicians were from rural areas and viewed music as an escape from farm work. When fiddler J. R. Chatwell approached Cliff Bruner for a job at a country dance, he exclaimed, "Man, get me out of this cotton patch!"[33] Fiddler Johnny Gimble, born in 1926 and raised on a farm east of Tyler, learned music from his brothers and performed with them from an early age. "I found out that picking cotton was a lot harder than playing the fiddle," he recalled.

> By the time I was twelve or thirteen years old, we were playing gigs for a flour company. You know, the Light Crust Doughboys were big on radio down there [Fort Worth]. So I guess a lot of the flour companies picked up the banner and did the same thing. We were playing for Peacemaker Flour from Morrison Milling Company in Sherman, Texas, and the old boy would pick us up at 5:30 in the morning on a Saturday and drive maybe a hundred miles down in East Texas, and we'd set up on a flatbed truck in front of a grocery store and play all day, and we'd get two dollars apiece. Which was about four times what I could make picking cotton.[34]

The larger cities offered opportunities for performing on radio and in dance halls—and perhaps in recording as well. After graduating from high school in 1943, Gimble went to Shreveport, Louisiana, to play with the Shelton Brothers. Gimble recalled:

> A hillbilly band, as they were called then, could . . . play for nothing if they'd let you advertise your dates. . . . So we were early in the morning, and we'd say, "We're gonna be down in Navasota, Texas, at the high school auditorium playing the 4H Club," or whoever sponsored it. And we'd go down and back every night; they would leave at two, three in the afternoon, drive down, play a show, come back and sleep a few hours and do an early-morning show and three times a week a noon show.[35]

The Shelton Brothers were also rural musicians, hailing from the northeast Texas community of Reilly Springs. Their real names were Robert and Joe Attlesey. Borrowing a family name, they performed as Bob and Joe Shelton. Bob was known as the "Hopkins County Firecracker" and frequently played the clown, complete with overalls and floppy hat. Together, the brothers started singing in Longview, Texas, in 1929, playing for tips at rootbeer and near-beer stands, and at Clint Aycock's cafe. In late 1929 the brothers moved to Tyler, where they played with Leon Chappalear and changed the name of their group to the Lone Star Cowboys. In Tyler their performances were broadcast live on KGKB radio. The Sheltons and the Lone Star Cowboys reflected the development of country music, though they were more conservative than most groups. As a duet, they performed with mandolin and guitar and played songs similar to those of their duet contemporaries elsewhere in the South. However, their repertoire had a blues element that was uncommon in mandolin-guitar duets and was clearly influenced by the African-American music of their day. In fact, the Shelton Brothers played Blind Lemon Jefferson's "Matchbox

Blues," as well as hokum jazz tunes such as "Sittin' on Top of the World" and "Four or Five Times."

During the 1930s the Shelton Brothers played often in Louisiana, performing on KWKH in Shreveport and on WWL in New Orleans, where they teamed with Lew Childre and Curly Fox. In 1934 they were one of the first groups to sign with the new Decca Company, and a year later, they released "Just Because" and "Deep Elem Blues." They followed up a few years later with a couple of spin-off tunes, "Just Because You're in Deep Ellum" and "What's the Matter with Deep Elm." With the success of "Deep Elem Blues," the Sheltons alternated between KWKH, where they were also billed as the Sunshine Boys, and WFAA in Dallas, where they became securely rooted in 1941. They also maintained close political and musical relations with singer Jimmie Davis. In fact, Joe Shelton fronted Davis's band from 1943 to 1949 and was involved in his successful race for governor of Louisiana in 1943.

Instrumentally, the Sheltons resisted the influence of the early western swing bands, and continued to maintain their distinctive hillbilly style. They even forbade their youngest brother, Merle, who often played with them after 1935, to play bar chords on his rhythm guitar. But as folklorist Bill Malone notes, they gradually incorporated more swing elements in their music, and by the late forties, they had become virtually indistinguishable from other swing-oriented country ensembles.[36]

Johnny Gimble joined the band that campaigned for Davis in 1943, a band that included fiddler Jimmy Thomasson, singer Curly Perrin and East Texas pianist Aubrey "Moon" Mullican, whose honky-tonk style later made him a rock 'n' roll pioneer. "I was getting to play with the big boys then," said Gimble. His career with the Sheltons was cut short in the spring of 1944, when he quit to prepare for military service.

The Shelton Brothers and the Light Crust Doughboys were among a number of popular bands in Dallas in the 1930s and 1940s. Others, as Montgomery has noted, included the bands of Roy Newman and Bill Boyd, brother of Jim Boyd. Neither Newman nor Bill Boyd worked much as a touring musician; instead, both were associated for many years with Dallas radio stations. Newman was a studio musician for both WRR and WFAA, while Boyd was an announcer and disc jockey on WRR. Both were part of a pool of musicians who played in varying combinations and remained popular in Dallas for more than twenty years.

Newman had been a radio staff pianist since the 1920s. He rarely played lead or solo passages in the bands he organized after 1931. Instead, he provided an unobtrusive rhythmic background and tended to feature the musicians in his band, such as those in Roy Newman and His Boys, which performed on WRR's "Noontime Varieties" after 1933. In this group, Newman produced what Malone has called "an infectious dance music which revealed little indebtedness to country music and much to blues and New Orleans jazz."[37]

Newman prided himself on enlisting hot fiddlers such as Art Davis, Thurman Neal, Jesse Ashlock and Carroll Hubbard, and sometimes used Jim Boyd on electric guitar. He emulated Milton Brown in his vocals and band arrangements, especially in his early recording sessions, but later, as Malone observed, moved in even jazzier directions. Bill Boyd's Cowboy Ramblers, on the other hand, remained essentially a country string band, though Boyd moved in more of a western swing direction after 1937 by augmenting his band in recording sessions with Doughboys such as Parker on piano, fiddler Kenneth Pitts, banjoist Montgomery and guitarist "Zeke" Campbell.

Bill and Jim Boyd were born in 1910 and 1914, respectively, on a cattle and cotton farm in Fannin County, Texas, and began performing country music on radio in Greenville in 1926. In 1929 they moved to Dallas, where they stayed, aside from periodic touring. Bill was a talented musician who became quickly involved in the burgeoning Dallas scene. In 1932 he participated in Jimmie Rodgers's Dallas recording session and during that same year formed the Cowboy Ramblers. The band included Bill and Jim Boyd (guitar and bass), Art Davis (fiddle), and Walker Kirkes (banjo); all were studio musicians at WRR. Together, they made their first recordings for the Victor label in 1934.

The beginning of what would eventually be called western swing is usually attributed to the 1929 duo that became the Light Crust Doughboys. Bob Wills moved from Turkey, in the Texas Panhandle, to Fort Worth, where he found work as a musician and blackface comedian in a medicine show. He and guitarist Herman Arnspiger formed the Wills Fiddle Band, which performed at dances around Fort Worth. In 1930, Wills and Arnspiger were joined by vocalist Milton Brown. The group became the Aladdin Laddies and appeared on radio station WBAP, sponsored by the Aladdin Mantle Lamp Company. By 1931 the trio had become the Fort Worth Doughboys, advertising Light Crust Flour for Burrus Mills on KFJZ in Fort Worth. In 1932, Arnspiger was replaced in the trio by Sleepy Johnson, who played guitar, fiddle, tenor guitar and tenor banjo. The group expanded and was renamed the Light Crust Doughboys, and soon gained widespread popularity through broadcasts on WBAP in Fort Worth.

However, by that time Wills and Brown had left the band over wage disputes with "Pappy" O'Daniel, soon after the band's first recording session for Victor in 1932. Brown formed his own band, Milton Brown and his Musical Brownies. The Doughboys continued working for O'Daniel, who started his own flour company and later had a political career that included election as Texas governor and U. S. senator. He formed another band, the Hillbilly Boys, to use in his campaigns. Brown and his band began performing on another Fort Worth station, KTAT. Brown was poised for stardom and negotiating for movie roles, according to biographer Cary Ginnell, when he was involved in a fatal car accident in Fort Worth in 1936. The band soon fell apart, though individual members went on to successful careers in other groups.

Wills moved to Waco, where he organized the Texas Playboys, and in 1934 relocated to Oklahoma. From 1934 to 1942 Wills and the Texas Playboys performed daily on KVOO in Tulsa and played dances at night around Oklahoma, Arkansas, Kansas and Texas.

Wills and the Texas Playboys quickly became the most innovative and popular of western swing bands, incorporating electric instruments as they became available as well as horns and reeds. The Texas Playboys group was a large, versatile band that combined a hot fiddle sound with blues and big band jazz. Wills was a gifted entertainer and an extraordinary band leader who hired top musicians and encouraged their creativity. He loved musicians who could improvise "hot" or "take-off" fiddle solos. Wills himself was unable to play in this style, being largely limited to the breakdowns he had played with his father, "Uncle John" Wills, at Panhandle house dances. But Wills hired musicians who could improvise and encouraged them to do so. Many talented players did stints with the Wills band, including Johnny Gimble.

The country music heard in taverns, dance halls and homes and over the radio in Dallas reflected the widespread popularity of western swing and other styles as well. The Sheltons' theme song was the pop tune "Let a Smile Be Your Umbrella." The music of Newman's and Boyd's bands ran the gamut. The Ramblers recorded, for instance, Western-themed songs such as "Ridin' Old Paint and Leadin' Old Ball" and "The Strawberry Roan," sentimental songs of mama, daddy and home such as "By a Window" ("There's a little light always shining bright in a window at the end of the lane/There is someone there in her rocking chair by that window at the end of the lane") and hot blues, hokum and western swing.

Newman's band played a similarly diverse repertoire. They recorded "(What Did I Do to Be) Black and Blue" as well as novelty songs such as "When There's Tears in the Eyes of a Potato." A September 1935 recording session produced "Shine on Harvest Moon," "Corrina, Corrina" and "Hot Dog Stomp," featuring Jim Boyd in what some researchers believe may be the first recorded use of an electric guitar.

Bands also performed and recorded double-entendre material such as Montgomery's Doughboy hit "Pussy, Pussy, Pussy," which began with Montgomery himself asking in falsetto, "Fellas, will you help me look for my cat?" The other members replied, "Sure. Here, pussy, pussy, pussy. . . ." Another such number was "Garbage Man Blues," recorded by Brown and later covered in a virtually identical treatment by Newman.

As Dallas continued to attract immigrants from rural Texas, interest in country music swelled. Live radio broadcasts on WFAA and KRLD attracted local, regional and national performers. According to the late former disc jockey Johnny Hicks, he and "Pappy" Hal Horton "had the country music radio scene pretty well tied up in 1946 to 1949, in Dallas on KRLD. Pappy Horton had four nights with the Hillbilly Hit Parade, then he and I did Cornbread Matinee daily stage show from the Arcadia Theater."[38] After Horton died in 1949, Hicks inherited his "Hillbilly Empire" and expanded it with Big D Jamboree, which he emceed until 1959. The Big D Jamboree, originally known as the Texas State Barn Dance, started in the early 1940s by Homer and Walter Callahan and Uncle Gus Foster, was a showcase for some of the biggest names in country music. It attracted more than 4,000 people every Saturday night at Dallas's Sportatorium on South Industrial Boulevard. About the Jamboree, Walter Callahan, still living in Dallas in 1993, said, "It was strictly country; it was just like the Grand Ole Opry. We had different acts every week . . . even Elvis Presley before he got famous. He was always country until that little shake changed him."[39]

Homer Callahan and his brother, Walter, were born in North Carolina in 1912 and 1910, respectively, and moved to Dallas in 1942. Homer performed as Bill Callahan, Walter as Joe Callahan. Their performance style resembled that of many brother duet acts of the 1930s: They combined guitar, mandolin, hillbilly singing and comedy routines. Like the Sheltons, they incorporated blues into their repertoire. "Rattle Snake Daddy," originally recorded in 1934, was a solo by Homer (who for a brief period also worked as a soloist on several nationally broadcast radio shows) and was one of the Callahans' most popular records. "Rattle Snake Daddy" was a mainstay of their act and was re-recorded for eight different labels, staying in print as late as 1951, around the time they began working as comedians for Lefty Frizzell.

The Callahan brothers sold their interest in the Big D Jamboree after two and a half years to Johnny Hicks. Foster went to Corsicana to become a disc jockey on KAND radio, and the Callahans went to Hollywood to work in Western movies, including *Springtime in Texas* and *Hell on Horseback*. Other country performers, including Jim Boyd and Bob Wills, also made Westerns, and the image of the movie cowboy was a powerful one in country music, known for years as country-western.

Dallas has always been a moviegoing town, and before theaters began moving to the suburbs they formed a glittering row on Elm Street. Indeed, Westerns were also popular fare in the black theaters in Deep Ellum just across Harwood Street from what African Americans sometimes sardonically referred to as "the great white way."

Dallas is often characterized as a town more concerned with image than reality, so it may be appropriate that it spawned not real but celluloid cowboys. Walker Kirkes recalled that when Roy Newman or Jim and Bill Boyd posed for promotional photographs, they usually had their bands rent cowboys costumes. Occasionally, a horse was brought in to heighten the effect. In one instance, Jim Boyd even smeared cow manure on his boot so it appeared that he had just come in out of the pasture.

When Bob Wills moved to Dallas in 1950 he opened a huge dance hall, the Bob Wills Ranch House, on Corinth Street not far from the Sportatorium. He often rode his horse, Punkin, onto the dance floor. The place drew large crowds, but Wills was a poor businessman; financial problems forced him to sell the Ranch House in 1952. The new owners included Jack Ruby, who a decade later became embroiled in the controversy surrounding the Kennedy assassination after he shot and killed Lee Harvey Oswald.

During the late forties and early fifties, Dallas became nationally known for its country music recording activity, primarily as a result of the studio started by the legendary Jim Beck in his home off Mockingbird Lane near Southern Methodist University. In

1948 or 1949 he moved to 1101 Ross Avenue. Songwriter Jimmy Fields (born in 1924 in Sherman, Texas) said that at that time Beck was recording Lefty Frizzell, Ray Price and Marty Robbins. "He recorded anybody and everybody. If he hadn't died in the mid-fifties, Dallas would have become Nashville, Tennessee. Paul Cohen from Decca brought his artists to Dallas. Don Law from Columbia brought his country artists, folks like Little Jimmie Dickens and others."[40]

Shortly before Beck's death, Fields started his own recording business. "I'd record both white and black musicians. I had three labels: Kick was for colored rhythm and blues, Felco was for contemporary-type white and black bands, and Jamaka, which was first intended for country and later for anything and everything." Fields used Beck's studio when it was available, but was forced to take his black bands to Fort Worth because "no one would let me record them in Dallas."[41]

Long before the fifties, of course, Deep Ellum's image had faded from the wild and dangerous place of the Shelton's "Deep Elem Blues." In 1939, the Sunshine Boys recorded "What's the Matter with Deep Elm" as a sort of musical postscript to the Sheltons' earlier hit. The Sunshine Boys were the Sheltons' backup band without the brothers, who were under contract to another record company. But the group sounded much the same as it did with the Sheltons and played in the same down-home string-band style, posing a call-and-response question-and-answer:

> What's the matter with Deep Ellum?
> Deep Ellum's just too doggone slow.

---

[1] In Bill C. Malone, *Country Music U.S.A.* (Austin: University of Texas, 1985), Charles R. Townsend, *San Antonio Rose: The Life and Music of Bob Wills* (Urbana: University of Illinois Press, 1986), and Cary Ginell, *Milton Brown and the Founding of Western Swing* (Urbana: University of Illinois Press, 1994), Marvin Montgomery is discussed in a cursory manner. Malone focuses his

attention primarily upon the five-string banjo, but fails to adequately explore the role of the tenor banjo in early hillbilly and western swing bands.

[2] Marvin Montgomery, interview with Alan Govenar, July 31, 1996.

[3] Marvin Montgomery, interview with Alan Govenar, August 1, 1996.

[4] Marvin Montgomery, interview with Alan Govenar, August 2, 1996.

[5] Montgomery, July 31, 1996.

[6] Marvin Montgomery, interview with Alan Govenar, August 8, 1996.

[7] Montgomery, July 31, 1996.

[8] Montgomery, August 2, 1996.

[9] Marvin Montgomery, interview with Jay Brakefield and Alan Govenar, July 15, 1996.

[10] Ibid.

[11] Marvin Montgomery interview with Alan Govenar, March 18, 1998.

[12] Ibid.

[13] Ibid.

[14] John "Knocky" Parker interview, August 28, 1963. Hogan Jazz Archive, Howard-Tilton Memorial Library, New Orleans.

[15] Ibid.

[16] Marvin Montgomery, interview with Alan Govenar, March 12, 1998.

[17] Montgomery, July 15, 1996.

[18] Ibid.

[19] Montgomery, March 18, 1998.

[20] Ibid.

[21] Ibid.

[22] Ibid.

[23] Ibid.

[24] Tim Schuller, "The Buster Smith Story," *CODA* (December–January 1987–88), 4.

[25] Walter Kirkes, interview with Alan Govenar, June 9, 1994.

[26] The presence of fiddlers in Texas has been traced to the period before the Civil War. These include Major L. Burns, who was born in Lexington, Tennessee in 1835 and moved to Montgomery County, Texas when he was ten; Reverend A. McCary, born in Huntsville, Texas, in 1846; Arch Bozzell of Parker County, a veteran of the Civil War; Jim Heffington, born on South Bear Creek in 1852; and Joe Robertson. Robertson's birthdate is unknown, but he was one of the earliest known Texas fiddlers and the grandfather of the legendary A. C. "Eck" Robertson, who was born in 1883.

From the mid-nineteenth century through the 1920s, the fiddle was played primarily at dances held on ranches and in homes and cities. Generally, it was accompanied by one or two guitars. As a dance music, traditional fiddling in Texas was highly rhythmic and was clearly derivative of its Appalachian roots. However, as fiddling became a contest music, a distinctive Texas sound began to develop. The origins of the "fiddle contest" are obscure. The first documented event of this kind was the annual Atlanta, Georgia, Old Fiddlers Convention, which apparently began in the 1880s. In Texas the earliest recorded fiddle contest was in Fort Worth in 1901. A photograph of the event by C. L. Swartz shows one woman and fifteen men, one of whom is black.

[27] Interview by Alan Govenar, May 23, 1984.

[28] For more information on John T. Samples, see Alan Govenar, *Daddy Double Do Love You* (Chicago: Jubilee Press, 1993), with the 45 rpm record *Daddy Double Do Love You* (Dallas: Documentary Arts, DA 1001).

[29] Alan Govenar, *Meeting the Blues* (Dallas: Taylor Publishing Company, 1988).

[30] "Eck" Robertson, Benny Thomasson, Ervin Solomon and Major Franklin are generally credited with introducing the Texas style of contest fiddling in the 1920s and 1930s, while Wills and his contemporaries are usually identified as progenitors of western swing.

[31] Townsend, 40.

[32] Patrick Carr, ed., *The Illustrated History of Country Music* (New York: Doubleday, 1979).

[33] Cliff Bruner, interview with Jay Brakefield and Allan Turner, June 7, 1981.

[34] Johnny Gimble, interview with Alan Govenar, September 22, 1994.
[35] Ibid.

[36] Malone, 168–70.

[37] Malone, 168.

[38] A.C. Greene, "Radio Recollections Keep on Rolling in," *The Dallas Morning News* (January 16, 1994), 44A.

[39] Walter Callahan, interview with Jay Brakefield, December 6, 1993.

[40] Jimmy Fields, interview with Alan Govenar, January 23, 1994.
[41] Ibid.

Neale Helvey and J. Doug Morgan Tent Show, 1933, in Iowa, where Marvin Montgomery started his musical career. *Courtesy* Marvin Montgomery.

Marvin Montgomery (left) and his cousin Orville Dooley, 1932, as traveling hoboes. Newton, Iowa. *Courtesy* Marvin Montgomery.

The Light Crust Doughboys at Republic Studios, 1936. Left to right: Zeke Campbell, Dick "Bashful" Reinhart, Marvin "Junior" Montgomery, Abner Pitts, Doctor Gross, Buddy Dodson. *Courtesy* Marvin Montgomery.

The Light Crust Doughboys, 1941, in Saginaw, Texas. *Courtesy* Marvin Montgomery.

Roy Newman and His Boys. Dallas, ca. 1930s. *Courtesy* Walker Kirkes.

Jim Boyd, ca. 1930s. *Courtesy* Walker Kirkes.

12

································

Benny Binion:
Gambling and
the Policy Racket

Prostitution and gambling had persisted in Dallas since its days as a frontier town, despite periodic reform efforts. In 1876, Mayor Ben Long's attempts to enforce the law spurred the gambling den proprietors to gather in the second story of a downtown building and defy Long and his deputies for three days and nights, until a truce was reached. In October 1883, when District Attorney Charles Clint mounted a campaign to drive gamblers out of town, a delegation of businessmen urged him to desist. They pointed out that Fort Worth was offering gamblers free rent and $3,500 cash to move. This attitude of unofficial tolerance persisted until after World War II.

In the 1920s, gambling in Dallas was controlled by a man with the appropriate name of Warren Diamond. His headquarters was in the Southland Hotel on Commerce Street, where high-stakes card and dice games were played. "The biggest crap game in town was there," said Johnny Moss, who was born in 1906 and grew up in Dallas. "The biggest poker game in town was at the Southland." Moss had been a childhood friend of Benny Binion, the city's future gambling boss, and learned to cheat at cards from a local gambler named Blackie Williams. "It was a bad town, Dallas," Moss said of the place when he was a young man. "That was Clyde Barrow days, you know."[1]

Binion, who got his start working for Diamond, was investigated in seven murders. But he was convicted in only one, the 1931 killing of a black liquor runner named Frank Bolding. Binion received a two-year suspended sentence. The killing earned him his nickname, "Cowboy," for the way he rolled off a box and came up shooting when Bolding pulled a knife. Binion went into business for himself in the late twenties. For a few years he had to deal with competition from Diamond and with occasional police raids. By the mid-1930s, he had gained a virtual monopoly over gambling in Dallas. When Diamond committed suicide in 1933, the city, anxious to boost revenues and to promote attendance at the State Fair of Texas, established a wide-open atmosphere, though the laws remained on the books.

The administration of Mayor Woodall Rodgers devised what amounted to a system of taxing and licensing the gambling industry. Police vice officers counted heads in the casinos, and these places paid a weekly "fine" of $10 per patron. Will Wilson, who put an end to this practice as Dallas's district attorney in the late forties, recalled that these fines netted the city about $250,000 annually. In addition to the casinos, which numbered as many as twenty-seven in downtown Dallas, there were open bookie joints. Many businesses and country clubs featured slot machines. Brothels flourished in walk-up hotels and other places with little interference from the law. People could gamble on horse races at Fair Park and at Arlington Downs in Arlington, halfway between Dallas and Fort Worth.

The flavor of the time is captured in an anecdote from Harmon Howze, who remembered a big win at the track as a young man in

Dallas. After a day's work at Dallas Power & Light, he often went to the horse races at Fair Park. His brother-in-law manned the back gate, and Howze got to know the men who worked at the track.

One day, one of the track employees told him, "Hey, I got us a deal today!" There was a horse in the seventh race, a little speck-led-looking filly named Thistle-Lucy, that was going to win. He asked Howze how much he could bet. Howze, who was making about $14 a week, said he could bet no more than $5; he had to keep some money to eat on till he got paid Friday. His friend offered to lend him $5 if he lost. Howze said:

> Anyway this little old horse comes in and paid $42 on a $2 ticket! You could figure that one out. I had ninety-something dollars. I was really rich! I got on a streetcar and went downtown. The Palace Theater had a little shop called National Shirt Shop, you could buy a shirt for a dollar. And then just across the street, there was a shoe outfit where you could buy a pair of shoes for $4.50. And I bought five shirts and I bought a new pair of shoes. I bought me a chamois jacket; that's when chamois jackets were really in. That was $14 I'd blown; that was a full week's work.
>
> And this kid working in there, I gave him a $50 bill 'cause that was the way they'd paid me off at the window, you know. He looked at it, and he didn't know what to do. And he went back in the back and called his boss and told him that I was in there, and he probably thought that I stole that fifty. And his boss told him to "take that fifty over there to the Palace Theater and let that gal that sells tickets look at it, and she'll tell you whether it's a bad fifty or not."
>
> So he came back and said, "Will you watch the store while l go over?" I could have carried off the cash register! I said, "Sure, go ahead."

> I was so rich I didn't know what to do with it.
> Room and board was $7 a week, and I was making
> $14 a week. That's the richest I've ever been.[2]

Many low-income Dallasites favored the numbers game known as policy, another of Binion's rackets. Essentially an illegal lottery, policy flourished in the black community, and bets were taken in virtually every cafe and in many other small, black-owned businesses on Central Track and in North Dallas. Betting slips reflected the names of the various "wheels" where winners were selected: White and Green, Texas and Louisiana, Harlem Queen, High Noon, Grand Prize, East West and so forth. The White and Green wheel was located in a heavily guarded room over the White and Green Cafe in the 2400 block of Elm, in the heart of Deep Ellum.

Runners who stole from Binion were known to end up dead, and the police made little effort to find the killers. But Binion also provided employment for black men when times were tough. Dr. Emerson Emory, a black Dallas physician, said his father, Cory Bates Emory, was a numbers salesman during the Depression and was glad to have the job.

> That was a big employment thing for black men back in the late twenties and thirties. They had what they called the policy houses, where you would go and turn in the numbers. In North Dallas, there was one behind the Powell Hotel, which was over on State Street, and there was one behind the State Theater. They had one in Deep Ellum, upstairs, over the White and Green Cafe, and that's what this policy was called, White and Green. The policy slip was much like one of those Lotto slips. It was long, and it had twelve numbers down each side. You could play any amount. The most common play was for ten cents. And my father earned the nickname of "Tackem" because he would tell the people, "How about tackin' 'em down for a nickel?" So if you

played, say, numbers 22, 13, 44, something like that, and they all came out on one side, you would win $10 for your ten cents. If you did what they called flatsaddle, which meant they came out on either side in that combination, you would still win, but not as much: $5. Then later, they had three numbers across the bottom that were called various things. And they picked the numbers the same way they do in the present Lotto, with a big barrel with the numbers in it, and they would turn it, and the number would fall out. That was the wheel.[3]

Policy provided a measure of hope during rough times. Binion distributed "dream books," which assigned numbers to the subjects of dreams to guide people in making their bets.

Other illegal businesses flourished, too. There seems to have been little in the way of hard drugs, but there was plenty of alcohol, during and after Prohibition. In cafes, soda water stands and social clubs, liquor and beer flowed, and homemade chock liquor was popular. One popular spot pictured in *The WPA Dallas Guide and History* bore the intriguing name Gypsy Tea Room, which in the late 1990s became the name of a club in the new Deep Ellum.

By the forties, marijuana was plentiful in Deep Ellum, too, sold by the stick. Writer Terry Southern recalled seeing the band, The Clouds of Joy, perform in a Central Track joint and assuming that they got their name because they were always wreathed in marijuana smoke. Retired police officer Gus Edwards, who patrolled the area from 1944–53, said police knew the supply was plentiful when the price of a marijuana cigarette dropped from a dollar to seventy-five cents. Edwards's foot patrol partner was an older cop named Harry Stewart. "We started there at Elm and Central and went through to Hall and Thomas," Edwards said. "Around Elm and Central was the hot spot. Boy, there on the weekend, we'd get [arrest] fifteen or twenty every eight-hour shift," mostly for public intoxication.[4]

Across the street, people would sit on railroad ties sunk in the ground, Edwards said.

> Those farmers, back in the cotton-picking days, they'd come in their trucks, trying to hire them people, load 'em up just like stock and go to West Texas to pick that cotton. There was one of them [farmers] come to us mad as an old wet hen, says, "Ain't there anything y'all can do about them people sitting out there on their butts and won't work?"
>
> One of the loungers asked, "Say, ain't this ground around here kinda rolling?"
>
> "Sure," said I, playing along with the joke.
>
> "Well, roll that cotton down here and we'll pick it," the man replied.[5]

Edwards said he was sympathetic to blacks, though he'd hardly met any before coming to Dallas. Raised in Sterling, Texas, west of San Angelo, he said:

> There's no black people there. And see, they put me right in colored town. And in fact I had officers to accuse me of being a nigger-lover. You know, I didn't have nothing against 'em. The ones that worked, and old ignorant country boys come in here, somebody mistreat 'em, I'd work to help 'em.
>
> You know, when Harry Truman run for re-election, they brought him in from Grand Prairie by road on Jefferson, and they had every officer they had at that intersection. And we was late getting up on the track that evening. And when we got up there, there was two dead ones in this one block. One of 'em was a gal, but I don't remember who the other one was. One of 'em they drug out of McMillan's, just like you'd kill a hog and drag it out. She'd rolled under a car and died.

> We'd go in there when they were shooting those
> dice, and there were knives and guns on the table.
> They'd pitch them old East Dallas shankers on there,
> and we'd go to the wall and stick 'em in there and
> break them old long blades off. Pitch the knives back
> on the table and walk out.[6]

Those who carried the long, thin knives, also known as "Deep Ellum specials," sometimes propped the blade open slightly with a matchstick so they could be opened quickly. Edwards recalled at least one occasion when his partner saved him from being stabbed in the back.

During World War II, Dallas was a party town for servicemen on liberty in Texas and neighboring states. C. S. McMillan's wife told a friend that their cafe was so busy they didn't have time to count the money; they'd throw it in big jars and count it later. But the end of the war brought a new mood.

When Will Wilson ran for district attorney in 1946, he ran against "organized crime," which everybody knew meant Benny Binion. Incumbent Dean Gaulding chose not to run for re-election. Wilson's opponent in the general election was a tough lawyer named Priest, also a powerful revival preacher, who ran a scare campaign based on the fact that Wilson had black support. "My opponent is voting Negroes like running sheep through a dipping vat," he told *The Dallas Morning News*. Years later, Wilson recalled, "I ran against Benny Binion, and my opponent ran against the blacks."[7]

Benny Binion knew when to fold. He shut his casinos on New Year's Day, 1947, the day Wilson took office. Binion packed suitcases with cash and headed for Las Vegas with his chauffeur, a large black man called "Gold Dollar." Borrowing the name of one of his Dallas bars, he started Binion's Golden Horseshoe casino there, but he didn't give up the Dallas policy racket. He left it in the keeping of a confederate named Harry Urban.

Binion's reign over the Dallas underworld had competition from Herbert Noble, who earned the nickname "the Cat" because he survived numerous assassination attempts. Once when Noble was wounded, Will Wilson recalled, Binion's men rented an apartment across the street from the hospital and tried to shoot him through the window. In late 1949, a car bomb killed Noble's wife when she started the car he usually drove. The distraught Noble was arrested while loading his plane with bombs he planned to drop on Binion's home in Las Vegas. Two years later, Noble's luck finally ran out. He was killed by a bomb planted near the mailbox of his ranch in Tarrant County.

Wilson was determined to bring Binion to justice. Working with police chief Carl Hansson, he had vice officers follow Binion's salesmen as they made their rounds and turned their money and betting slips over to "pickup men." These employees took the slips and cash to a counting house in a remodeled barn on a farm Urban owned in Irving, just west of the Trinity River near the present site of Texas Stadium.

In late 1949, Wilson oversaw a series of police raids on the policy operation. Police seized $2,000, which Wilson said was a conservative estimate of the daily net take. Police also raided Urban's vending-machine business in the 2800 block of Main, near Deep Ellum, as well as a room at the Southland Hotel, two black Deep Ellum cafes and a shine parlor on Central Track. Sheriff Bill Decker was a friend of Binion's, and Wilson feared that a police officer or deputy sheriff might warn the gambler's men that a raid was coming. So the officers weren't told until the last minute where they were going. After reporting for duty, they were watched closely and weren't allowed to use the phone.

A safe deposit box yielded Binion's income tax returns, and Henry Wade, Wilson's successor, prosecuted Binion for income tax evasion and gambling violations after he was extradited from Nevada. He served four years in federal prison. After his release in 1957, he returned to Las Vegas, where he lived out his life. Not long before Binion's death at age eighty-five, he received a visit from Dr. Emory and others from Dallas who were in town for a medical convention. They reminisced about the old days in Dallas.[8]

The breakup of Binion's empire hardly ended gambling in Deep Ellum. Alto McGowan operated The Sportsman's Club in the 2400 block of Elm in the early fifties, foiling police raids with a lookout who pushed an outside button to flash the lights. The place was upstairs from the club and liquor store run by C. S. McMillan, son of restaurant owner Quitman McMillan.

McGowan was a smart businessman who could be tough when he needed to be. Once, when "Lone Wolf" Gonzaulles, the famed Texas Ranger, raided his place and broke a radio, McGowan told him, "White man, you're going to buy me a new radio, or one of us is going to hell." Gonzaulles went down a few doors and bought him a radio. McGowan said that at one time, he was clearing $1,200 to $1,300 a week out of his gambling joint. In 1953 he joined a church, gave the club away and opened a funeral home.[9]

Even so, dice and card games continued in the cafes and beer joints from Deep Ellum to North Dallas. Eddie Goldstein, son of pawnbroker "Honest Joe" Goldstein, recalled crossing Central Track as a child in the 1940s and seeing men shooting dice on the sidewalk. Goldstein and others also remembered a huge man called "Open the Door" Richard who sold liquor after hours and on weekends out of his shine stand on Central, around the corner from the Harlem Theater.[10]

Nevertheless, when Will Wilson left office, Dallas was quite a different place from the wide-open town of the thirties and forties. Interestingly, the last case he prosecuted was that of Tommie Schwartz of Day and Night Pawn Shop. Schwartz went to prison for masterminding the robbery of a doctor's home, then turning in the men he'd hired for the job. Newspaper accounts of his trial called him "the pudgy pawnbroker." According to Wilson, Schwartz had been allowed to operate illegal activities for years because he was a regular police informant. His prosecution was one more signal that things would no longer be done the old way.

Although gambling and vice were clearly spread throughout the city, their early association with Deep Ellum has persisted. In fact, Deep Ellum still has this reputation and is seen as an area of the city where lewd and illegal pleasures predominate. However, Deep Ellum was and is much more than that. Gambling and vice were ultimately only peripheral to the day-to-day lives of the people who worked in the Deep Ellum area.

[1] John H. Moss, interview with Alan Govenar, August 12, 1993.
[2] William Howze, interview with Harmon Howze, October 10, 1984.
[3] Emerson Emory, interview with Jay Brakefield, December 5, 1992.
[4] C. W. "Gus" Edwards, interview with Jay Brakefield, May 1, 1992.
[5] Ibid.
[6] Ibid.
[7] Will Wilson, interview with Jay Brakefield, May, 1993.
[8] Emory interview.
[9] Alto McGowan, interview with Jay Brakefield, April 15, 1992.
[10] Eddie Goldstein, interview with Jay Brakefield, April 3, 1992.

Postcard showing Fair Park racetrack, 1930s. *Courtesy* Documentary Arts.

"Deep Ellum's Just Too Doggone Slow": Decline and Rebirth

Ernestine Claunch came to Dallas with a friend from Norman, Oklahoma in January, 1940, to work for the Frito Company. It was the end of the Depression; she had finished school and there were still no jobs in Oklahoma. Her brother Marion was a Frito distributor and he recommended that she come to Dallas to be interviewed by the company's founder and president, Elmer Doolin.

At that time, the Frito Company was located on North Haskell Avenue at the corner of Bryan Street with about eighteen employees in the office and approximately thirty in the plant. "It was just like a big family," Ernestine said. "They ran a very strict office during business hours, and then when we played, we played because they would take us to lunch and have parties. We were part of a neighborhood." She continued:

On the corner there was a city service station. Next to the Frito office was Carolyn's Beauty Shop, then a Foster's Family Grocery and at 1411 Haskell was the Frito plant. Directly across the street was Sun Drugstore and on Bryan Street was the telephone exchange in a three or four story building. There was a lot of activity at that building because all of the long distance was handled by operators, and people came to and from work on the street car. . . . Bryan Street was residential for working people and Ursuline Academy was in that area. There were small businesses scattered around and some houses, some apartments and what were called light-housekeeping rooms that might be converted in someone's home where, for example, a couple might live downstairs or in a different part of the house.[1]

Ernestine lived at first with her brother on Mary Street in East Dallas and then moved to the YWCA in the 1200 block of North Haskell. "It was called Proctor Hall," she said, "and it was filled with working women who worked all over town." Ernestine lived there for two years and then got an apartment on Swiss Avenue which she shared with three friends. "We figured out how we could afford it," she remembered. "The rent was forty-five dollars a month and at they 'Y' it was six dollars a week for room and board." Ernestine kept that apartment until 1950, when she married Jack Putnam, who operated Dallas Office Machines in Deep Ellum, located in the former Pythian Temple. They met in 1947; Putnam had the Frito account, and Ernestine was responsible for ordering office supplies.

While they were dating, they sometimes met in Deep Ellum. She elaborated:

Everyone rode the street car everywhere you went. We didn't have a car. The street car went up Bryan and then crossed over to Main. On Elm they had electric buses.

Deep Ellum was very active, lots of people and lots of pawnshops. Smith's Furniture and Model Tailors were there. That kind of activity. The part I remember the most was that the merchants had all of their wares out on the street. Not all of them, but a lot of them did. Families were down there with children. The merchants kind of hawked their things. They had clothes on racks and they tried to get you to come into their shops. And there was one cafe that was in the same block where my husband's shop was. I don't remember the address, but they had great food. For years and years we made chili from the recipe we got at this restaurant. Everybody went to lunch at this cafe. Maybe it would cost twenty-five cents. Jack had many friends there, all of the shopkeepers.

Everyone worked until Saturday noon and then went downtown for shopping. On pay day you usually went some place pretty nice for lunch and you met other people. And then you did your shopping. At that time in the early forties when you went to town, you always dressed. You wore white gloves in the summer whether you went to church or shopping or wherever. And the girls who worked with me wore gloves and hats to work because they worked downtown. I didn't have to because I was only walking over to Haskell.

The only problem that Ernestine remembered her husband having in Deep Ellum was with the "winos" and homeless people who used the parking lot next to his building. "There were several small fires that were started and that type of thing. First of all, you don't want that kind of person near your place of business. Back then, people were more frightened than they are today."

By all accounts, Deep Ellum deteriorated in the 1950s and slowly the small businesses began to close. Although her husband sold his business in the mid-1950s, however, the office supply company itself remained in Deep Ellum until the 1970s. Ernestine, receiving several promotions, continued to work at the Frito Company through all its transitions for forty-two years. In assessing the growth and demise of Deep Ellum, it is difficult to assess how and why the area declined. Ernestine speculates that the growth of strip shopping centers and later, malls, changed the shopping patterns of the people who patronized the small businesses. Moreover, integration and the upward mobility of African Americans and Jews created new business and housing opportunities.

History conspired against Deep Ellum and Central Track. The 1911 Kessler master plan for Dallas called for replacing the tracks with a central highway—a goal that was accomplished almost forty years later with the building of Central Expressway.

The area had acquired an unsavory reputation early on. J. D. Smith established his furniture store in Deep Ellum in 1904 because he thought the city's growth to the east would help the business prosper. After all, Union Station was nearby. When he tried to borrow money to construct his own building in 1912, however, the first bank he approached wouldn't lend it to him because he was building east of the station.[2] He got the money and built anyway, in the 2500 block of Elm. But in 1916, Union Station was moved to the other end of town, the corner of Young and Houston, where it still stands as the Amtrak station. The Central Tracks remained, carrying freight trains that served the heavy industries north and south of the area.

Even in its heyday during the 1920s, people were foreseeing the end of Deep Ellum. A 1925 *Dallas Morning News* article intoned, "The towers of industry, represented by the ever-extending sky line, are gradually crawling farther toward the vitals of 'Deep Ellum' and it won't be long until the picturesque highway will be history." What happened, of course, was more complex than that. The Depression spelled the end of institutions like the Ella B. Moore

Theater and made money for entertainment scarce. Starting in the late twenties, many black community institutions—stores, dance halls, professionals such as doctors and lawyers—moved north from Deep Ellum into the thriving community around Thomas and Hall, the old Freedmantown. The Green Parrot dance hall left Deep Ellum around 1927 and was re-established under a different ownership on Hall. Few recall now that it was ever located in Deep Ellum. Also in 1927, the State Theater opened on Hall, giving African Americans a movie house outside Deep Ellum for the first time since the 1920s. In the 1930s, Dr. Walter R. McMillan, a relative of restauranteur Quitman McMillan, established a clinic in North Dallas. Later in that decade, the black population was moving again, this time into previously all-white areas of South Dallas. Some homes were bombed after African Americans moved in. Again, there was a movement of entertainment facilities and professionals. In 1937, the Queen Theater was opened in the old Queen City area. The building is now a church.

The new hot spots included the Hummingbird dance hall and Cafe Drugs, which opened in September 1938 at 3214 Thomas, next to Peoples Drug Store. The Rose Room opened on Hall in 1942 with a performance by Buster Smith and his band. The Empire later closed and reopened as the Empire Room, where Ray Charles regularly performed early in his career, in the 1950s. Movie theaters moved, too. The Harlem remained in the 2400 block of Elm, but acquired a reputation as a rowdy spot. Dr. Emerson Emory, a black psychiatrist who grew up in North Dallas near Central Track, recalled his sole trip to the Harlem, in the forties. "The show started at two, and between noon and two, everything happened except murder," he said. "It was called the house of action, and it *was* the house of action."[3]

Deep Ellum was left with the lower-rent places and the Goodwill store. *The WPA Guide* says of Deep Ellum:

There are second-hand clothing stores, job-lot sales emporiums, gun and locksmith shops, pawnshops, tattoo studios, barber shops, drug stores. Sales here are not the matter-of-fact transactions of other retail districts, but negotiations involving critical examination, head-shaking and loud argument by both seller and buyer. . . . Pitchmen hawk their wares. Street evangelists exhort, their frenzied appeals often but little noticed.

An Indian herb store flourishes on the sale of a verminifuge made on the premises. This is not a place for the squeamish; the emporium's decorative motif is somewhat startling. A mangy bull-moose head towers amid stuffed, coiled rattlesnakes, armadillos, a boa-constrictor and snarling bobcats. On a wall among Indian relics are some beautiful prints of tribal life. But the main attraction here is a collection of ex-stomach worms, neatly preserved to posterity in jars of alcohol. . . .

Clothing, like liquor and fighting equipment, is cheap. . . . New clothing and foodstuffs, bought in job lots, from unclaimed freight sales and bankrupt stocks, find their way to consumers at amazingly low prices. But the second-hand store is the backbone of the clothing business. Suits may be bought for $3. Battered hats and caps start at fifteen cents; good overcoats sell from $4 up; the badly worn for much less. Shoes are to be had for twenty-five cents and fifty cents; new footwear from $1.25. Three pairs of men's socks are offered for ten cents. Women's dresses start at fifty cents and $1; hats for the feminine head at fifteen cents.[4]

According to *The WPA Dallas Guide and History,* the most notorious nightspot had recently closed, the Cotton Club, a cabaret accessible by separate tunnels for male and female patrons.[5]

Some of the vivid street life remained. David Goldstein, son of pawnbroker Isaac "Rocky" Goldstein, said that when he went to his father's store in the forties, "Saturday was like the State Fair."[6] Eddie Goldstein recalled a man with a guitar who stood at the corner of Elm and Hawkins in the late forties and early fifties and a saxophonist who played on a nearby corner.[7] The streets still rang at times with the sounds of street preachers and gospel groups. And blues musicians such as Frankie Lee Sims still played outdoors around Central Track. Jack Richardson, better known as "Black Ghost," said a man called "Worm" played bucket with Sims, "and he got music out of that bucket, too."[8]

Clifford McMillan, known as C. S., operated several businesses in Deep Ellum into the late 1940s. Rudolph McMillan said his older brother had a soft spot in his heart for their father's old locations.[9] C. S. bought two of them and established businesses: a cafe in the 200 block of Central Track, and the Mirror Bar and a liquor store at 2413 Elm, site of his father's old McMillan's Cafe.

In 1947, police officer Gus Edwards shot and killed Travis Lee Morgan, a laborer, while trying to arrest him outside the Harlem Theater. The killing merited a two-paragraph story in the *Morning News* under the headline "Negro Shot Fatally in Resisting Arrest." The slaying of M. L. Patton, owner of the Patton Hotel on Central Track, by a holdup man, was also covered in a couple of inside paragraphs. In an interview, Edwards said he and his partner had to protect the killer from an angry crowd, but this wasn't reported in the *Morning News*, which tended to cover news of the African-American community in a perfunctory way, if at all.

One of the more interesting late-comers to Central Track was known as "Open the Door" Richard. "Open the Door" was a huge man who weighed at least 350 pounds. His real name was Edward George Laffiton, though few knew that. A lot of other people around Deep Ellum and Central Track were known by their nick-names. In his Central Track days, Willard Watson was called "Pretty Boy." A con man who haunted the area was called "Walkie-Talkie." Richardson was known to everyone as "Ghost" or "Black Ghost," a nickname he had earned for his speed at football when he was one of the first blacks to attend Lincoln High School in South Dallas. Deep Ellum stores regularly cashed checks for him made out to "Black Ghost."

"Open the Door" came from Springfield, Missouri, a racially troubled town in the Ozarks. In 1906, four years before he was born, the apparent calm of the place had been shattered by the lynchings of three black men. Many African Americans left immediately, following the railroad tracks out of town to avoid being seen.[10] The Laffiton family left, too, but it's not certain when. Richardson recalled once driving with his boss to Honey Grove, in East Texas, to visit "Open the Door's" family, but there is apparently no one in town by that name now, and the name doesn't ring a bell with black or white citizens.

There had been Laffitons in Dallas since at least 1878, when a Richard Laffiton, "colored barber," shows up in city directories with a shop on Main Street. Edward Laffiton, apparently related to the Dallas Laffitons, moved to Dallas in the late thirties. He worked at a succession of jobs, including a stint as a porter at the Lakewood Country Club. In 1947 he went into business for himself, establishing Open the Door Richard Shoe Shiners in the 100 block of Central, between Elm and Main.

The name he chose for his business is a history lesson in itself; it was a routine performed by vaudeville comedian Clinton "Dusty" Fletcher. The performer would come onstage feigning intoxication, carrying a ladder. He would repeatedly try to climb the ladder, only to fall to the floor, all the time inveighing his friend, "Open the door, Richard." But Richard, apparently more pleasantly engaged, would fail to heed the summons.[11] In 1947, the same year Laffiton's business first shows up in the Dallas City Directory, a song called "Open the Door Richard" became a huge hit for rhythm-and-blues artist Louis Jordan. The song was based on the old comedy routine, and Dusty Fletcher was listed as one of the writers. It was such a big hit that some radio stations eventually banned DJs from using "Open the Door Richard" gags on the air.

Dallas's "Open the Door" Richard lived on Pennsylvania Avenue, in the Queen City section of South Dallas, with his second wife, Brunetta, and her mother, Minnie Mae Clinton. Open's wife was big, too. They had no children, but there was a stepson and they took in the troubled "Black Ghost," who lived with them for several years as a teen-ager. But Laffiton had a rougher side, too, Gus Edwards remembered. "Open the Door" once hit his mistress with a gun butt and knocked her down the steps of the Patton Hotel.[12]

The shoe-shine stand was the locus of several businesses, legal and otherwise. "Open the Door" and "Ghost" bought liquor from a store on Elm Street and sold it after hours and on Sundays. Sometimes, when the police were cracking down, the whiskey would be kept in a garbage can with a false lid on the sidewalk outside the stand. Laffiton shows up in court records for a string of liquor violations. Some of the customers were white, "Ghost" recalled, but the police made sure they got their booze and left immediately. "They didn't have no business down there," he said.[13]

Ed Doran recalled tearing down "Open the Door" Richard's place after Doran Chevrolet, located in the 2200 block of Main, bought the property for expansion. "The area out back was two feet deep in broken wine bottles," he said. "Open the Door" also operated a moving business. Doran recalled a truck with lettering that read, "If it's light, I'll move it right." And Laffiton operated a barbershop for a while, though he wasn't a barber.[14]

Ghost said his boss stayed clear of gambling, though some retired police officers and other veterans of the area think he was involved at least in steering people to dice games. Retired officer Edwards remembered that once during World War II, a prostitute stole a serviceman's money. Edwards told her that if she'd give the money back, he wouldn't put her in jail. She excused herself, ducked behind the curtain at Open the Door Richard's and retrieved the money from her private parts.[15]

"Open the Door" survived the coming of Central Expressway, staying in business on Central until 1963. Toward the end of his life, he worked doing odd jobs for a group of black doctors in South Dallas that included Dr. Robert Prince. A few years before his death in 1965, he accidentally shot himself while cleaning a pistol at the shine stand. His resulting long illness drained his funds, and he died broke. He and his wife lie in unmarked graves in South Dallas's Lincoln Memorial Cemetery, not far from the graves of C. S. McMillan and his wife and Dr. P. M. Sunday, the physician who once had an office in the Pythian Temple.

Dave and Dora Goldstein and their six children moved out of their store in 1940 to a house in South Dallas. They prospered during World War II, in part because Dave had bought up a lot of radios and other merchandise that he knew would become scarce in wartime.[16]

The mood changed after the war. Reform District Attorney Will Wilson hired a bunch of young hotshots like himself, got the office moved to nicer, more spacious quarters and cracked down on vice. Gus Edwards said that toward the end of his Central Track days, in the late forties or early fifties, Police Chief Carl Hansson told him and Harry Stewart to crack down on violent crime on their beat and not to worry about complaints. "We got to figuring that every murder we'd had either tied in with a pimp or a dice hustler or a whore," Edwards said. "We went to work on them whores. We didn't have no more murders up there for ages. I mean, that stopped it. Them whores and pimps, they was on the run. Some of 'em would beat the paddy wagon back up there; we'd grab 'em again and back they'd go. It didn't take long, I think, hittin' 'em $30 a lick, they didn't tarry long. I told them gals . . . as long as you sell them the meat and get on that bed and deliver it, long as you don't get 'em drunk and roll 'em, you're not gonna get no complaint from me."[17]

The new mood of reform coincided roughly with the building of the long-discussed Central Expressway. The first leg of the expressway opened in 1949. Retired police officer Sam Tuck recalled chasing a suspect in the area during the expressway construction. The man disappeared, and officers were baffled until they shined a flashlight and realized that he had fallen into a hole dug for an expressway pillar.[18]

Deep Ellum may well have been on its last legs anyway, victim of a changing world. "I don't think Central Expressway killed Deep Ellum as much as two things: television and integration," said Eddie Goldstein.[19] But Central Expressway did begin sealing the area off from the rest of downtown Dallas. In the mid-fifties, the city installed parking meters in Deep Ellum and changed Elm to a one-way street, routing traffic to the west, back toward downtown. The merchants, led by Gene Smith of Smith Furniture, banded together in protest and staged a march up Elm carrying a coffin.

In the fifties, Good-Latimer Expressway replaced Good Street, and the building that had housed the Indian Herb Store was demolished. In 1955, Dave and Dora Goldstein closed their pawn business and switched to selling guns exclusively. Dave died in 1964 after lapsing into a diabetic coma, and Dora and her sons moved the business to a site north of downtown, where they kept it going until the early nineties. Doran Chevrolet moved to North Dallas in 1960 after "thank God, they condemned the building," Ed Doran said.[20]

C. S. McMillan sold his liquor store to Label Feldman, whose pawnshop was across the street, and went into real estate and other businesses. McMillan bought the old Peoples Undertaking established by the Starks family. He became, according to his brother, the first black Republican precinct chairman in Dallas since Reconstruction. Ironically, C. S. McMillan profited from the white resistance to blacks moving into South Dallas, working for apartment developers buying up white homes. Rudolph McMillan recalled accompanying his brother on his rounds. A white homeowner angrily told them, "You niggers get off my property." C. S. McMillan calmly replied, "Don't you want to make some money?" and ended up getting the man to sign a contract.[21]

After Feldman bought the liquor store, an old carnival fighter named Ed "Cornbread" Smith ran a gym upstairs where he trained Curtis Cokes, who later became world welterweight boxing champion. Cornbread went to the gym after his day's work at a nearby pawnshop and often stayed there late, gambling with his friends. "He stayed till his wife came and got him," Cokes recalled.[22]

The real killing blow was the elevation of Central Expressway in 1969. The city bought up the 2300 and 2400 blocks of Elm Street and razed the buildings. The elevated freeway passed so close to Honest Joe's, in the 2500 block, that part of the top floor had to be removed, exposing a portion of the building that Eddie Goldstein had never seen before. Inside was an old speakeasy, complete with antique pool table.[23]

Honest Joe and some of the other stalwarts hung on, though business became scarce. Honest Joe's business peaked about 1952. During his last few years, he sold off rent houses and other investments to keep the store alive. When he died in 1972, his son insisted that the funeral procession pass the store. This, he said, would honor the Jewish tradition of carrying the body past the temple, since the store was Honest Joe's temple. A *Dallas Morning News* story referred to Goldstein as "the Pascha of pawn" and quoted him as frankly describing much of his merchandise as junk.[24] A gallery owner hired by the family years later to clean the place out reported removing twenty-eight industrial dumpsters of scrap metal.[25] Eddie Goldstein said the first time he walked in and saw the place empty, he was shocked at how small it was. Full of junk, it had seemed huge, cavernous.

In the 1980s, the area was being reborn in a way the pawnbrokers and hustlers could hardly have imagined. The old buildings rang with music—loud rock that owed its existence to the blues and jazz that had been played there years before. Sometimes new and old crossed paths. In their final performing days, in the 1980s, Buster Smith and Herbie Cowens played in Deep Ellum clubs, not far from where they had started more than sixty years before. Again the sidewalks were crowded. These nighttime crowds consisted mostly of young whites in trendy black clothing. Dave's Pawn Shop for a time became a coffeehouse called Dave's Art Pawnshop. The area also became home to art galleries, with some of the artists living in lofts over the old stores. Wild artwork and graffiti decorated the walls of the brick buildings. Trendy restaurants and boutiques sprang up. Survivors like C. A. Spain seemed like creatures from another world. Spain finally closed his store in 1992. In early 1994, a dry-goods store owned by Holocaust survivors Henry and Frances Kirzner closed. The Polish immigrant couple had run the store in the 2200 block of Elm, once the western edge of Deep Ellum, for more than thirty-five years. Rocky Goldstein died in late 1995, and is best-remembered today as the man who sold John Hinckley the gun that he used to shoot President Ronald Reagan and his press secretary, James Brady. The last Elm Street pawnshops closed or moved in the 1980s. Label Feldman, whose shop had stayed in the 2400 block of Elm until it was razed, remained in business in the 2200 block of Commerce until April 1997, when he sold out to another pawnbroker.

Today, a few longtime businesses survive. In the 2500 block of Elm, the old Pythian Temple faces the vacant buildings that once housed Dave's and Honest Joe's pawnshops, though the latter is plain now, stripped of its gaudy trappings. If you walk around the back and stand among broken bottles under a freeway underpass, you can read part of an old painted sign on the brick identifying the building as Honest Joe's. Other odd scraps of old Deep Ellum remain as well, like the tiles from Doran Chevrolet's showroom floor that are now part of a parking lot. There's a restaurant/club called Blind Lemon, though its owners say they were drawn to the name more because of its sound and graphic possibilities than to any real connection to the musician. His photo is not among the historic pictures on the walls.

Some of the old illicit excitement remains in Deep Ellum. Drugs, it is said, can be had in some of the clubs, and in 1993 police broke up a call-girl racket operating out of a Deep Ellum lingerie store. Some Dallasites are afraid to go to the area because of occasional incidents of violence, though it is probably safer than many other areas of Dallas.

To get some feel of what Deep Ellum was like in its heyday, you have to go to Grand Avenue in East Dallas, where Eddie Goldstein has made his King Edward Swap Shop a shrine to his father's place. Signs on the outside proclaim "Little Honest Joe's on Deep East Grand," and inside is an amazing collection of merchandise and junk, everything from tools to fishing poles. Many of the customers are African Americans, and the banter and haggling that goes on is probably as close to old Deep Ellum as one can find. But in fact, nothing is going to revive Deep Ellum because it was a different world, one that existed because of an odd confluence of racism and tolerance, hard luck and opportunity, sadness and hope, desperate poverty and good-time Saturday nights. It is a world that will not come again, but one whose development attests to its enduring legacy.

[1] Ernestine Putnam, interview with Alan Govenar, September 10, 1993. All subsequent quotes by Putnam are from this interview.

[2] Junious and Jay Smith, interviews with Jay Brakefield, July 11, 1992.

[3] Emerson Emory, interview with Jay Brakefield, December 5, 1992.

[4] *The WPA Dallas Guide*, 295.

[5] Ibid., 296.

[6] David and Isaac Goldstein, interview with Jay Brakefield, March 22, 1992.

[7] Eddie Goldstein, interview with Jay Brakefield, April 3, 1992.

[8] Jack Richardson, interview with Jay Brakefield, May 23, 1992.

[9] Rudolph McMillan, interview with Jay Brakefield, April 9, 1993.

[10] Katherine Lederer, "And Then They Sang a Sabbath Song," *Springfield* (April–June, 1981), 26–28, 33–36, 24–26.

[11] Ted Fox, *Showtime at the Apollo* (New York: Holt, Rinehart and Winston 1983), 96.

[12] C. W. "Gus" Edwards, interview with Jay Brakefield, May 1, 1992.

[13] Richardson interview.

[14] Ed Doran, interview with Jay Brakefield, April 24, 1992.

[15] C. W. Edwards interview.

[16] Dora Goldstein, interview with Jay Brakefield, May 1, 1992.

[17] C. W. Edwards interview.

[18] Sam Tuck, interview with Jay Brakefield, June 15, 1992.

[19] Eddie Goldstein interview.

[20] Ed Doran interview.

[21] McMillan interview.

[22] Curtis Cokes, interview with Jay Brakefield, August 7, 1992.

[23] Eddie Goldstein interview.

[24] "'Honest Joe' Goldstein, Pawn Shop Owner, Dies," *The Dallas Morning News*, September 4, 1972.

[25] Bret Stout, interview with Jay Brakefield, June, 1993.

Officers Harry Stewart (left) and C. W. "Gus" Edwards pretend to arrest "Open the Door" Richard, ca. late 1940s. *Courtesy* C. W. Edwards.

McMILLAN ENTERPRISES

Mack's Liquor Store

ALL LEADING BRANDS

2413 A Elm St.   R-1584

C. S. McMILLAN, Owner

The Mirror Bar

"Where Dining is a Pleasure"

Southern Fried Chicken a Specialty

STEAKS   SHORT   ORDERS

— BEER —

205 No. Central   DALLAS

Mack's Sports Palace

"Downtown Recreation Center for Negroes"
2413 Elm St.

Mirror Bar No. 2

2413½ Elm St.   C-0829

DALLAS

Advertisement for businesses owned by C. S. McMillan, Quitman McMillan's son. 1947 *Negro City Directory.*

Honest Joe (seated) and his son Eddie Goldstein (in doorway), at Honest
Joe's Pawn Shop in Deep Ellum, ca. 1960s. *Courtesy* Eddie Goldstein.

Eddie Goldstein at King Edward Swap Shop, late 1990s. Photo by Jay Brakefield.

King Edward Swap Shop on East Grand, late 1990s. Eddie Goldstein, son of "Honest Joe," has made this store a replica of his father's old pawn shop. Photo by Jay Brakefield.

C. A. Spain (left) with customers. Deep Ellum, 1990. Photo by Alan Govenar.

Appendix 1
Selected Blues, Jazz, Gospel and Country Discography

The following discography includes artists who recorded in Dallas and/or had strong ties to the city. The information was gathered from existing recordings and standard discographies, including John Godrich, Robert M. W. Dixon, and Howard Rye, *Blues & Gospel Records, 1890–1943* (Oxford: Clarendon Press, 1997), Brian Rust, *Jazz Records 1897–1942* (Chigwell, Essex: Storyville Publications, 1982), Brian Rust, *The American Dance Band Discography 1917–1942* (New Rochelle, New York: Arlington House Publishers, 1975), Cary Ginell, *The Decca Hillbilly Discography* (Westport, Connecticut: Greenwood Press, 1989), and Joe Nicholas, *Country Directory* (Cheswold, Delaware: International Hillbilly Record Collector Exchange, 1962). Additional discographical information was provided by Marvin Montgomery, Kevin Coffey, and Cary Ginell. A list of abbreviations follows the discography, on pp. 278–80.

BILL BOYD & HIS COWBOY RAMBLERS

Bill Boyd, gtr, vcl; Jim Boyd, b, vcl; Art Davis, fid; Walker Kirkes, tbj.
Texas Hotel, San Antonio, Texas, August 7, 1934

BVE-83822	I'm Gonna Hop off the Train	BB B-5740
BVE-83823	Rambler's Rag	BB B-5740
BVE-83824	The Lost Wagon	BB B-5788
BVE-83825	Way Down in Missouri	BB B-5788
BVE 83826	Ridin' on a Humpback Mule	BB B-5608
BVE 83827	The Broken Man	BB B-5819
BVE-83828	The Strawberry Roan	BB B-5667
BVE-83829	When I Find My Dear Daddy Is Waiting	BB B-5819
BVE-83830	On the Texas Plains	BB B-5608
BVE-83831	Ridin' Old Paint and Leadin' Old Ball	BB B-5667

As above plus Slomie Creel, pno.
Texas Hotel, San Antonio, January 27, 1935

BVE-87718-2	St. Louis Blues	BB B-5828
BVE-87719-2	Thousand Mile Blues	BB B-5828
BVE- 87720-2	The Wind Swept Desert	BB B-5855
BVE-87721	Song Bird Yodel	BB B-5894
BVE-87722	Watching the World Go By	BB B-5923
BVE-87723	Going Back to My Texas Home	BB B-5923
BVE- 87724-2	Mama Don't Like No Music	BB B-5855

BVE-87725-2	The Train Song	BB B-5945
BVE-87726	Harvest Time	BB B-5894
BVE-87727-2	Under the Double Eagle	BB B-5945

Bill Boyd, gtr, vcl; Jim Boyd, b, vcl; Art Davis, fid, md; J. Fred McCord, gtr; unknown pno.

Texas Hotel, San Antonio, August 12, 1935

BS-94436	By a Window	BB B-6119
BS-94437	Evil in You Children	BB B-6068
BS-94438-2	Barn Dance Rag	BB B-6177
BS-94439-2	When the Sun Goes Down Again	BB B-6085
BS-94440-2	On Top of the Hill	BB B-6119
BS-94441	Old Fashioned Love	BB B-6177
BS-94442-2	Boyd's Blues	BB B-6109
BS-94443	The Sweetest Girl	BB B-6161
BS-94444-2	David Blues	BB B-6109
BS-94445	Rio Grande Waltz	BB B-6161
BS-94446	I Can't Tame Wild Women	BB B-6068
BS-94447	Get Aboard That Southland Train	BB B-6085

Bill Boyd, gtr, vcl; Jim Boyd, vcl; Jesse Ashlock, fid; unknown pno; Walker Kirkes, tbj; Lefty Perkins, stg.

Texas Hotel, San Antonio, February 24, 1936

BS-99313-2	Tumbling Tumbleweeds (vcl BB & JB)	BB B-6346
BS-99314-2	Eyes of Texas (vcl BB & JB)	BB B-6384
BS-99315-2	When It's Twilight in Sweetheart Lane (vcl BB & JB)	
		BB B-6346
BS-99316-2	Oh, No She Don't (vcl JB & JA)	BB B-6323
BS-99317	Cheatin' on Your Baby (vcl BB)	BB B-6351
BS-99318	Hold on Little Doggies (vcl BB & JB)	BB B-8198
BS-99319-2	Wah-Hoo (vcl JB)	BB B-6308
BS-99320	Floatin' Down (to Cotton Town)	BB B-6492
BS-99321-2	Beale Street Blues (vcl JA)	BB B-6492
BS-99322	Lone Star (vcl JB)	BB B-6384
BS-99323	My Ball and Chain (vcl BB)	BB B-6308
BS-99324-2	Mama's Getting Hot & Papa's Getting Cold (vcl BB)	
		BB B-6323
BS-99325	(Ready for the) River Blues (vcl JA)	BB B-6443
BS-99326	When the Sun Sets on My Swiss Chalet (vcl BB & JB)	
		BB B-6599
BS-99327	Must I Hesitate (vcl JA)	BB B-6351
BS-99328	Jesse Blues (vcl JA)	BB B-6420

BS-99329	I Need One Sweet Letter from You (vcl JA)	BB B-6486
BS-99330	That Ramshackle Shack (vcl BB)	BB B-6523
BS-99331-2	Hobo's Paradise (Big Rock Candy Mt.) (vcl BB)	BB B-6523
BS-99332-2	When They Play Rural Rhythm (vcl BB & JB)	BB B-6420
BS-99333	Black & Tan Rag (instrumental)	BB B-6328
BS-99334-2	Goofus (instrumental)	BB B-6328
BS-99335-2	Saturday Night Rag	BB B-6599
BS-99336	Prickley Heat	Unissued

Bill Boyd, gtr, vcl; Jim Boyd, b, vcl; Cecil Brower, fid; Jack Hinson, pno; Walker Kirkes, bj; Curly Perrin, gtr, vcl, unknown second fiddler, probably Pitts.
Texas Hotel, San Antonio, Texas, October 27, 1936

BS-02946-2	Fan It (vcl BB & group)	BB B-7128
BS-02947-2	Somebody's Been Using It	BB B-8246
BS-02948-2	You Can't Come In	BB B-6772
BS-02949	Deed I Do	BB B-7006
BS-02950	You're Tired of Me (vcl Perrin)	BB B-6807
BS-02951	Way Out There (vcl BB & CP)	BB B-6670
BS-02958-2	An Old Water Mill by a Waterfall	BB B-6715
BS-02959-2	Draggin' It Around (Draggin' the Bow)	BB B-6731
BS-02960-2	Ain't She Coming Out Tonight	BB B-6694
BS-02961-2	You Shall Be Free Monah (vcl BB & group)	BB B-6694
BS-02962	Show Me the Way to Go Home	BB B-6715
BS-02963-2	Guess Who's in Town (vcl CP)	BB B-7006
BS-02964	Right or Wrong	BB B-6731
BS-02965-2	That Makes Me Give in	BB B-8198
BS-02966	Jennie Lee	BB B-6807
BS-02967	Put Me in Your Pocket	BB B-6670
BS-02968	Yellow Rose of Texas	BB B-7088
BS-02969	Blues Is Nothing	BB B-6772

Bill Boyd, gtr, vcl; Jim Boyd, b, vcl; Cecil Brower, fid; John Boyd, stg; John W. "Knocky" Parker, pno; Rankin Moler, bj; unknown cl, second fid, (may be H. Hebert, cl, and J. R. Chatwell, fiddler)
March 1, 1937

BS 07415-2	Beaumont Rag	BB B-6959
BS-07416	What's the Use	BB B-7004
BS-07417-2	Dance to Those Sobbin' Blues	BB B-7053
BS-07418-2	She's Doggin' Me (vcl JB)	BB B-6889
BS-07419	Van Buben	BB B-6959
BS-07420-2	Pretty Little Dream Girl (vcl, sax CP)	BB B-7088
BS-07421-2	She's Killin' Me (vcl CP)	BB B-6889

BS-07422	Little Wooden Whistle (vcl CP)	BB B-7053
BS-07423	Red Lips (vcl JB)*	BB B-7507
BS-07424	I'll Find You	BB B-7507
BS-07425	Cemetery Sal (vcl JB)	BB B-7867
BS-07426-2	Madeira (may be Chatwell fid)	BB B-7004
BS-07427	Meant for Me (vcl JB)	BB B-8100
BS-07428	Mississippi Mud (vcl JB)	BB B-8125
BS-07429	That's Why I'm Jealous of You (vcl JB & CP)	BB B-7435
BS-07430	New Six or Seven Times (vcl BB)	BB B-7128

* "Red Lips" was redubbed on May 31, 1950 to delete the cl solo and was issued on Vi 21-0351-B as "Red Lips Kiss My Blues Away."

Bill Boyd, gtr, vcl; Jim Boyd, b, vcl; Zeke Campbell, gtr; Carroll Hubbard, fid; Marvin Montgomery, tbj; Knocky Parker, pno; Lefty Perkins, stg; Curly Perrin, gtr; Kenneth Pitts, fid; unknown d.

Dallas Athletic Club, Dallas, September 12, 1937

BS-014038	Jungle Town	BB B-7347
BS-014049	Come Easy, Go Easy	BB B-7800
BS-014050	Frosty Morning	BB B-7800
BS-014051	I Saw Your Face (in the Moon)	BB B-7260
BS-014052	An Ace	BB B-7435
BS-014053	Cross-eyed Gal on the Hill	BB B-7299
BS-014054	Can't Use Each Other	BB B-7347
BS-014055	My Wonderful One	BB B-7260
BS-01456-2	New Steel Guitar Rag	BB B-7691
BS-01457	Devilish Mary	BB B-7299
BS-014058	Sister Lucy Lee	BB B-7189
BS-014059	Won't You Please Come Home	BB B-7910
BS-014060	So Tired of Waiting Alone	BB B-7910
BS-014061	I'm a High Steppin' Daddy	BB B-7521
BS-014062	If I Can Count on You	BB B-7189
BS-014063	(You Gotta) See Mama Every Night	BB B-7521
BS-014064	Alice Blue Gown	BB B-8141

Bill Boyd, gtr, vcl; Jim Boyd, b, vcl; John Boyd, stg; Curly Perrin, gtr, vcl; Butch Gibson, cl; Carroll Hubbard, fid; Marvin Montgomery, tbj; Knocky Parker, pno, acd; Kenneth Pitts, fid; Gail Whitney, vcl.

Blue Bonnet Hotel, San Antonio, April 9, 1938

BS-022304	Like You (vcl Gail Whitney)	BB B-8100
BS-022305	Annie Laurie Swing (vcl Gail Whitney)	BB B-7531
BS-022306-2	I'm Jealous of the Twinkle in Your Eye (vcl CP)	BB B-7624
BS-022307	Someone in Heaven is Thinking of You (vcl JB & CP)	BB B-7754

BS-022308-2	Song of the Waterfall (vcl JB)	BB B-8112
BS-022309	Don't Drop a Slug in the Slot (vcl JB & CP)	BB B-7573
BS-022310	When My Dreams Come True (vcl CP)	BB B-7739
BS-022311-2	Ridin' on the Old Ferris Wheel (vcl CP)	BB B-7573
BS-022312-2	I'm in Love with You Honey (vcl CP)	BB B-7624
BS-022313	You're Just about Right (vcl BB)	BB B-7531
BS-022314	Broadway Mama (Vcl BB)	BB B-7739
BS-022315-2	Blues When It Rains (vcl JB & CP)	BB B-7788
BS-022316-2	Tableau Clog Dance	BB B-7662
BS-022317-2	Pedestal Clog Dance	BB B-7662
BS-022318	Boyd's Tin Roof Blues	BB B-7788
BS-022319	Home in Indiana (vcl JB)	BB B-8125
BS-022320	I've Got Those Oklahoma Blues (vcl JB)	BB B-7754
BS-022321-2	Jig	BB B-7691

Bill Boyd, gtr, vcl; Jim Boyd, b, vcl; Carroll Hubbard, fid; Kenneth Pitts, fid; John Boyd, stg; Knocky Parker, pno; Marvin Montgomery, tbj; Curly Perrin, gtr.
Blue Bonnet Hotel, San Antonio, October 30, 1938

BS-028801	My Baby Loves Me I Know	BB B-8081
BS-028802	New Spanish Two Step	BB B-7921
BS-028803	Spanish Fandango	BB B-7921
BS-028804	I Love My Baby	BB B-8013
BS-028805-2	Singing and Swinging for Me (vcl BB)	BB B-7971
BS-028806	Tom Cat Rag	BB B-7940
BS-028807	Here Comes Pappy	BB B-7940
BS-028808	One Thing at a Time	BB B-7971
BS-028809	Weeping Blues	BB B-7989
BS-028810	Boyd's Kelly Waltz	BB B-7989
BS-028811	Never Let You Cry Over Me	BB B-8013
BS-028812	La Colondrina	BB B-8070
BS-028813	Troubles	BB B-8112
BS-028814	I Get the Blues for Mamy	BB B-8053
BS-028815	I Want to Go Back	BB B-8070
BS-028816	Mill Blues (Gin Mill Blues)	BB B-8053

Bill Boyd, gtr, vcl; Jim Boyd, b, vcl; Kenneth Pitts, fid; Cecil Brower, fid; Marvin Montgomery, bj; Knocky Parker, pno; unknown md.
Jefferson Hotel, Dallas, February 12, 1940

BS-047659	The Sunset Trail to Texas	BB B-8394
BS-047660	Drink the Barrel Dry	BB B-8394
BS-047661	Pussy, Pussy, Pussy	BB B-8414

BS-047662	I Wish You Knew the Way I feel	BB B-8458
BS-047663	You Take It	BB B-8458
BS-047664	I'll Take You Back Again	BB B-8498
BS-047665	You Better Stop That Cattin' 'Round	BB B-8414
BS-047666	I Want a Feller (vcl JB & BB)	BB B-8498
BS-047667	If You'll Come BAck	BB B-8533
BS-047668	The Xenda Waltz	BB B-8409
BS-047669	Down at Polka Joe's	BB B-8409
BS-047670	There's a Light Shining Bright	BB B-8533

Bill Boyd, gtr, vcl; unknown b; Marvin Montgomery, bj; Bob Dunn, stg; Knocky Parker, pno. The fids may be Pitts, Brower or Hubbard. Jim Boyd indicates he didn't participate.

Jefferson Hotel, Dallas, April 9, 1941

BS-063074	Flower of Texas	BB B-8769
BS-063075	I'll Be Back in a Year, Little Darlin'	BB B-8721
BS-063076	Jitterbug Jive	BB B-8787
BS-063077	I Can't Forget (No Matter How I Try)	BB B-8769
BS-063078	They Go Goo-Ga-Ga-Goofy over Gobs	BB B-8747
BS-063079	I Guess You Don't Care Anymore	BB B-8787

April 10, 1941

BS-063084	Swing Steel Swing	BB B-8721
BS-063085	Sweethearts or Strangers	BB B-8728
BS-063086	Don't Let the Barrel Go Dry Polka	BB B-8747
BS-063087	Now I Feel the Way You Do	BB B-8728
BS-063088	No Dice	BB B-8823
BS-063089	Hold on to That Thing	BB B-8823

Bill Boyd, gtr, vcl; Jim Boyd, b, vcl; Kenneth Pitts & Cecil Brower, fids; Marvin Montgomery, bj; unknown stg; Kenneth Pitts on acd.

Jefferson Hotel, Dallas, October 12, 1941

BS-071180	Tell Me Why My Daddy Don't Come Home	BB B-8910
BS-071181	Rollin' down the Great Divide	BB B-8885
BS-071182	My Birmingham Rose	BB B-9014
BS-071183	The Letter I Never Did Mail	BB B-8910
BS-071184	(When I Had) My Pony on the Range	BB B-8885
BS-071185	Jennie Lou	BB 33-0501
BS-071186	Tumbleweed Trail	BB B-9014
BS-071187	Put Your Troubles Down the Hatch	BB 33-0501
BS-071188	Home Coming Waltz	BB B-8900
BS-071189	Over the Waves (Waltz)	BB B-8900

Frank Novak, Jr., ldr; John Tom Cali & Andy Sannella, gtr; Richard von Hallberg, b; Frank Pinero & Milan Hartz, fid; Eugen von Hallberg, acd; Bill Boyd, vcl.

New York City, June 19, 1945

D5-AB-0422	At Mail Call Today	BB 330-530
D5-AB-0423	No Time for Tears	BB 33-0533
D5-AB-0424	Shame on You	BB 33-0530
D5-AB-0425	I Just Don't Know Why But I Do	Vi 20-1888

New York City, June 20, 1945

D5-AB-0426	Tellin' Lies (vcl BB)	Vi 20-2379
D5-AB-9427	Highways Are Happy Ways (vcl BB)	BB 33-0533
D5-AB-0428	Dream Train (vcl BB)	Vi 20-2270
D5-AB-0429	Don't Turn My Picture to the Wall (vcl BB)	Vi 20-2562

Bill Boyd, gtr, vcl; Jim Boyd b; Kenneth Pitts & Cecil Brower, fid; Marvin Montgomery, bj; Andy Schroeder, stg; unknown cl.

Jefferson Hotel, Dallas, Texas, November 19, 1945

D5-AB-0849	(Down the) Trail to San Antone (vcl BB w/trio)	Vi 20-1888
D5-AB-0850	I Wish We'd Never Met (vcl BB w/trio)	Vi 20-2172
D5-AB-0851	Roadside Rag	Vi 20-1793
D5-AB-0852	These Tears Are Not for You (vcl BB)	Vi 20-1793

Kenneth Pitts, ldrr, acd, fid; Jim Boyd, gtr; William B. Campbell, gtr; William D. Woodward, gtr; Cecil Brower, fid; Andy Schroeder, stg; Asa Lee Woodward, b; Bill Boyd vcl.

National Radio Studios, New Orleans, October 3, 1946

D6-VB-2988	Jim's Polka	Vi 20-2050
D6-VB-2989	Oklahoma Bound (vcl BB)	Vi 20-2050
D6-VB-2990-2	New Fort Worth Rag	Vi 20-2270
D6-VB-2991	Out in the Rain Again (vcl BB)	Vi 20-2562
D6-VB-2992	Now or Never (vcl BB & trio)	Vi 20-2379
D6-VB-2993-2	Palace in Dallas (vcl BB & trio)	Vi 20-2172

W. Hill & H. Simevits (Sims), fid; Miton DeLugg, acd; Jim Boyd, gtr; Melvin Osborne, gtr; Noel Boggs, stg; Victor Davis, pno; Stanley Puls, b; Chester Ricord, d; Bill & Jim Boyd, vcl.

Hollywood, November 7, 1947

D7-VB-1856-2	Mean, Mean, Mean (Clear Thru) (vcl BB & trio)	
		Vi 21-0410
D7-VB-1857	Closed for Repairs (vcl BB)	Vi 20-2833
D7-VB-1858	I'm Writing a Letter to Heaven (vcl BB & JB)	Vi 20-2697

D7-VB-1859	Too Blue to Care (vcl JB)	Vi 21-0000
D7-VB-1860	I Always Lose (vcl BB)	Vi 21-0000
D7-VB-1861-2	American Patrol	Vi 20-2833
D7-VB-1862	You're Laughing Up Your Sleeve (vcl BB)	Vi 20-3190
D7-VB-1863	Yes You Did (vcl BB)	Vi 21-6164
D7-VB-1864-2	Come and Get It (vcl BB)	Vi 21-6335
D7-VB-1865-2	Southern Steel Guitar	Vi 20-3190
D7-VB-1866-2	The Skaters Waltz	Vi 20-3067
D7-VB-1867-2	Texas Blues	Vi 21-0164

As above, except Richard Anderson, pno; Melvin Mountjoy, d.
Hollywood, November 11, 1947

D7-VB-1885	Never Break Your Promise to a Woman (vcl BB & JB)	
		Vi 20-3067
D7-VB-1886	Vacant Heart (vcl BB)	Vi 20-2697
D7-VB-1887	Pull Down the Shades and Lock the Door (vcl BB)	
		Vi 20-2960
D7-VB-1888-2	Monterey Polka	Vi 20-2960

Bill Boyd, gtr, vcl; Jim Boyd, b, vcl; Art Davis, fid; D. Bohme, fid; Paul Blunt, stg; Marvin Montgomery, bj.
Chicago, March 10, 1949

D9-VB-0427	Lone Star Rag	Vi 21-0045
D9-VB-0428	Without a Woman's Love (vcl BB & JB)	Vi 21-0045
D9-VB-0429	Pass the Turnip Greens (vcl BB & JB)	Vi 21-0109
D9-VB-0430	Poison Ivy	Vi 21-0109
D9-VB-0431	Up on the House Top (vcl BB)	Vi 21-0126
D9-VB-0432	Varsoviana	Vi 21-0071
D9-VB-0433	Jingle Bells Polka (vcl BB & band)	Vi 21-0126
D9-VB-0434	Blue Danube Waltz	Vi 21-0071

Bill Boyd, gtr; Paul Blunt, stg; Art Davis, fid; Fred Calhoun, pno; Wanna Coffman, b; Marvin Montgomery, bj; Kenneth Pitts, acd, fid.
Sellers Studioes, Dallas, February 7, 1950

EO-VB-3222	Letters Have No Arms (vcl BB)	Vi 21-0208
EO-VB-3223	Domino Rag	Unissued
EO-VB-3224	Red River Rag	Vi 21-0335
EO-VB-3225	The Bandera Waltz (vcl JB & PP)	Vi 21-0208

Bill Boyd, gtr; Jim Boyd, b; Kenneth Pitts & Art Davis, fid; Paul Blunt, stg, pno; Marvin Montgomery, bj.
Sellers Studios, Dallas, May 28, 1950

EO-VB-4724	Bill Boyd Rag	Vi 21-0375
EO-VB-4725	Cuckoo Waltz	Vi 21-0410
EO-VB-4726	Why Don't You Love Me (vcl BB)	Vi 21-0351
EO-VB-4727	Yes I do, Yes I do, Yes I Do (vcl BB)	Vi 21-0375

Bill & Jim Boyd, gtr; A. Casares & Art Davis, fid; Paul Blunt, stg; C. H. Gilliam, acd; B. Parker, b.
WFAA Studios, Dallas, February 24, 1951*

E1-VB-1310	Step (Polka)	Vi 21-0449
E1-VB-1311	Gladiola Waltz	Vi 21-0482
E1-VB-1312	Why Do You Punish Me? (vcl BB)	Vi 21-0482
E1-VB-1313	Drifting Texas Sand (vcl BB)	Vi 21-0449

*After 1951 Bill Boyd did four more singles. Recording dates and most personnel are unknown.

HATTIE BURLESON (See also Hattie Hudson, who may have been the same singer)

Hattie Burleson, vcl; Don Albert, tp; Siki Collins, ss; Allen Van, pno; John Henry Bragg, bj; Charlie Dixon, bb.
Dallas, c. October 1928

DAL-706-A	Jim Nappy	Br 7054
DAL-707-A	Bye Bye Baby	Br 7054
DAL-744-A	Superstitious Blues	Br 7042
DAL-745-A	Sadie's Servant Room Blues	Br 7042

Possibly Bob Call, pno.
Grafton, Wisconsin, c. November 1930

L 614-1	Clearin' House Blues	Pm 13050
L 615-1	High Five Blues	Pm 13050
L 616-1	Dead Lover Blues*	Pm 13138

*Other side of Pm 13138 is by Laura Rucker

BUSSE'S BUZZARDS

Henry Busse, tp, dir; Roy Maxon, tb; Chester Hazlett, Hal McLean, cl, as; Charles Stricklfaden, ss, bar; E. Lyle Sharp, cl, ts; Willard Robison (composer), pno; Mike Pingitore, bj; John Sperzel, bb; George Marsh, d.
Camden, New Jersey, July 9, 1925

9115-A	Deep Elm (You Tell 'Em I'm Blue)	OK 40379

BOBBY (BOBBIE) CADILLAC

Vcl acc by unknown pno; gtr, c effects prob. by Billiken Johnston.
Dallas, December 6, 1928
147576-2   Tom Cat Blues   Co unissued

Acd; unknown pno.
Dallas, December 8, 1928
147599-2   Carbolic Acid Blues   Co 14413-D

BOBBY (BOBBI) CADILLAC AND COLEY JONES

Vcl duets acc by Coley Jones, gtr, poss. Alex Moore, pno; Jones, gtr.
Dallas, December 5, 1929
149536-2   I Can't Stand That   Co 14604-D
149537-1   He Throws That Thing   Co 14604-D

Dallas, December 6, 1929
149566-1   Listen Everybody   Co 14505-D
149567-1   Easin' in   Co 14505-D

GENE CAMPBELL

Vcl, gtr.
Dallas, November, 1929
DAL-515   Mama, You Don't Mean Me No Good No How   Br 7139
DAL 516   Bended Knee Blues   Br 7139

Chicago, May 1930
C-5701-A   Wandering Blues   Br 7170
C-5702   Somebody's Been Playin' Papa   Br 7177
C-5703   Wash and Iron Woman Blues   Br 7177
C-5704-B   Robbin' and Stealin' Blues   Br 7170
C-5705   I Wish I Could Die   Br 7184
C-5706   Lazy Woman Blues   Br 7184
C-5707-A   Levee Camp Man Blues   Br 7154
C-5708   Western Plain Blues   Br 7154
C-5709   Freight Train Yodeling Blues-Part 1   Br 7161
C-5710   Freight Train Yodeling Blues-Part 2   Br 7161

Dallas, November 1930

DAL-6789-A	Don't Leave Me Blue Blues	Br 7214
DAL-6790-A	Doggone Mean Blues	Br 7214
DAL-6791-A	Married Life Blues	Br 7227
DAL-6792-A	Fair Weather Woman Blues	Br 7227

Chicago, January 22, 1931

C-7250	Lonesome Nights Blues	Br 7197
C-7251	Wedding Day Blues	Br 7197
C-7252-A	Main Papa's Blues	Br 7206
C-7253-A	Face To Face Blues	Br 7206

Chicago, January 23, 1931

C-7257-A	Crooked Woman Blues	Br 7225
C-7258-A	Overalls Papa Blues	Br 7225
C-7255-A	"Toby" Woman Blues	Br 7226
C-7256-A	Turned Out Blues	Br 7226

CAROLINA COTTON PICKERS

John Williams, Thad Seabrooks, Joseph Williams, tp; Leroy Hardison or Ben Martin, Julius Watson, tb; Eugene Earl, tb, bb; Booker Starks, Albert Martin, as; Lew Williams, Walter Bash, ts; Cliff Smalls, pno; W. J. Edwards, gtr; Lee Thurman, sb; Otis Walker, d, vcl.
Birmingham, Alabama, March 24, 1937

B-23-1	Western Swing	Vo 03539

HERBERT "KAT" COWENS

Eddie Heywood's Kansas City Blackbirds, probably: James White, c; Levi Milligan, tb; Edward Alexander, as; Eddie Heywood, pno; Clarence Phillips, bj; Herbert Cowens, d.
New York, September 19, 1927

81541-A, B	Black Bottom Blues	OK rejected
81452-A, B, C	What Have I Done?	OK rejected

Stuff Smith and His Orchestra: Jonah Jones, tp, vcl; George Clark, ts; Stuff Smith, vn, vcl; Sam Allen, pno; Bernard Addison, gtr; John Brown, sb; Herbert Cowens, d.

US-7792-3	Sam the Vegetable Man	Vs 8063
US-7793-2	My Thoughts	Vs 8081

| US-7794-2 | My Blue Heaven | Vs 8081 |
| US-7795-3 | When Paw Was Courtin' Ma | Vs 8063 |

Eric Henry, pno, replaces Allen; Luke Stewart, gtr, replaces Addison; Stella Brooks, vcl.
New York, week of March 18–22, 1940

US-1506-1	It's Up to You	Vs 8251
US-1507-1	I've Got You under My Skin	Vs 8242
US-1508-1	Crescendo in Drums	Vs 8242
US-1509-1	Joshua	Vs 8251

Johnnie Temple, acc by Buster Bailey, cl; Sam Price, pno; Albert Casey, gtr; Herbert Cowens, d.
New York, April 4, 1940

67489-A	Good Woman Blues	De 7735
67490-A	Skin and Bones Woman	De 7750
67491-A	I'm Cuttin' Out	De 7772
67492-A	Fireman Blues	De 7782
67493-A	Lovin' Woman Blues	De 7772
67494-A	Roomin' House Blues	De 7782
67495-A	Sugar Bowl Blues	De 7735
67496-A	Stick Up Woman (Let Me Make This Trip with You)	De 7750

Billie Holiday, acc. by Roy Eldridge, tp; Ernie Powell, Lester Boone, Jimmy Powell, as; Eddie Heywood, pno; Paul Chapman, gtr; Grachan Moncur, sb; Herbert Cowens, d.
New York, May 9, 1941

30457-1	I'm in a Low-Down Groove	OK 6451
30458-1	God Bless the Child	OK 6270
30459-1	Am I Blue?	Co 37586
30460-1	Solitude	OK 6270

Sam Price and His Texas Bluesicians: Chester Boone, tp; Floyd Brady, tb; Don Stovall, as; Skippy Willliams, ts; Sam Price, pno, vcl; Ernest Hill, sb; Herbert Cowens, d.
New York, June 13, 1941

69365-A	Do You Dig My Jive?	De 8575
69366-A	I Know How To Do It	De 8566
69367-A	Valetta (vcl, SP)	De 8566
69368-	Boogie Woogie Moan	De 8575

DALLAS STRING BAND

Coley Jones, md, vcl; prob. Sam Harris, gtr; prob. Marco Washington, sb.
Dallas, December 6, 1927

145343-2	Dallas Rag	Co 14290-D
153444-3	Sweet Mama Blues (with group vcl)	Co 14290-D

Same musicians as above, plus group vcl.
Dallas, December 8, 1928

147612-1	So Tired	Co 14389-D
147613-1	Hokum	Co 14389-D

Dallas, December 9, 1928

147622-2	Chasin' Rainbows	Co 14401-D
147623-2	I Used to Call Her Baby	Co 14401-D

Coley Jones, md, vcl; prob. Sam Harris, gtr; prob. Marco Washington, sb; Harris or Washington, second vcl.
Dallas, December 6, 1929

149568-2	Shine	Co 14574-D
149569-1	Sugar Blues	Co 14574-D

CARL DAVIS & THE DALLAS JAMBOREE JUG BAND

Carl Davis, vcl, k, gtr; unknown, 2nd gtr; "Shorty," sb; Charles "Chicken" Jackson, wb, prob. jug.
Dallas, September 20, 1935

DAL-103	Elm Street Woman Blues	Vo 03092
DAL-104-2	Tyler Texas Stomp	ARC unissued

Dallas, September 25, 1935

DAL- 152-1	It May Be My Last Night	Vo 03232
DAL-153-2	Dusting the Frets	Vo 03092
DAL-157-2	Flying Crow Blues	Vo 03132
DAL-2-158-2	Tuxedo Stomp	ARC unissued

TEXAS BILL DAY* and BILLIKEN JOHNSON

Texas Bill Day, vcl, pno; Coley Jones, gtr.
Dallas, December 4, 1929

149512-1	Goin' Back To My Baby	Co 14494-D
149513-2	Don't Get Love in Your Mind	Co 14494-D
149514-2	Good Mornin' Blues	Co 14587-D
149515-2	Burn the Trestle Down	Co 14587-D

Texas Bill Day, vcl, pno; Billiken Johnson, k, vcl effects; Coley Jones, gtr.
Dallas, December 25, 1929

| 149538-2 | Elm Street Blues | Co 14514-D |
| 149539-2 | Billiken's Weary Blues | Co 14514-D |

*Note: Texas Bill Day may be the same man as Will Day, but lacking definitive confirmation, we have listed them separately.

WILL DAY*

vcl; acc. by unknown cl, gtr; Willis Haris, vcl-1, or Alberta Brown, vcl-2.
New Orleans, April 25, 1928

146185-2	West Texas Blues-1	Co unissued
146186-2	Central Avenue Blues	Co 14318-D
146187-2	Unnamed Title-2	Co unissued
146191-2	Sunrise Blues	Co 14318-D

*Note: Texas Bill Day may be the same man as Will Day, but lacking definitive confirmation, we have listed them separately.

REV. EMMETT DICKINSON

Sermon without congregation despite contrary labeling.
Grafton, Wis. c. March 1930

| L-277-4 | Death of Blind Lemon | Pm 12945 |

ARIZONA DRANES

vcl, pno; with Sara Martin.
Chicago, June 17, 1926

| 9737-A | In That Day | OK 8380 |
| 9738-A | It's All Right Now | OK 8353 |

vcl, pno; with Sara Martin; Richard M. Jones, vcl.
Chicago, June 17, 1926

| 9739-A | John Said He Saw A Number | OK 8352 |
| 9740-A | My Soul Is A Witness for the Lord | OK 8352 |

pno solo.
Chicago, June 17, 1926

| 9741-A | Crucifixion | OK 8380 |
| 9742-A | Sweet Heaven Is My Home | OK 8353 |

vcl, pno; with Rev. F. W. McGee and Jubilee Singers
Chicago, November 15, 1926

9877-A	Bye and Bye We're Going to See the King	OK 8438
9878-A	I'm Going Home on the Morning Train	OK 8419
9879-A	Lamb's Blood Has Washed Me Clean	OK 8419
9880-B	I'm Glad My Lord Saved Me	OK 8438

vcl, pno; poss. Coley Jones, md; several female vcl.
Chicago, July 3, 1928

400980-A	I Shall Wear a Crown	OK 8600
400981-A	God's Got a Crown	OK unissued
400982-B	He Is My Story	OK unissued
400983-B	Just Look	OK 8646

vcl, pno; several female vcl.
Chicago, July 3, 1928

| 400984-A | I'll Go Where You Want Me To Go | OK 8600 |
| 400985-B | Don't You Want To Go? | OK 8646 |

TROY FLOYD

Troy Floyd and His Plaza Hotel Orchestra: Troy Floyd, cl, as, dir; Don Albert, Willie Long, tp; Benny Long, tb; N. J. "Siki" Collins, cl, as; Scott Bagby, cl, ts; Allen Vann, pno; John H. Braggs, bj; Charlie Dixon, bb, tb; John Humphries, d; Kellough Jefferson, vcl.
San Antonio, March 14, 1928

400507-A	Shadowland Blues, Part 1	OK 8571
500508-C	Shadowland Blues, Part 2	OK 8571
400509-B	Wabash Blues	Par PMC-7082 (LP)

Troy Floyd and His Shadowland Orchestra: as above, but Herschel Evans, cl, ts, replaces Bagby.

San Antonio, June 21, 1929

402696-B	Dreamland Blues, Part 1	OK 8719
402697-B	Dreamland Blues, Part 2	OK 8719

LOUIS FORBSTEIN'S ROYAL SYNCOPATORS

Louis Forbstein; Rex Newman, vcl; unknown musicians: 2tp, tb, cl, as, vn, ts, pno, bj, bb, d.
Kansas City, c. May 15, 1925

9115-A	Deep Elm (You Tell 'Em I'm Blue)	OK 40379

FRENCHY'S STRING BAND

Christian "Frenchy" Polite, c; unknown gtr; Percy Darensbourg, bj; prob. Octave Gaspard, sb (bowed); prob. Jesse Hooker, cl; prob. Hooker vcl on Sunshine Special.

147566-1	Texas and Pacific Blues	Co 14387-D
147567-1	Sunshine Special	Co 14387

CHARLIE FRY AND HIS MILLION-DOLLAR PIER ORCHESTRA

Charlie Fry, as, vn, dir; Julian Kurtzman, Theo Wohleben, tp; Ben Morgan, tb; Ray Thwaite, Oscar Moldaur, cl, ss, as; John Baviton, cl, ts; Ray Allen, pno; Frank Kriell, bj, vcl; Herman Schmidt, bb; Fred Niehardt, d.
New York, July 23, 1925

10514	Deep Elm (You Tell 'Em I'm Blue)	Ed 51574

LILLIAN GLINN

Vcl acc by Willie Tyson, pno; with Octave Gaspard, bb-1, or unknown gtr.
Dallas, December 2, 1927

145312-1	All Alone and Blue-1	Co 14300-D
145313-2	Come Home Daddy-1	Co 14300-D
145314-1	Doggin' Me Blues-1	Co 14275-D
145315-1, -2	Brownskin Blues	Co 14275-D

Acc by Willie Tyson, pno; with unknown c and bb-1
New Orleans, April 24, 1928

146176-3	The Man I Love Is Worth Talking About	Co 14330-D
146177-2	Best Friend Blues	Co 14330-D
146178-2	Lost Letter Blues	Co 14360-D
146179-2	Packing House Blues	Co 14360-D
146180-1	Shake It Down-1	Co 14315-D

Acc by unknown c; cl; pno; bb.
New Orleans, April 25, 1928

| 146190-2 | Where Have All the Black Men Gone | Co 14315-D |

Acc poss. Pete Underwood, tp; Taylor Flanagan, pno; Perry Bechtel, gtr.
Atlanta, April 9, 1929

148212-1	I'm a Front Door Woman with a Back Door Man	
		Co 14433-D
148213-2	Atlanta Blues	Co 14421-D
148214-1	All the Week Blues	Co 14421-D
148215-2	Cannon Ball Blues	Co 14617-D

Atlanta, April 10, 1929

| 148225-2 | Wobble It a Little Daddy | Co 14617-D |
| 148226-2 | Black Man Blues | Co 14433-D |

Acc by unknown pno; bjo: poss Octave Gaspard, bb.
Dallas, December 6, 1929

149550-2	I'm Through (Shedding Tears over You)	Co 14559-D
149551-2	I Love That Thing	Co 14559-D
149552-1	Don't Leave Me Daddy	Co 14493-D
149553-2	Shreveport Blues	Co 14519-D
149556-2	Moanin' Blues	Co 14493-D
149557-2	Cravin' a Man Blues	Co 14519-D

OTIS HARRIS

vcl, gtr.
Dallas, December 8, 1928

| 147608-1 | Waking Blues | Co 14428-D |
| 147609-2 | You'll Like My Loving | Co 14428-D |

SAMMY HILL

vcl, gtr; prob. Keno Pipes, gtr.
Dallas, August 9, 1929

55319-1	Cryin' for You Blues	Vi V38588
55320-2	Needin' My Woman Blues	Vi V38588

HATTIE HUDSON (possibly a pseudonym for Hattie Burleson)

vcl; acc. by Willie Tyson, pno.
Dallas, December 6, 1927

145338-2	Doggone My Good Luck Soul	Co 14279-D
145339-2	Black Hand Blues	Co 14279-D

BLIND LEMON JEFFERSON

(as by Deacon L. J. Bates); vcl, gtr.
Chicago, c. December 1925–January 1926

11040-1	I Want to Be Like Jesus in My Heart	Pm 12386
11041-1	All I Want Is That Pure Religion	Pm 12386

vcl, gtr.
Chicago, c. March 1926

2471-1, -2	Got the Blues	Pm 12354
2472-1, -2	Long Lonesome Blues	Pm 12354
2474-1	Booster Blues	Pm 12347
2475-1	Dry Southern Blues	Pm 12347

vcl, gtr.
Chicago, c. April 1926

2543-1	Black Horse Blues	Pm 12367
2544-1, -2	Corinna Blues	Pm 12367

vcl, gtr.
Chicago, c. May/June 1926

1053	Got the Blues	Pm 12354
1054	Long Lonesome Blues	Pm 12354
2557-1	Jack O'Diamond Blues	Pm 12373
2557-2	Jack O'Diamond Blues	Pm 12373
2558-2	Chock House Blues	Pm 12373

216

vcl, gtr.
Chicago, c. August 1926

| 2016-4 | Beggin' Back | Pm 12394 |
| 2018-1 | Old Rounders Blues | Pm 12394 |

vcl, gtr.
Chicago, c. November 1926

3066-1, -2	Stocking Feet Blues	Pm 12407
3067-1, -2	That Black Snake Moan	Pm 12407
3070-1	Wartime Blues	Pm 12425
3076-1, -2	Broke and Hungry	Pm 12443
3077-1, -2	Shuckin' Sugar Blues	Pm 12454

vcl, gtr.
Chicago, c. December, 1926

3088-2	Booger Rooger Blues	Pm 12425
3089-1	Rabbit Foot Blues	Pm 12454
3090-2	Bad Luck Blues	Pm 12443

vcl, gtr.
Atlanta, March 14, 1927

80523-B	Black Snake Moan	OK 8455
80524-B	Match Box Blues	OK 8455
80525-B	'Stillery Blues	OK unissued
80526-B	Woman Labor Man	OK unissued
80527-B	My Easy Rider	OK unissued
80528-B	Elder Green's in Town	OK unissued
80529-B	English Stop Time	OK unissued

Atlanta, March 15, 1927

| 80536-B | Laboring Man Away from Home | OK unissued |

vcl, gtr.
Chicago, c. April 1927

4423-2	Easy Rider Blues	Pm 12474
4424-2	Match Box Blues	Pm 12474
4446-4	Match Box Blues	Pm 12474

vcl, gtr.; George Perkins, pno.
Chicago, c. May 1927

| 4491-5 | Rising High Water Blues (pno only, no gtr) | Pm 12487 |

vcl, gtr.
Chicago, c. May 1927

4514-4	Weary Dogs Blues	Pm 12493
4515-2	Right of Way Blues	Pm 12510

vcl; acc. George Perkins, pno.
Chicago, c. June 1927

4567-1, -2	Teddy Bear Blues (no gtr)	Pm 12487

vcl, gtr.; George Perkins, pno.
Chicago, c. June 1927

4577-2	Black Snake Dream Blues	Pm 12510

comments, tap dancing, gtr.
Chicago, c. June 1927

4578-3	Hot Dogs	Pm 12493

(as by Deacon L. J. Bates); gtr.
Chicago, c. June 1927

4579-1	He Arose From the Dead	Pm 12585

vcl, gtr.
Chicago, c. September 1927

20039-2	Struck Sorrow Blues	Pm 12541
20040-2	Rambler Blues	Pm 12541

vcl, gtr.
Chicago, c. October 1927

20064-1	Chinch Bug Blues	Pm 12551
20065-2	Deceitful Brownskin Blues	Pm 12551
20066-1	Sunshine Special	Pm 12593
20070-2	Gone Dead on You Blues	Pm 12578
20073-2	Where Shall I Be?	Pm 12585
20074-2	See That My Grave Is Kept Clean	Pm 12585
20075-2	One Dime Blues	Pm 12578
20076-2	Lonesome House Blues	Pm 12593

vcl, gtr.
Chicago, c. February, 1928

20363-2	Blind Lemon's Penitentiary Blues	Pm 12666
20364-2	'Lectric Chair Blues	Pm 12608
20374-1	See That My Grave Is Kept Clean	Pm 12608

20375-3	Lemon's Worried Blues	Pm 12622
20380-2	Mean Jumper Blues	Pm 12631
20381-3	Balky Mule Blues	Pm 12631
20387-2	Change My Luck Blues	Pm 12639
20388-2	Prison Cell Blues	Pm 12622

vcl, gtr.
Chicago, c. March 1928

20401-1	Lemon's Cannon Ball Blues	Pm 12639
20402	Low Down Mojo Blues	Pm unissued
20407-2	Long Lastin' Lovin'	Pm 12666
20408-2	Piney Woods Money Mama	Pm 12650

vcl, gtr.
Chicago, c. June 1928

| 20636-1 | Low Down Mojo Blues | Pm 12650 |

vcl, gtr.
Chicago, c. July/August 1928

20479-2	Competition Bed Blues	Pm 12728
20750-2/		
20815-2	Lock Step Blues	Pm 12679
20751-1, -2/		
20816-2	Hangman's Blues	Pm 12679
20772-2	Sad News Blues	Pm 12728

vcl, gtr.; unknown, pno.
Chicago, c. July 1928

| 20788-1 | How Long How Long | Pm 12685 |

vcl, gtr.
Chicago, c. August 1928

20818-2	Christmas Eve Blues	Pm 12692
20819-2	Happy New Year Blues	Pm 12692
20820-1	Maltese Cat Blues	Pm 12712
20821-1	D B Blues	Pm 12712

vcl, gtr.
Chicago, c. January 1929

21095-3	Eagle Eyed Mama	Pm 12739
21096-1	Dynamite Blues	Pm 12739
21110-2	Disgusted Blues	Pm 12933

| 21132-1 | Competition Bed Blues | Pm 12728 |
| 21133-1 | Sad News Blues | Pm 12728 |

vcl, gtr.
Chicago, c. March 1929

21196-1	Peach Orchard Mama	Pm 12801
21197-1	Oil Well Blues	Pm 12771
21198-1	Tin Cup Blues	Pm 12756
21199-1	Big Night Blues	Pm 12801
21200-1	Empty House Blues	Pm 12946
21201-2	Saturday Night Spender Blues	Pm 12771
21202-1	That Black Snake Moan No. 2	Pm 12756

Chicago, c. August 1929, vcl, gtr

| 21400-2 | Peach Orchard Mama | Pm 12801 |
| 21402-2 | Big Night Blues | Pm 12801 |

vcl, gtr.
Richmond, Indiana, September 24, 1929

15664-	Bed Springs Blues	Pm 12872
15665-	Yo Yo Blues	Pm 12872
15666-	Mosquito Moan	Pm 12899
15667-	Southern Women Blues	Pm 12899
15668-	Bakershop Blues	Pm 12582
15669-	Pneumonia Blues	Pm 12880
15670-A	Long Distance Moan	Pm 12852
15671-	That Crawlin' Baby Blues	Pm 12880
15672-	Fence Breakin' Yellin' Blues	Pm 12921
15673-	Cat Man Blues	Pm 12921
15674-	The Cheaters Spell	Pm 12933
15675-	Bootin' Me 'Bout	Pm 12946

ALBERT "BUDD" JOHNSON

Julia Lee, acc by George E. Lee's Novelty Singing Orchestra: Harold Knox, tp; Jimmy Jones, tb; Clarence Taylor, as; Budd Johnson, ts; Jesse Stone, pno; Charles Russo, bj, gtr; Pete Woods, d.
Kansas City, November 8, 1929

| KC-602 | He's Tall and Dark and Handsome | Br 4761 |
| KC-603 | Won't You Come Over to My House? | Br 4761 |

Louis Armstrong and His Orchestra: Louis Armstrong, tp, vcl, ldr; Ellis Whitlock, Zilmer Randolph, tp; Keg Johnson, tb; Scoville Brown, George Oldham, cl, as; Albert "Budd" Johnson, cl, ts; Teddy Wilson, pno; Mike McKendrick, bj, gtr; Bill Oldham, bb; Yank Porter, d.

Chicago, January 26, 1933

74891-1	I've Got the World on a String	Vi 24245
74892-1	I Gotta Right to Sing the Blues	Vi 24233
74893-1	Hustlin' and Bustlin' for Baby	Vi 24233
74894-1	Sittin' in the Dark	Vi 24245
74895-1	High Society	Vi 24232
74896-1	He's a Son of the South	Vi 24257

Chicago, January 27, 1933

75102-1	Some Sweet Day	Vi 24257
75103-1	Basin Street Blues (Zilmer Randolph, as)	Vi 24351
75104-1	Honey, Do I	Vi 24369

Chicago, January 28, 1933

75105-1	Snowball	Vi 24369
75106-1	Mahogany Hall Stomp	Vi 24232
75107-1	Swing, You Cats	BB B 10225

Charlie Beal, pno, replaces Wilson; Sid Catlett, d, replaces Porter
Chicago, April 24, 1933

75420-1	Honey, Don't You Love Me Any More?	Vi 24335
75421-1	Mississippi Basin	Vi 24321
75422-1-2	Laughin' Louie	BB B 5363
75423-1	Tomorrow Night (After Tonight)	Vi 68-0774
752424-1	Dusky Stevedore	Vi 24320

Louis Armstrong and His Orchestra. Henry Dial, d, replaces Sid Catlett; Budd Johnson, vcl
Chicago, April 26, 1933

75478-1	Sweet Sue, Just You (vcl, LA, BJ)	Vi 24321

Earl Hines and His Orchestra: Earl Hines, pno, dir; Charlie Allen, Wilson Fletcher, tp; Walter Fuller, tp, w; Louis Taylor, Kenneth Stuart, Trummy Young, tb; Darnell Howard, cl, as, vn; Omer Simeon, as, bar; Budd Johnson, ts; Lawrence Dixon, gtr; Quinn Wilson, sb, as; Wallace Bishop, d; Henry Woodip, as; Ida Mae James, vcl.
Chicago, February 10, 1937

C-1814-1	Flany Doodle Swing	Vo 3501

C-1815-2	Pianology	Vo S-78
C-1816-1	Rhythm Sundae (as, Cecil Irwin)	Vo 3467
C-1817-2	Inspiration	Vo 3586
C-1818-2	I Can't Believe That You're in Love with Me (vcl, IMJ)	
		Vo 3467

Gus Arnehim and His Orchestra: Johnny Carlson, Les Beigel, tp; Ray Foster, tp, vcl; Don Daniels, Ralph Copsey, tb; Irving Fazola, cl; Bill Covery, Jack Shoop, as; Johnny Hamilton, ts; Stan Kenton, pno; Lloyd Ranier, gtr; Manny Stein, sb; Lou Singer, d; Jimmy Farrell, vcl; some titles, poss. all, arr. by Buddy Johnson.

New York, June 23, 1937

21298-1	So Rare	Br 7919
21299-2	Dancing Under the Stars	Br 7919
21300-1	High, Wide and Handsome	Br 7922
21301-2	The Folks Who Live on the Hill	Br 7922

New York, July 22, 1937

21419-1	My Cabin of Dreams	Br 7933
21420-1	All You Want to Do Is Dance	Br 7933
21421-1	Have You Got AnyCastles, Baby?	Br 7937
21422-1	On with the Dance	Br 7937

Madeline Green, vcl

Chicago, August 10, 1937

C-1979-1	Blue Skies (vcl, MG)	JA 2 (LP)
C-1980-1	Hines Rhythm	JA 2 (LP)
C-1980-2	Hines Rhythm	Epic LN 3223
C-1981-1-2	Rhythm Rhapsody	Rejected
C-1982-1	A Mellow Bit of Rhythm	JA 2 (LP)
C-1983-1	Ridin' a Riff	Epic LN-3223

Earl Hines, pno, dir; Freddy Webster, George Dixon, tp; Ray Nancy, tp, vcl; Louis Taylor, Kennth Stuart, Joe McLewis, tb; Leroy Harris, cl, as, vcl; Budd Johnson, William Randall, Leon Washington, cl, ts; Claude Roberts, gtr; Quinn Wilson, sb, a; Oliver Coleman, d; Ida Mae James, vcl; Jimmy Mundy, a.

New York, March 7, 1938

22517-1	Solid Mama (vcl, JM)	Vo 4143
22518-1	Please Be Kind (vcl, IMJ)	Vo 4008
22519-1	Good Night, Sweet Dreams, Goodnight	Vo 4008

| 22520-1 | Tippin' at The Terrace | Vo 4143 |
| 22521-1 | Dominick Swing | Vo 4032 |

New York, March 17, 1938

| 22578-1 | Jezebel (vcl, LH) | Vo 4032 |
| 22579-1 | Jack Climbed a Beanstalk (vcl, RN) | Vo 4272 |

Henry Jackson, tp, and Kathryn Perry, vcl, added (All titles are on Jazz Panorama Jp-19 and Swing Classics ET-5; those marked * are on Almanac QSR-2418, all microgrooves.)

Chicago, Grand Terrace Ballroom, August 3, 1938

Deep Forest
*Limehouse Blues
Teacher's Pet
Hi-Yo Silver
Colorado Sunset (vcl, LH)
So Help Me
A Little Kiss at Twilight
Bambina
A-Tisket, A-Tasket (vcl, KP & ch)
*St. Louis Blues
Cavernism
Beside a Moonlit Stream (vcl, LH)   Unissued

Lionel Hampton and His Orchestra: Walter Fuller, tp; Omer Simeon, cl, as; George Oldham, as; Budd Johnson, Robert Crowder, ts; Spencer Odun, pno; James Simpkins, sb; Alvin Burroughs, d; Lionel Hampton, vib, vcl, pno.

Chicago, October 11, 1938

025866-1	Down Home Jump	Vi 26114
025867-1	Rock Hill Special (pno, LH)	Vi 26114
025868-1	Fiddle Diddle (vcl, LH)	Vi 26173

Lionel Hampton and His Orchestra: Ziggy Elman, tp; Toots Mondello, Buff Estes, as; Jerry Jerome, Budd Johnson, ts; Spencer Odun, pno; Ernest Ashely, gtr; Artie Bernstein, sb; Nick Fatool, d; Lionel Hampton, vib.

Chicago, February 26, 1940

044724-1	Shades of Jade	Vi 26604
044275-1	Till Tom Special	Vi 26604
044726-1	Flying Home	Vi 26595
044727-1	Save It, Pretty mama	Vi 26595
044278-1	Tempo and Swing	Vi 26608

Earl Hines and His Orchestra: Earl Hines, pno, dir; Walter Fuller, tp, vcl; Milton Fletcher, Edward Sims, tp; George Dixon, tp, as; Edward Burke, John Ewing, Joe McLewis, tb; Claude Roberts, gtr; Quinn Wilson, sb, a; Alvin Burroughs, d; Horace Henderson, Jimmy Mundy, Skippy Williams, a; Omer Simean, cl, bari; Leroy Harris, as, vcl; Budd Johnson, cl, as, ts, a; Robert Crowder, ts.

New York, July 12, 1939

038255-1	Indiana	BB B-10391
038256-1	G.T. Stomp	BB B-10391
038256-2	G.T. Stomp	Vi LPV-512
038257-1	Ridin' and Jivin'	BB B-10351
038258-1	Grand Terrace Shuffle (a, BJ)	BB B-10351
038259-1	Father Steps in (a, BJ)	BB B 10377
038260-1	Piano Man (vcl, WF; a, BJ)	BB B-10377

Laura Rucker, vcl, added

Chicago, October 6, 1939

040474-1	Riff Medley (a, BJ)	BB B-10531
040475-1	Me and Columbus (vlc, LR)	BB B-10467
040476-1	XYZ (a, BJ)	BB B-10531
040477-1	Gator Swing	BB B-10763
040478-1	After All I've Been to You	BB B-10467
040479-1	Lightly and Politely	BB B-10727

Shirley Clay, tp, replaces Fletcher; Buster Hardin, Edgar Battle, as.

New York, June 19, 1940

051521-1	Wait 'Til It Happens to You (vcl, BE)	BB B 10985
050522-1	Call Me Happy (as, BH)	BB B-10835
051523-1	Ann (vcl, BE)	BB B-10870
051524-1	Topsy-Turvy (vcl, WF; as, EB)	HMV EA-3168
050525-1	Blue Because of You (vcl, LH)	BB B -10835
050526-1	You Can Depend on Me (vcl, WF)	BB B-10792
050527-1	Tantalizing a Cuban	BB B-10792

Earl Hines and His Orchestra: Earl Hines, pno, dir; Harry Jackson, Rostello Reese, Leroy White, tp; Joe McLewis, John Ewing, Edward Fant, tb; Leroy Harris, as, vcl; Scoops Carey, as; William Randall, Budd Johnson, ts; Franz Jackson, ts, a; Hurley Ramey, gtr; Truck Parham, sb; Alvin Burroughs, d; Billy Eckstine, Madeline Greene, The Three Varieties, vcl; Jimmy Mundy, Bingie Madison, a.

Hollywood, December 2, 1940

055175-1	Easy Rhythm	BB B 10985

055176-1	In Swamp Lands	BB B-10036
055177-1	I'm Falling For You (vcl, BE)	BB B-11065,
055178-1	Everything Depends on You (vcl, MG, 3V)	BB B-11036
055179-1	Comin' in Home	BB B-11199
055180-1	Jelly, Jelly (vcl, BE)	BB B-11065

Earl Hines, dir, pno; George Dixon, tp, as; Harry Jackson, Tommy Enoch, Benny Harris, tp; Joe McLewis, George Hunt, Edward Fant, tb; Leroy Harris, cl, as; Scoops Carey, cl, as; William Randall, Budd Johnson, ts; Franz Jackson, ts; Hurley Ramey, gtr; Truck Parham, sb; Rudolph Taylor, d; Jimmy Mundy, Eddie Durham, Buster Harding, Avery Robinson, Edgar Battle, a; Billy Eckstine, Madeline Greene, The Three Varities, vcl. *New York, April 3, 1941*

063328-1	Up Jumped the Devil	BB B 11237
063329-1	Sally, Won't You Please Come Back?	BB B-11126
063330-1	Jersey Bounce	BB B-1126
063331-1	Julia (vcl, BE)	BB B-11199

Wonderland Park, London, Ontario, Canada, c. July 1941
Call Me Happy
That Rhythm Man
Honeysuckle Rose
Up Jumped the Devil
Jumpin' Up and Down
Pick-A-Rib
All six titles are on Almanac QSR-2418 (LP)

Freddy Webster, tp, replaces Harris; John Ewing, tb, replaces Fant.
Hollywood, August 20, 1941

061540-1	It Had To Be You (vcl, MG, 3V)	BB B-11308
061541-1	Windy City Jive	BB B-11329
061542-1	Straight To Love (vcl, LH)	BB B-11374
061543-1	Water Boy (vcl, BE)	BB B-11329
061544-1	Swingin' On C	BB B-11465
061545-1	Yellow Fire	BB B-11308

Jesse Miller, tp, replaces Webster; Nat Atkinson, tb, replaces Ewing.
Chicago, October 28, 1941

070332-1	Somehow (vcl, BE)	BB B-11432.
070333-1	I Got It Bad and That Ain't Good (vcl, BE, 3V, MG)	
		BB B-11374
070334-1	I Never Dreamt (vcl, MG, 3V)	BB B-11465

070335-1   The Father Jumps   BB B-11535

Gerald Valentine, tb, a, replaces Atkinson; Robert Crowder, ts, a, replaces Jackson; Mel Powell, a.
New York, November 17, 1941
068400-1   The Boy with the Wistful Eyes (vcl, MG, EV)   BB B-11394
068401-1   The Jitney Man (vcl, BE)   BB B 11535
068401-1   The Earl   BB B-11432
068403-1   You Don't Know What Love Is (vcl, BE)   BB B-11394

Earl Hines and His Orchestra: Earl Hines, pno, dir; George Dixon, tp, as; Harry Jackson, Maurice McConnell, Jesse Miller, tp; George Hunt, Joe McLewis, tb; Gerald Valentine, tb, a; Leroy Harris, Scoops Carey, cl, as; William Randall, Budd Johnson, ts; Robert Crowder, ts, a; Clifton Best, gtr; Truck Parham, sb; Rudolph Taylor, d; Billy Eckstine, Madeline Greene, The Three Varieities, vcl.
New York, March 19, 1942
073459-1   She'll Always Remember   BB B-11512
073460-1   Skylark   BB B-11512
073461-1   Second Balcony Jump   BB B-11567
073462-1   Stormy Monday Blues   BB B-11567

Benny Goodman and His Orchestra: Benny Goodman, cl, dir; Ziggy Elman, Jimmy Maxwell, Irving Goodman, tp; Red Ballard, Vernon Brown, Ted Vesely, tb; Toots Mondello, Buff Estes, as; Bus Bassey, Jerry Jerome, ts; Johnny Guarnieri, pno; Arnold Covey, gtr; Artie Bernstein, sb; Nick Fatool, d; Helen Forrest, vcl.
Chicago, March 1, 1940
WC-2972-A   Be Sure   Co 35426
WC-2976-A   Once More (a, BJ; vcl, HF)   Co 35543

"BILLIKEN" JOHNSON

Fred Adams, vcl; Billiken Johnson, vcl, vcl effects, whistling; Willie Tyson, pno; Octave Gaspard, bb.
Dallas, December 3, 1927
145322-1   Sun Beam Blues   Co 14293-D
145323-2   Interurban Blues   Co 14293-D

Billiken Johnson with Neal Roberts: Billiken Johnson, vcl, train whistle and mule imitations; Neal Roberts, pno, vcl.

Dallas, December 8, 1928

| 147606-2 | Frisco Blues | Co 14405-D |
| 147607-1, -2 | Wild Jack Blues | Co 14405-D |

BLIND WILLIE JOHNSON

Vcl acc by own gtr; humming and moaning without vcl (-1).
Dallas, December 3, 1927

145316-1, -2	I Know His Blood Can Make Me Whole	Co 14276-D
145317-2	Jesus Make Up My Dying Bed	Co 14276-D
145318-1, -2	Nobody's Fault But Mine	Co 14303-D
145319-2	Mother's Children Have a Hard Time	Co 14343-D
145320-1	Dark Was the Night, Cold Was the Ground, 1	Co 14303-D
145321-3	If I Had My Way I'd Tear the Building Down	Co 14343-D

Angeline Johnson, vcl added. There is evidence that this is instead Johnson's first wife, Willie B. Harris.
Dallas, December 5, 1928

147568-1	I'm Gonna Run to the City of Refuge	Co 14391-D
147569-2	Jesus Is Coming Soon	Co 14391-D
147570-2	Lord, I Just Can't Keep from Crying	Co 14425-D
147571-1, -2	Keep Your Lamp Trimmed and Burning	Co 14425-D

Angeline Johnson omitted.
New Orleans, December 10, 1929

149578-2	Let Your Light Shine On Me	Co 14490-D
149579-1	God Don't Never Change	Co 14490-D
149580-2	Bye and Bye I'm Goin' to See the King	Co 14504-D
149581-2	Sweeter As the Years Roll By	Co 14624-D

Angeline Johnson, vcl added except*
New Orleans, December 11, 1929

149594-1	You'll Need Somebody on Your Bond	Co 14504-D
149595-2	When the War Was On	Co 14545-D
149596-2	Praise God I'm Satisfied	Co 14545-D
149597-1	Take Your Burden to the Lord and Leave It There	
		Co 14520-D
149598-2	Take Your Stand*	Co 14624-D
145599-1	God Moves on the Water*	Co 14520-D

Atlanta, April 20, 1930

150307-/		
194926-2	Can't Nobody Hide From God	Co 14556-D
150308-/		
194927-1	If It Had Not Been for Jesus	Co 14556-D
150309-/		
194928-2	Go With Me To That Land	Co 15497-D
150310-2/		
194929-2	The Rain Don't Fall on Me	Co 14537-D
150311-2/		
194930-2	Trouble Will Soon Be Over	Co 14537-D
150312-/		
194931-3	The Soul of a Man	Co 14582-D
150313-/		
194897-2	Everybody Ought to Treat a Stranger Right	Co 14597-D
150314-/		
194890-3	Church, I'm Fully Saved To-day	Co 14582-D
150315-2	John the Revelator	Co 14530-D
150316-2	You're Gonna Need Somebody on Your Bond	Co 14530-D

Note: Co 14530-D was withdrawn shortly after issue.

WILLIAM J. "KEG" JOHNSON (see also Louis Armstrong sessions listed under Albert "Budd" Johnson)

Benny Carter and His Orchestra: Benny Carter, cl, as, dir; Eddie Mallory, Bill Dillard, Dick Clark, tp; J. C. Higginbortham, Fred Robinson, Keg Johnson, tb; Waymon Carver, as, f; Glyn Paque, as; Johnny Russell, ts; Teddy Wilson, pno; Lawrence Lucie, gtr; Ernest Hill, sb; Sid Catlett, d.
New York, October 16, 1933

265160-1	Devil's Holiday	Co 2898
265161-1	Lonesome Nights	OK 41467
265162-2	Symphony in Riffs	Co 2898-D
265163-2	Blue Lou	OK 41567

Benny Carter, cl, as, dir; Russell Smith, Otis Johnson, irving Randolph, tp; Benny Morton, Keg Johnson, tb; Ben Smith, Russell Procope, as; Ben Webster, ts; Teddy Wilson, pno; Clarence Holiday, gtr; Elmer Jones, sb; Walter Johnson, d; Charles Holland, vcl.
New York, December 13, 1934

16412-1	Shoot the Works	Vo 2898
16413-1	Dream Lullaby	Vo 2898
16414-1	Everybody Shuffle	Vo 2870

16415-1	Synthetic Love (vcl, CH)	Vo 2870

Fletcher Henderson and His Orchestra: Fletcher Henderson, pno, a, dir; Russell Smith, Joe Thomas, Henry Allen, tp; Claude Jones, Keg Johnson, tb; Buster Bailey, cl; Russell Procope, Hilton Jefferson, cl, as; Coleman Hawkins, ts; Bernard Addison, gtr; John Kirby, sb; Vic Engle, d; Charles Holland, vcl; Russ Morgan, poss. Will Hudson, a.

New York, March 6, 1934

81787-1	Hocus Pocus (a, WH)	BB B-5682
81787-2	Hocus Pocus (a, WH)	Vi LPV-556 (LP)
81788-2	Phantom Fanasies	Vi 24699
81789-2	Harlem Madness (vcl, CH; a, FH)	Vi 24699
81790-1	Tidal Wave	BB B-5682

Fletcher Henderson, pno (first title only), a, dir; Russell Smith, Irving Randolph, Henry Allen, tp; Claude Jones, Keg Johnson, tb; Buster Bailey, cl; Russell Procope, Hilton Jefferson, as; Ben Webster, ts; Horace Henderson, pno (last three titles); Lawrence Lucie, gtr; Elmer Jones, sb; Walter Johnson, d; Benny Carter, a.

New York, September 11, 1934

38598-A	Limehouse Blues (a, BC)	De 157
38599-A	Shanghai Shuffle (a, FH)	De 158
38600-A	Big John's Shuffle (a, HH)	De 214
38601-B	Happy As the Day Is Long (a,BC)	De 214

Fletcher Henderson, pno on the first two titles; Horace Henderson, pno, on the last two; Procope and Jefferson db cl; Russ Morgan, a.

New York, September 12, 1934

38602-A	Tidal Wave (a, RM)	De 213
38603-A	Down South Camp Meetin' (a, FH)	De 213
38604-B	Wrappin' It Up (a, FH)	De 157
38605-B	Memphis Blues (a, FH)	De 158

Benny Carter, as, added for the fourth title, possibly for the others; Fletcher Henderson, pno on all but the first title, Horace Henderson, pno, first and fourth.

New York, September 25, 1934

38723-A	Wild Party	De 342
38724-A	Rug Cutter's Swing (a, HH)	De 342
38725-A	Hotter Than 'Ell (a, HH)	De 555
38728-A	Liza (All the Clouds'll Roll Away)	De 555
		(unissued)

Henry Allen and His Orchestra: Henry Allen, tp, vcl; Keg Johnson tb; Buster Bailey, cl; Hilton Jefferson, as; Horace Henderson, pno; Lawrence Lucie, gtr; Elmer James, sb; Walter Johnson, d
New York, July 28, 1934

15471-1	There's a House in Harlem for Sale	Ban 33178
15472-1	Pardon My Southern Accent (vcl, HA)	Ban 33129
15473-1	Rug Cutter Swing	Ban 33178
15474-1	How's about Tomorrow Night?	Ban 33129

Chu Berry and His Stompy Stevedores: Irving Randolph, tp; Keg Johnson, tb; chu Berry, ts; Benny Payne, pno, vcl; Danny Barker, gtr; Milton Hinton, sb; Leroy Maxey, d.
New York, September 10, 1937

M-622-1	Chuberry Jam	Co 37571
M-623-1	Maelstrom	Co 37571
M-624-1	My Secret Love Affair	Vri 657
M-625-1	Ebb Tide	Vri 657

Cab Calloway and His Orchestra: Cab Calloway, vcl, dir; Shad Collins, Irving Randolph, Lammar Wright, tp; Claude Jones, Keg Johnson, DePriest Wheeler, tb; Garvin Bushell, Andrew Brown, cl, as; Ben Webster, Walter Thomas, ts; Bennie Payne, pno; Morris White, gtr; Milton Hinton, sb; Leroy Maxey, d.
New York, May 21, 1936

B-19304-1	Love Is the Reason	Br 7677
B-19035-1	When You're Smiling	Br 7685
B-19306-a	Jes' Natch'ully Lazy	Br 7677
B-19307-1	Are You in Love with Me Again	Br 7685

Cab Calloway, vcl, dir; Shad Collins, Irving Randolph, Lammar Wright, tp; Claude Jones, Keg Johnson, DePriest Wheeler, tb; Garvin Bushell, Andrew Brown, cl, as; Ben Webster, Walter Thomas, ts; Bennie Payne, pno; Morris White, gtr; Milton Hinton, sb; Leroy Maxey, d.
New York, September 15, 1936

B-19875-1	Copper-Colored Gal	Br 7748
B-19876-1	Frisco Flo	Br 7756
B-19877-1	The Wedding of Mr. and Mrs. Swing	Br 7748
B-19878-1	The Hi-De-Ho Miracle Man	Br 7756

New York, March 3, 1937

M-145-1	Don't Know If I'm Comin' or Goin'	Vri 535
M-146-2	My Gal Mezzanine	Vri 593
M-147-1	That Man Is Here Again	Vri 501

M-156-1	Peckin'	Vri 612
M-157-1	Congo	Vri 593
M-158-2	Swing, Swing, Swing	Vri 501

New York, March 17, 1937

M-266-1	Wake Up and Live	Vri 535
M-267-1-2	Goodnight, Baby	Rejected
M-268-1	Manhattan Jam	Vri 612

Doc Cheatham, tp, replaces Collins; Chu Berry, ts, replaces Webster
New York, August 24, 1937

M-606-1-2	Moon at Sea	Vri 651
M-607-1	I'm Always in the Mood for You	Vri 643
M-608-1	She's Tall, She's Tan, She's Terrific	Vri 643

New York, August 31, 1937

M-617-1	Go South, Young Man	Vri 644
M-618-1	Mama, I Wanna Make Rhythm	Vri 644
M-619-1	Hi-De-Ho Romeo	Vri 651
M-620-2	Queen Isabelle	Vri 662
M-621-2	Savage Rhythms	Vri 662

Shad Collins, tp, added; Chauncey Haughton, cl, as, replaces Bushell; Danny Barker, gtr, replaces White
New York, December 10, 1937

M-690-1-3	Every Day's a Holiday	Vo 3896
M-691-2-3	Jubilee	Vo 3896
M-692-1	In an Old English Village	Vo 3912
M-693-1	(Just an) Error in the News	Vo 3912
M-694-1	A Minor Breakdown (Rustle of Swing)	Rejected
M-695-1	Bugle Blues	Vo 4019

New York, January 26, 1938

M-743-1	One Big Union for Two	Vo 3970
M-744-1	Doing the Reactionary	Vo 3970
M-745-2	Rustle of Swing	Vo 4144
M-746-1	Three Swings and Out	Vo 3995
M-747-1	I Like Music (with a Swing Like That)	Vo 3995
M-748-1	Foolin' with You	Vo 4019

Payne db, vb.
New York, March 23, 1938

M-787-1	Azure	Vo 4100
M-788-1	Skrontch [sic]	Vo 4045
M-789-1	We're Breakin' up a Lovely Affair	Vo 4045
M-790-1	Peck-a-Doodle-Do	Vo 4100
M-791-1	At the Clambake Carnival	Vo 4437
M-792-1-2	Hoy-Hoy	Vo 4144

New York, August 30, 1938

M-891-1	Miss Hallelujah Brown	Vo 4400
M-892-1	The Congo-Conga	Vo 4411
M-893-1	The Boogie-Woogie	Vo 4400
M-894-1	There's a Sunny Side to Everything	Vo 4411
M-895-1	Shout, Shout, Shout	Vo 4369
M-896-1	Mister Paganine, Swing for Minnie	Vo 4369
M-897-1	Jive (Page One of the Hepster's Dictionary)	Vo 4437

New York, October 27, 1938

M-904-1	Do You Wanna Jump, Children?	Vo 4477
M-905-1	I'm Madly in Love with You	Vo 4511
M-906-2	April in My Heart	Vo 4477
M-907-1	Blue Interlude	Vo 4538

June Richmond, vcl
New York, November 2, 1938

M-908-1	F. D. R. Jones	Vo 4498
M-909-1	Deep in a Dream	Vo 4511
M-910-1	Tee-Um, Tee-Um, Tee-I, Tahiti	Vo 4538
M-911-1	Angels with Dirty Faces	Voc 4498

Cozy Cole, d, replaces Maxey; Edgar Battle, a.
New York, February 20, 1939

M-970-1	Long, Long Ago	Vo 4905
M-971-1	Afraid of Love	Vo 4905
M-972-1	Ratamacue	Vo 4700
M-973-1	Ad-De-Dey	Vo 4700

New York, March 28, 1939

WM-1009-1	A New Moon and an Old Serenade	Vo 4767
WM-1010-1	One Look at You	Vo 4767
WM-1011-1	The Ghost of Smokey Joe	Vo/OK 4807
WM-1012-1, -2	Floogie Walk	Vo/OK 4807

Mario Bauza, tp, replaces Randolph; Chappie Willett, a.
New York, July 17, 1939

WM-1054-A	Trylon Swing	Vo/OK 5005
WM-1055-A	Utt-Da-Zay	Vo/OK 5062
WM-1056-A	Crescendo in Drums	Vo/OK 5062
WM-1057-A	(Hep! Hep!) The Jumpin' Jive	Vo/OK 5005

Dizzy Gillespie, tp, replaces Randolph; Chappie Willett, a.
New York, August 30, 1939

WM-1065-A	For the Last Time I Cried over You	Vo 5126
WM-1066-A	Twee-Twee-Tweet	Vo 5126
WM-1067-A	Pluckin' the Bass	Vo/OK 5406
WM-1068-A	I Ain't Gettin' Nowhere Fast	Vo/OK 5195

New York, October 17, 1939

WM-1101-A	Chili Con Conga	Vo/OK 5315
WM-1102-A	Tarzan of Harlem	Vo/OK 5267
WM-1103-A	Jiveformation, Please	Vo/OK 5195
WM-1104-A	Vuelva	Vo/OK 5315

New York, November 29, 1939

WM-1113-A	A Bee Gezindt	Vo/OK 5267
WM-1114-A	Give, Baby, Give	Vo/OK 5406
WM-1115-A	Sincere Love	Vo/OK 5364
WM-1116-A	Do It Again	Vo/OK 5364

Cab Calloway, vcl, dir; Mario Bauza, Dizzy Gillespie, Lammar Wright, tp; Tyree Glenn, tb, vib; Quentin Jackson, Keg Johnson, tb; Jerry Blake (alias Jacinto Chabani), cl, as; Hilton Jefferson, as; Andrew Brown, as, bar; Chu Berry, Walter Thomas, ts; Bennie Payne, pno; Danny Barker, gtr; Milton Hinton, sb; Cozy Cole, d; Andy Gibson, Benny Carter, Edgar Battle, Buster Harding, Don Redman, a.
Chicago, March 8, 1940

WM-2983-A	Pickin' the Cabbage	Vo/OK 5467
WM-2984-A	Chop, Chop, Charlie Chan	Vo/OK 5444
WM-2985-A	Paradiddle	Vo/OK 5467
Wm-2986-A	Boog It	Vo/OK 5444

New York, May 15, 1940

27295-1	Calling All Bars	OK 5731
27295-2	Calling All Bars	JA 8 (LP)
27296-1	Do I Care? No, No	Vo/OK 5591

27297-1	The Lone Arranger	Rejected
27298-1	Feelin' Tip Top	OK 5874
27299-1	Topsy Turvy (Hard Times)	Vo/OK 5566
27300-1	Hi-De-Ho Serenade	Vo/OK 5591
27301-1	Who's Yehoodi?	Vo/OK 5566
27301-2	Who's Yehoodi?	JA 8 (LP)

Chicago, June 27, 1940

WC-3160-A	Fifteen Minute Intermission	OK 5644
WC-3161-A	Rhapsody in Rhumba	OK 5644
WE-3162-A	Come on with the "Come on"	OK 5687
WC-3163-A	A Ghost of a Chance	OK 5687
WC-3164-A	Bye Bye Blues	OK 6084
WC-3164-B	Bye Bye Blues	JA 8 (LP)

Meadowbrook, Cedar Grove, New Jersey, July 27, 1940
Minnie the Moocher; Limehouse Blues; I Can't Resist You; Hard Times (Topsy Turvy); Fifteen Minute Intermission; Boog It; Cupid's Nightmare; King Porter Stomp. All JP LP-16.

New York, August 5, 1940

27801-1	Papa's in Bed with His Britches on	OK 5731
27802-1	Silly Old Moon	OK 5774
27803-1	Boo-Wah Boo-Wah	OK 5774
27804-2	Sunset	OK 5804
27805	Yo eta cansa	OK 5827

New York, August 28, 1940

28513-1	Cupid's Nightmare	OK 6035
28514-1	Levee Lullaby	OK 5950
28515-1	Are You Hep to the Jive?	OK 5804
28516-1	Goin' Conga	OK 5911
28517-1	Hot Air	OK 5950
28518-1	Lonesome Nights	OK 5827

New York, October 14, 1940

28863-1	A Chicken Ain't Nothin' But a Bird	OK 5847
28864-1	The Workers' Train	OK 5874
28865-1	North of the Mohawk Trail	OK 5911
28866-1	Make Yourself at Home	OK 5847

Chicago, January 16, 1941

C-3518-1	Run, Little Rabbut	OK 6084
C-3519	Willow, Weep for Me	OK 6109
C-3520-1	You Are the One in My Heart	OK 6391
C-3521-1	Are You All Reet?	OK 6035
C-3522-1	Ebony Silhouette	OK 6192

Jonah Jones, tp, replaces Bauza
New York, March 15, 1941

29866-1	Hep Cat Love Song	OK 6192
29867-1-2	Jonah Joins the Cab	OK 6109
29868-1-2	Geechee Joe	OK 6147
29869-1-3	Special Delivery	OK 6147

New York, July 3, 1941

30835-1	Take the "A" Train	OK 6305
30836-1	Chattanooga Choo-Choo	OK 6305
30837-1	My Gal	Co 32593
30838-1	St. James Infirmary	OK 6391

New York, July 4, 1941

30838-4	St. James Infirmary	OK 6391
30938-1	We Go Well Together	OK 6341
30939-1	Hey Doc	OK 6354
30940-1	I See a Million People	OK 6341
30941-1	Conchita (Cares Nothing about Love)	OK 6354

The Palmer Brothers, vcl.
New York, September 10, 1941

31300-1	Blues in the Night	OK 6422
31300-2	Blues in the Night	Epic LN-3265 (LP)
31301-1	Mrs. Finnigan	OK 6459
31302-1	My Coo-Coo Bird (Could Sing)	OK 6459
31303-1	Says Who? Says You, Says I!	OK 6422

The Cabaliers, vcl.
New York, December 24, 1941

32037-1	The Moment I Laid Eyes on You	OK 6574 (unissued)
32038-1	Virginia, Georgia, and Caroline	OK 6574 (unissued)
32039-1	Blue Moonlight	Rejected
32040-1	Lordy	Co 36751

Chicago, February 2, 1942

C-4179-1	I Want to Rock	OK 6616
C-4180-1	What's Buzzin' Cousin?	Rejected
C-4181-1	I'll Be Around	OK 6717
C-4182-1	'Tain't No Good	OK 6616
C-4183-1	Minnie the Moocher	OK 6634

Hollywood, July 27, 1942

HCO-884-1	Let's Go, Joe	OK 6720
HCO-885-1-2	Ogeechee River Lullaby	Co 36662
HCO-886-1	I Get the Neck of the Chicken	Co 36662
HCO-887-1	Chant of the Jungle	Rejected

COLEY JONES

Vcl acc by own gtr.
Dallas, December 3, 1927

145324-1	Army Mule in No Man's Land	Co 14288-D
145325-2	That's My Man	Co unissued
145326-2	Papa Coley's Past Life Blues	Co unissued
145327-2	You Go Ahead, I'll Stay Right Here	Co unissued
145328-3	O Death, Where Is Thy Sting	Co unissued

Note: The unissued sides are credited to COALIE JONES in the Columbia files.

Dallas, December 4, 1927

145329-1, -2	Traveling Man	Co 14288-D

Dallas, December 6, 1927

145342-2	Frankie and Albert	Co unissued

JAKE JONES & THE GOLD FRONT BOYS

Jake Jones, vcl; acc the Gold Front Boys: unknown, cl; unknown, bj; unknown, gtr.
Dallas, October 27, 1929

DAL-473	Monkeyin' Around	Br 7130
DAL-474	Southern Sea Blues	Br 7130

REV. JOE LENLEY

Sermons with singing; acc poss. Arizona Dranes, pno, vcl.
Dallas, December 5, 1929

149546-2	Let Us Therefore Come	Co 14521-D
149547-2	Lord Who Shall Abide in Thy Tabernacle	Co 14521-D

THE LITTLE RAMBLERS

Roy Johnston, tp; Tommy Dorsey, tb; Bobby Davis, cl, ss, as; Sam Ruby or Freddy Cusick, ts; Adrian Rollini, bsx, gfs; Irving Brodsky, pno; Tommy Felline, bj; Stan King, d, k.
New York, July 14, 1925

140759-2	Deep Elm (You Tell 'Em I'm Blue)	Co 423-D

LONE STAR COWBOYS (see also Shelton Brothers)

Jimmie Davis, vcl; Leon Chappelear gtr; Bob Attlesey, u; Joe Attlesey, md.
Chicago, August 4, 1933

76862-1	It's All Coming Home to You	BB B-5156
76863-1	I Wonder If She's Blue	BB B-5187
76864-1	When It's Round-Up Time in Heven	BB B-5187
76865-1	Would You? (jug, BA)	BB B-5359
76866-1	You've Been Tom-Cattin' Around	BB B-5425
76867-1	Alimony Blues	BB B-5425

Leon Chappelear, gtr; Bob Attlesey, u; Joe Attlesey, md.
Chicago, August 4, 1933

76868-1	Hang Out the Front Door Key	Vi 23843
76869-1	Deep Elm Blues	Vi 23843
76870-1	Will There Be Any Cowboys in Heaven?	Vi 23850
76871-1	Wonderful Child	Vi 23850

Jimmie Davis, vcl; Leon Chappelear, gtr; Bob Attlesey, u, jug; Joe Attlesey, md.
Chicago, August 5, 1933

76872-1	The Keyhole in the Door	BB B-5156
76873-1	Beautiful Texas	BB B-5394
76874-1	Triflin' Mama Blues	BB B-5635
76875-1	I Want Her Tailor-Made	BB B-5359

76876-1	Alimony Blues	BB B-5635
76877-1	There Ain't Gonna Be No Afterwhile	BB B-5570
76878-1	Easy Rider Blues	BB B-5570

Leon Chappelear, gtr; Bob Attlesey, u, jug; Joe Attlesey, md.
Chicago, August 5, 1933

76879	Crawdad Song	BB B-6052
76880-1	Who Wouldn't Be Lonely?	BB B-5283
76881-1	Just Because	BB B-6052

LEON'S LONE STAR COWBOYS

Leon Chappelear, lead gtr, vcl; Leon "Lonnie" Hall, fid, vcl-1; Johnny Harvey, cl; Skipper Hawkins, b; Howard Oliver, tbj; Gene Sullivan, rhythm gtr, vcl, lead gtr-2.

Note: The Attlesey brothers assumed the surname Sheton for subsequent recordings.

Chicago, August 14, 1935

90225	Mama Don't Allow It	DE 5423
90226	Ben Wheeler Stomp	DE 5928
90227	Dinah -1	DE 5361
90228	Milenburg Joys	DE 5454
90229	Mistreated Blues	DE 5423
90230	I'm a Do Right Papa	DE 5361
90231	That Old Sweetheart of Mine	DE 5301
90232	Truly I Promise to Love You	DE 4914
90233	Tiger Rag	DE 5396
90235	by Jimmie Davis & Buddy Jones	

August 15, 1935

90236	My Gal Sal	DE 5301
90237	Sweet Georgia Brown	Unissued
90238	Weary Blues	DE 5323
90239	Just Forget	DE 5914
90240	Sweet Sue, Just You	DE 5328
90241	No Mama Blues	DE 5454
90242	I'm Sitting on Top of the World	DE 5328
90243	White River Stomp	DE 5433
90244	Kansas City Blues -2	DE 5396
90245	Four or Five Times -1	DE 5323
90246	Darktown Strutter's Ball	Unissued
90247	My Little Girl	DE 5433

Leon Chappelear, lead gtr, vcl; Leon "Lonnie" Hall, fid; Grundy "Slim" Harbert, b; Speck Haarrison, cl, alto sax; Howard Oliver, tbj; Gene Sullivan, rhythm gtr, vcl -1.

New Orleans, March 13, 1936

60715	31st Street Blues	DE 5280
60716	China Boy	DE 5280
60717	Mr. and Mrs. is the Name -1	DE 5289
60718	I'll Never Say "Never Again" Again -1	DE 5288
60719	Texas Plains	DE 5288
60720	(I Know I Love You But) I Don't Know Why	DE 5289
60721	Prairie Rose	DE 5530

Leon Chappelear, lead gtr, vcl; Hugh Berry, cl, Leon "Lonnie" Hall, fid; Grundy "Slim" Harbert, b; Howard Oliver, tbj; Carl Rainwater, amp stg.

Dallas, February 14, 1937

61775	Just a Blue Eyed Blonde	DE 5340
61776	Trouble in Mind	DE 5340
61777	Too Good to Be True	DE 5388
61778	Baby Won't You Come Along	DE 5416
61779	You're in My Heart to Stay	DE 5404
61780	Wild Cat Mama (The Answer to Do Right Papa)	DE 5404
61781	I'm Serving Days	DE 5449
61782	Who Walks in When I Walk Out	DE 5377
61783	Travelin' Blues	DE 5416
61784	In a Little Red Barn	DE 5377
61785	I Never Knew	DE 5697
61786	Angry	DE 5388
61787	The Empty Cradle	DE 5449
61788	The One Rose (That's Left in My Heart)	MW 8014

Note: artist credit on DE 5449 to "Leon Chappelear"

Leon Chappelear, lead gtr, vcl; Hezzie Bryant, b; J. R. Chatwell, fid; Leon "Lonnie" Hall, fid; Archie Lorante, pno; Howard Oliver, tbj.

December 12, 1937

63030	Dear Little Girl	DE 5481
63031	She's Got Me Worried	DE 5571
63032	New Do Right Daddy	DE 5481
63033	She's Runnin' Around	DE 5511
63034	Goin' Up to Dallas	DE 5551
63035	Toodle-Oo Sweet Mama	DE 5697
63036	Red Hot Mama from Way Out West	DE 5551
63037	You're a Million Miles from Nowhere	DE 5511

| 63038 | My Mother's Rosary | DE 5530 |
| 63039 | Sentimental Gentleman from Georgia | DE 5571 |

IDA MAY MACK

Vcl; acc. K.D. Johnson, pno.
Memphis, Tennessee, August 29, 1928

45438-1, -2	Wrong Doin' Daddy	Vi V38532
45438-2	Sunday Mornin' Blues	Vi V38532
45442-1	Elm Street Blues	Vi V38030
45443-2	Country Spaces	Vi unissued

Memphis, Tennessee, August 30, 1928

45446-1	Mr. Moore Blues	Vi 21690
45447-1	When You Lose Your Daddy	Vi 21690
45450-1	Mr. Forty-Nine Blues	Vi V38532
45451-1	Goodbye, Rider	Vi V38030

WILLIAM McCOY

H solo, speech
Dallas, December 6, 1927

| 145334-2 | Mama Blues | Co 14302-D |
| 145335-1 | Train Imitations and the Fox Chase | Co 14302-D |

H solo; acc. poss. Sam Harris, gtr.
Dallas, December 7, 1928

| 147593-2 | Just It | Co 14393-D |
| 147594-1 | How Long Baby | Co 14393-D |

vcl, h; poss. Jesse Hooker, cl; poss. Sam Harris, gtr.
Dallas, December 8, 1928

| 147610-1, -2 | Out Of Doors Blues | Co 14453-D |
| 147611-1 | Central Tracks Blues | Co 14453-D |

WHISTLIN' ALEX MOORE (also known as Alex Moore)

vcl; acc by own pno.
Dallas, December 5, 1929

149530-1	They May Not Be My Toes	Co 14596-D
149531-2	West Texas Woman	Co 14496-D
149534-2	Heart Wrecked Blues	Co 14518-D
149535-2	Ice Pick Blues	Co 14518-D

Poss. Blind Norris, gtr.

| 149562-2 | It Wouldn't Be So Hard | Co 14496-D |
| 149563-2 | Blue Bloomer Blues | Co 14596-D |

Alex Moore: vcl; unknown gtr, vb.
Chicago, February 18, 1937

61852-A	Blue Bloomer Blues	De 7288
61853-A	Come Back Baby	De 7288
61854-A	Bull Con Blues	De 7552
61855-A	Hard Hearted Woman	De 7552

Vcl, pno.
Dallas, June 30, 1960
Whistlin' Alex Moore's Blues
Pretty Woman With a Sack Dress On
Rubber Tired Hack
You Say I'm a Bad Feller
From North Dallas to the East Side
New Miss No-Good Weed
Black-Eyed Peas and Hog Jowls
Boogie in the Barrel
Going Back to Froggy Bottom
July Boogie
West Texas Woman
Frisky Gal
Chock House Boogie
(All on *From North Dallas to the East Side*, Arhoolie CD 408.)

Radio station KLIF, Dallas, 1947
Miss No-Good Weed
Alex's Boogie
You Got Me Dissatisfied
Alex's Rag
Alex's Blues
Alex's Wild Blues
Sometime I feel Worried
I Love You Baby

Stuttgart, Germany, October 23, 1969
Rock and Roll Bed
Boogiein' in Strassburg

Vcl, pno.
Dallas, February 3, 1988
Wiggle Tail
Everybody Have a Good Time
Chasin' Rainbows
Newest Blue Bloomer Blues
Elephant Brain Man
(All on Rounder 2091, record title *Wiggle Tail.*)

Dallas, 1947, Dallas, 1988
Then and Now, Untitled Piano Blues　　　　　　　　　　DA 105

ROY NEWMAN AND HIS BOYS

Roy Newman, pno; Jim Boyd, gtr, vcl; Earl Brown, b, vcl; Art Davis, fid, vcl; Walker Kirkes, tenor banjo; Ish Irwin, b; Thurman Neal, fid; Buddy Neal, gtr.
Fort Worth, Texas, September 30, 1934

FW 1140	Messin' Around (instrumental)	Vo 02906
FW 1141	Tiger Rag	Vo 02906
FW 1142	Weary Blues(instrumental)	Vo 02864
FW 1143	Red Wing	Unissued
FW 1144	Drag Along Blues (instrumental)	Vo 02864
FW 1145	Chicken Reel (instrumental)	Vo 02883
FW 1146	Way Down Yonder in Carolina	Unissued
FW 1147	Git Along Home, Cindy	Vo 02883

Roy Newman, pno; Holly Horton, cl; Jim Boyd, gtr; Thurman Neal, fid; Buddy Neal, gtr; Art Davis, fid; Earl Brown, b; Ish Irwin, b; Walker Kirkes, tenjor bj; Holly Horton, cl.
Fort Worth, Texas, June 26, 1935

FW 1222	Tin Roof Blues	Vo 02994
FW 1223	Garbage Man Blues	Vo 02994
FW 1224	Somebody Loves Me	Vo 03000
FW 1225	Barn Dance Rag (instrumental)	Vo 03000

Earl Brown, gtr; Art Davis, md; Jim Boyd, elg.

Dallas, Texas, September 27, 1935

DAL 172	Rhythm Is Our Business	Vo 03103
DAL 173	Dinah	Vo 03183
DAL 174	I Can't Dance	Vo/OK 03117
DAL 175	Slow and Easy	Vo 03103

Dallas, September 28, 1935

DAL 178	Hot Dog Stomp	Vo 03371
DAL 179	The Lonesome Road	Vo 03212
DAL 180	Shine on Harvest Moon	Vo 03272
DAL 181	Corrine, Corrina	Vo/OK 03117

Dallas, October 1, 1935

DAL 191	How Many Times?	Vo 03151
DAL 192	Sadie Green	Vo 03151
DAL 193	Rock-a-Bye Moon	Vo 03272
DAL 194	A Good Man Is Hard to Find	Vo 03325
DAL 195	Some of These Days	Vo 03183
DAL 196	There'll Be Some Changes Made	Vo 03325

Dallas, October 4, 1935

DAL 201	Birmingham Jail	Vo 03212
DAL 202	(What Did I Do to Be) So Black and Blue	Vo 03240
DAL 203	12th Street Rag	Vo 03240
DAL 204	Wonderful One	Vo 03371

Fort Worth, November 8, 1936

FW 1278	Hot Potato Stomp	Unissued
FW 1279	Everybody's blues	Unissued
FW 1280	There's a Silver Moon on the Golden Gate	Unissued
FW 1281	Too Busy	Unissued

Dallas, June 6, 1937

DAL 205	I Love My Baby	Unissued
DAL 206	Long Long Ago	Unissued
DAL 207	When You and I Were Young, Maggie	Vo 03598
DAL 208	We'll Meet by the Bend in the River	Vo 03598
DAL 209	Everybody's Blues	Vo 03878
DAL 210	She's Doggin' Me	Vo 03672
DAL 211	Match Box Blues	Unissued

Dallas, June 14, 1937

DAL 308	Takin' Off	Vo 04025
DAL 309	Who Calls You Sweet Mama Now?	Vo 03631
DAL 310	The Night That You Nestled (in My Arms)	Vo 03631
DAL 311	Drifting and Dreaming	Unissued
DAL 312	Mississippi Mud	Vo 04025
DAL 313	When There's Tears in the Eyes of a Potato	Vo 03878
DAL 314	Cemetery Sal	Unissued
DAL 315	Dust Off That Old Piano	Vo 03938
DAL 316	Mary Lou	Vo/OK 03752
DAL 317	Railroad Blues	Unissued

Dallas, June 18, 1937

DAL 363	I'm Saving Saturday Night for You	Vo/OK 03752
DAL 364	Catch on and Let's Go	Vo 03672
DAL 365	Back in Your Own Backyard	Vo 03938
DAL 366	Graveyard Blues	Vo 03963
DAL 367	Better Get Off Your High Horse, Baby	Vo 03963
DAL 368	Everywhere You Go	Vo 03999
DAL 369	Tamiami Trail	Vo 03999

Dallas, December 1, 1938

DAL 660	Down Hearted Blues	Vo/OK 04959
DAL 661	Kansas City Blues	Vo/OK 04959
DAL 662	Nagasaki	Unissued
DAL 663	Match Box Blues	Vo/OK 04578
DAL 664	I Cried for You	Vo/OK 04792
DAL 665	Texas Stomp	Vo/OK 04866
DAL 666	Take Me Back to My Home in the Mountains	Vo/OK 05486
DAL 667	My Baby Rocks Me (with One Steady Roll)	Vo/OK 04578
DAL 668	I've Got It	Vo/OK 04639
DAL 669	Everybody's Trying to Be My Baby	Vo/OK 04866

Dallas, December 5, 1938

DAL 722	Eleven Pounds of Heaven	Vo/OK 04792
DAL 723	I Don't Love Anyone But You	Vo/OK 04740
DAL 724	I Used to Love You (But It's All Over Now)	Vo/OK 04639
DAL 725	Where Morning Glories Grow	Vo 05379
DAL 726	Cemetery Sal	Unissued
DAL 727	I Love My Baby (My Baby Loves Me)	Vo/OK 05486
DAL 728	Boog-A-Boo Baby	Vo/OK 04740

Dallas, June 19, 1939

DAL 856	The Devil with the Devil	Vo 05066
DAL 857	Blues, Why Don't You Let Me Alone?	Vo/OK 05320
DAL 858	Round the World on a Dime	Vo 05066
DAL 859	I've Got the Walkin' Blues	Vo 05379
DAL 860	Kentucky, Sure As You're Born	Vo/OK 05242
DAL 861	If I Ever Get to Heaven	Vo 05014

Dallas, June 20, 1939

DAL 871	Don't Let Me Stand in Your Way	Vo/OK 05320
DAL 872	Out of Place	Unissued
DAL 873	Love Burning Love	Vo 05175
DAL 874	Everything Is Peaches	Vo/OK 05242
DAL 875	I Ought to Break Your Neck	Vo 05175

ORAN "HOT LIPS" PAGE

Bennie Moten's Kansas City Orchestra: Bennie Moten, dir; Count Basie, pno; Ed Lewis, Booker Washington, c; Thamon Hayes, tb; Harlan Leonard, cl, ss, as; Jack Washington, cl, as, bar; Woody Walder, cl, ts; Ira "Buster" Moten, pac, 2nd pno; Leroy Berry, bj; Vernon Page, bb; Willie McWashington, d; Bob Clemmons, vcl; Hot Lips Page, tp; Jimmy Rushing, vcl; Eddie Durham, tb, gtr, a.

Kansas City, October 27, 1930

| 62909-1 | Won't You Be My Baby? (vcl, JR) | Vi LPV-514 (LP) |
| 62909-2 | Won't You Be My Baby? (vcl, JR) | Vi 2302 |

Kansas City, October 28, 1930

62910-2	I Wish I Could Be Blue	Vi 22734
62911-2	Oh! Eddie	Vi 22958
62912-1	That Too, Do (vcl, JR)	Vi LPM-100023(LP)
62912-2	That Too, Do (vcl, JR)	Vi 22793
62913-1	Mack's Rhythm	Vi LPM-10023(LP)
62914-1	You Made Me Happy	Pirate MPC-521(LP)
62915-1	Here Comes Marjorie	Vi 23391
62916-1	The Count	Vi 23391

Kansas City, October 29, 1930

62921-1	Liza Lee (vcl, JR)	Vi 23023

Buster Moten switches to pac.

Kansas City, October 30, 1930

62922-2	Get Goin' (Get Ready to Love) (vcl, JR)	Vi 23023
62923-1	Professor Hot Stuff	Vi 23429
62994-2	When I'm Alone (vcl, JR)	Vi 22734
62925-2	New Moten Stomp	Vi 23030
62926-2	As Long As I Love You (Jeanette) (vcl, JR)	Vi 22660

Kansas City, October 31, 1930

62927-1	Somebody Stole My Gal (vcl, CB)	Vi 23028
62928-2	New That I Need You (vcl, JR)	BB B-6711
62929-2	Bouncin' Round	Vi 23030
62930-1	Break a Day Schuffle	Rejected

New York, April 15, 1931

53012-2	Ya Got Love (vcl, JR)	Vi 22680
68900-2	I Wanna Be Around My Baby All the Time (vcl, JR)	Vi 22680

Bennie Moten, dir; Hot Lips Page, Joe Keyes, Dee Stewart, tp; Dan Minor, tb; Eddie Durham, tb, gtr, a; Eddie Barefield, cl, as; Jack Washington, as, bar; Ben Webster, ts; Count Basie, pno; Leroy Berry, gtr; Sterling Russell Trio (Sterling Russell, Hamilton Stewart, Clifton Armstrong), vcl.

Camden, New Jersey, December 13, 1932

74846-1	Toby	Vi 23384
74847-1	Moten Swing	Vi 23384
74848-1	The Blue Room (Curatito de Dichas*)	Vi 24381
74849-1	Imagination (vcl, SR3)	Vi 23378
74850-1	New Orleans (vcl, JR)	Vi 24216
74851-1	The Only Girl I Ever Loved (vcl, SR3)	Vi 23378
74852-1	Milenberg Joys (Estrambotico*)	Vi 24381
74853-1	Lafayette	Vi 24216
74854-1	Prince of Wails	Vi 23393
74855-1	Two Times* (vcl, JG)	Vi 23393

*Hot Lips Page, Barefield, Basie, Durham, gtr, Walter Page, Willie McWashington only.

Chu Berry and His Stompy Stevedores: Hot Lips Page, tp,vcl; George Matthews, tb; Buster Bailey, cl; Chu Berry, ts; Horace Henderson, pno; Laurence Lucie, gtr; Israel Crosby, sb; Cozy Cole, d.

New York, March 23, 1937

M-293-2	New You're Talking My Language (vcl, HLP)	Vri 532
M-294-1-2	Indiana	Vri 587,
		Vo 3824
M-295-1	Too Marvelous For Words (vcl, HLP)	Vri 532
M-295-2	Too Marvelous For Words (vcl, HLP)	Swing 358
M-296-1	Limehouse Blues	Vri 587

Teddy Wilson and His Orchestra: Hot Lips Page, tp; Pee Wee Russell, cl; Chu Berry, ts; Teddy Wilson, pno; Allan Reuss, gtr; Sally Gooding, vcl; unknown sb, d.

New York, December 17, 1937

B-22192-1-2	My First Impressions of You	Rejected
B-22193-1-2	With a Smile and a Song	Rejected
B-22194-1-2	When You're Smiling	Rejected
B-22195-2	I Can't Believe That You're in Love with Me	Rejected

Hot Lips Page and His Band: Hot Lips Page, tp, vcl; Ben Smith, cl, as; Sam Simmons, ts; Jimmy Reynolds, pno; Connie Wainwright, gtr; Wellman Braud, sb; Alfred Taylor, d.

New York, Mach 10, 1938

63393-A	Good Old Bosom Bread (vcl, HLP)	De 7451
63394-A	He's Pulling His Whiskers	De 7451
63395-B	Down on the Levee (Levee Lullaby) (vcl, HLP)	De 7433
63396-A	Old Man Ben (vcl, HLP)	De 7433

Hot Lips Page, tp, vcl, dir; Eddie Mullens, Bobby Moore, tp; George Stevenson, tb; Harry White, tb, a; Ulysses Scott, as; Ben Smith, cl, as; Benny Waters, Ernie Powell, ts; Jimmy Reynolds, pno; Connie Wainwright, gtr; Abe Bolar, sb; Alfred Taylor, d.

New York, April 27, 1938

022293-1	Jumpin'	BB B-7583
022924-1	Feelin' High and Happy (vcl, HLP)	BB B-7569
022925-1	At Your Beck and Call (vcl, HLP)	BB B-7569
922926-1	Rock It for Me (vcl, HLP)	BB B-7567
022927-1	Skull Duggery (a, HW)	BB B-7583
022928-1	I Let a Song Go Out of My Heart	BB B-7567

Dave Page, tp, replaces Mullens; Ben Williams, as, ts, replaces Scott; Delores Payne, Ben Bowers, vcl.

New York, June 24, 1938

023732-1	If I Were You (vcl, DP)	BB B-7684

023733-1	(A Sky of Blue, with You) and So Forth (vcl, DP)	
		BB B-7680
023734-1	The Pied Piper (vcl, HLP)	BB B-7682
023735-1	Small Fry (vcl, HLP)	BB B-7684
023736-1	I'm Gonna Lock My Heart and Throw Away the Key (vcl, HLP)	
		BB B-7682
023737-1	Will You Remember Tonight Tomorrow? (vcl, BB)	
		BB B-7680

Hot Lips Page, a, tp; Eddie Barefield, cl, as; Don Stovall, as; Don Byas, ts; Pete Johnson, pno; John Collins, gtr; Abe Bolar, sb; A.G. Godley, d.
New York, November 11, 1940

| 68334-A | Lafayette | De 18124 |
| 68335-A | South | De 18124 |

Hot Lips Page and His Band: Hot Lips Page, tp; Eddie Barefield, cl, as; Don Stovall, as; Don Byas, ts; Pete Johnson, pno; John Collins, gtr; Abe Bolar, sb; A.G. Godley, d; Be Morton, vcl.
New York, December 3, 1940

| 68435-A | Harlem Rhumbain' the Blues | De 8531 |
| 68436-A | No Matter Where You Are (When Evening Draws Her Curtain) (vcl, BM) | De 8531 |

Hot Lips Page Trio: Hot Lips Page, tp, mel, vcl; Leonard Feather, pno; Teddy Bunn, gtr, vcl; Ernest Hll, bb, sb.

058149-1	Thirsty Mama Blues (vcl, HLP)	BB B-8981
058150-1	Just Another Woman (vcl, HLP)	BB B-8660
058151	My Fightin' Gal (vcl, HLP)	BB B-8660
058152-1	Evil Man's Blues (vcl, TB)	BB B-8634
058153-1	Do It If You Wanna	BB B-8634

Chu Berry and His Jazz Ensemble: Hot Lips Page, tp, vcl; Chu Berry, ts; Clyde Hart, pno; Alberty Casey, gtr; Al Morgan, sb; Harry Jaeger, d.
New York, September 1941

R-4178	Blowing Up a Breeze	Com 541
R-4180	Monday At Minton's (What's It to You?)	Com 541
R-4181	Gee, Ain't I Good to You? (vcl, HLP)	Com 1508

(Page does not play on R-4179)

Ida Cox and Her Al-Star Band: Hot Lips Page, tp; J.C. Higginbotham, tb unless marked *; Edmond Hall, cl unless marked *; James P. Johnson, pno;

Charlie Christian, elg; Artie Bernstein, sb; Lionel Hampton, d, unless marked *

New York, October 31, 1939

25509-1	Deep Sea Blues	Vo 05336
25510-1	Death Letter Blues*	Vo 05336
25511	One Hour Mama	Vo 05232
		unissued

Fletcher Henderson, pno, replaces Johnson.

New York, October 31, 1939

26239-A	Four Day Creep	Vo 05298
26240-A	Pink Slip Blues	Vo 05258
26241-A	Hard Time Blues	Vo 95298
26242-A	Take Him off My Mind	Vo 05258

Pete Johnson's Band: Hot Lips Page, tp; Eddie Barefield, cl, as; Don Stovall, as; Don Byas, ts; Pete Johnson, pno; John Collins, gtr; Abe Bolar, sb; A. G. Godley, d.

New York, November 11, 1940

| 68332-A | 627 Stomp | De 18121 |

Joe Turner and His Fly Cats: Joe Turner, vcl; Hot Lips Page, tp; Don Byas, ts; Pete Johnson, pno; John Collins, gtr; Abe Bolar, sb; A. G. Godley, d.

New York, November 11, 1940

| 68333-A | Piney Brown Blues | De 18121 |

Billie Holiday and Her Orchestra: Billie Holiday, vcl, acc by Hot Lips Page, tp; Tab Smith, as, ss; Kenneth Hollon, Stanley Payne, ts; Kenneth Kersey, pno; Jimmy McLin, gtr; John Williams, sb; Eddie Dougherty, d.

New York, March 21, 1939

24245-1	You're Too Lovely to Last	Vo/OK 4834
24246-1	Under a Blue Jungle Moon	Vo/OK 4786
24247-1	Everything Happens for the Best	Vo/OK 4786
24248-1	Why Did I Always Depend on You?	Vo/OK 4834
24249-1	Long Gone Blues	Co 37586

Billie Holiday, acc by Hot Lips Page, tp; Coleman Hawkins, Lester Young, Charlie Barnet, ts; Teddy Wilson, pno, gtr, sb, d.

New York, December 19, 1940

| The Man I Love | Saga ERO-8014(LP) |

The Men from Minton's: Hot Lips Page, Victor Coulson and unknown player, tp; Rudy Williams, as; Don Byas, ts; Alan "Pee Wee" Tinney, pno; Charlie Christian, elg; Ebenezer Paul, sb; possibly Taps Miller, or unknown* d.
Monroe's Uptown House, New York, 1941
Guy's Got to Go
On With Charlie C*
Up on Teddy's Hill*   Esoteric,
                                                                       ESJ-4

(See also Pete Johnson and His Boogie Woogie Boys session under Buster Smith.)

Artie Shaw and His Orchestra: Artie Shaw, cl, dir; Lee Castle, Max Kaminsky, Steve Lipkins, tp; Hot Lips Page, tp, vcl; Jack Jenney, Morey Samuel, Ray Conniff, tb; Charlie di Maggio, Lee Robinson, as; George Auld, Mickey Folus, ts; Johnny Guarnieri, pno; Mike Bryan, gtr; Eddie McKimmey, sb; Dave Tough,d; Paula Kelly, vcl; Paul Jordan, a; 15 vn, vl, vc.
New York, November 12, 1941

068194-1	To a Broadway Rose	Vi 27838
068195-1-2	St. James Infirmary, Part 1 (vcl, HLP)	Vi 27895
068196-2	St. James Infirmary, Part 2	Vi 27895
068197-1	Deuces Wild	Vi 27838

New York, December 23, 1941

068803-1	Dusk	Vi 28-0405
068804-1	Suite No. 8	Vi 28-0405
068805-1	Somebody's Rocking My Dreamboat	Vi 27746
068806-1	I Don't Want to Walk without You	Vi 27746

Fredda Gibson (alias Georgia Gibbs), vcl.
New York, January 20, 1942

071701-1	Somebody Nobody Loves	Vi 27798
071702-1	Not Mine	Vi 27779
071703-1	Absent-Minded Moon	Vi 27779
071704-1	Hinustan	Vi 27798

New York, January 21, 1942

071709-1	Carnival	Vi 27860
071710-1	Needlenose	Vi 27860
071711-1	Two in One Blues	Vi 20-1526
071712-1	Sometimes I Feel Like a Motherless Child	Vi 27806

Fats Waller and His Rhythm: Waller, pno solo and comments, with Hot Lips Page, tp.
Carnegie Hall, New York, January 14, 1942
Blues in B flat   PC 09 (LP)

Jam session: Max Kaminsky, Yank Lawson, Hot Lips Page, Marty Masala, tp; Bobby Hackett, c; Tommy Dorsey, tb; Mezz Mezzrow, Pee Wee Russell, Joe Marsala, cl; Sidney Bechet, ss; Bud Freeman, ts; Jass [sic] Stacy, Joe Bushkin, pno; Carmen Mastren, Eddie Condon, gtr; Artie Shapiro, sb; Zutty Singleton, Dave Tough, d.
St. Regis Hotel, New York, November 5, 1938
Keep Smiling at Trouble
Just the Blues
China Boy
Someday Sweetheart
St. Louis Blues   JP LP-9

BILL NEELY

Vcl, gtr
Blackland Farm Boy, 1974   Arhoolie 5014
Satan's Burning Hell
Crying the Blues Over You
Austin Breakdown
Lonely Breakdown
Pflugerville Boogie
Law and Justice
Don't Waste Your Tears over Me
Blackland Farm
Big Yellow Moon over Texas
My Tennessee Home
Deep Elm Blues
Sun Setting in Your Life

CHARLIE "BIRD" PARKER

Jay McShann and His Orchestra: Jay McShann, pno, dir; Harold Bruce, Orville Minor, Bernard Anderson, tp; Joe Baird, tb; Charlie Parker, as, a; John Jackson, as; Bob Marane, Harry Fergguson, ts; Gene Ramey, sb; Gus Johnson, d; Walter Brown, vcl; William J. Scott, a.

Dallas, April 30, 1941

93730-A	Swingmatism (a, WJS)	De 8570
93731-A	Hootie Blues (vcl,WB; a, CP)	De 8559
73732-A	Dexter Blues (a, WJS)	De 8583

Parker continued to record extensively; this session is included because it took place in Dallas.

BOOKER PITTMAN

Blanche Calloway: Joe Keyes, tp; Edgar Battle, tp, a; Clarence Smith, tp, vcl; Alton Moore, tb; Booker Pittman, cl, as; Leroy Hard, as; Ben Webster, ts; Clyde Hart, pno; Andy Jackson, bj, gtr; Joe Durham, bb; Cozy Cole, d; Blanche Calloway, Billy Massey, vcl.

Camden, New Jersey, Mach 27, 1931

68938-2	Just a Crazy Song (Hi-Hi-Hi) (vcl, BC)	Vi 22661
68939-2	Sugar Blues (vcl, BM)	Vi 22661
68940-1	Sugar Blues (vcl, CS, BM)	TT C-1587
68941-1	I'm Gettin' Myself Ready For You (v, BC)	Vi 22659
68942-2	Loveless Love (vcl, BC)	Vi 22659

Note: Timely Tunes C-1587 as Fred Armstrong and His Syncopators

Camden, New Jersey, May 8, 1931

69025-3	Misery (vcl, BC)	Vi 22717
69026-2	It's Right Here For You (vcl, BC)	Vi 22717
69027-1-2	Make Me Know It (vcl, BC)	Rejected

Herb Alvis, tb, added.
Camden, New Jersey, June 11, 1931

68234-3	It Looks Like Susie (vcl, BC)	Vi 22733
68235-1	Without That Gal! (vcl, BC)	Vi 22733
68236-1	When I Can't Be with You (vcl, BC)	TT C-1578
69027-4	Make Me Know It (If You Mean What You Say!) (vcl, BC)	Vi 22736

Note: Timely Tunes c-1578 as Fred Armstrong and His Syncopators

Freddy Johnson and His Harlemites: Arthur Briggs, Bobby Jones, tp; Billy Burns, Herb Flemming, tb; Booker Pittman, cl, as; Cle Saddler, as; Roy Butler, as, bar; Alfred Pratt, ts; Freddy Johnson, pno, a; Sterling Conaway, gtr; Juan Fernandez, sb; Billy Taylor-d.
Paris, December 7, 1933

| 66451/2bkp | I Got Rhythm | Br A-500341 |
| 6646bkp | Tiger Rag | Br A-500344 |

BEN POLLACK AND HIS ORCHESTRA

Ben Pollack, d, vcl, dir; Harry James, Shorty Sherock, Charlie Spivak, tp; Bruce Squires, Glenn Miller, tb; Irving Fazola, cl; Opie Cates, as; Dave Matthews, ts, a; Ray Cohen, vn; Freddy Slack, pno; Frank Frederico, gtr; Thurman Teague, sb; Sammy Taylor, d; Carol Mackay, Lois Still, vcl. Hollywood, December 18, 1936

| B-4373-B | Deep Ellum Blues | Vri 504 |

SAM "SAMMY" PRICE

Douglas Finnell and His Royal Stompers: Douglas Finnell, tp; Bert Johnson, tb; Sammy Price, pno, vcl; Percy Darensbourgh, bj.
Dallas, September 29, 1929

| DAL-466 | The Right String But the Wrong Yo Yo (vcl, SP) Br 7123 |
| DAL-467 | Sweet Sweet Mama (vcl, SP) | Br 7123 |

Bert Johnson, tb solo, acc by Sammy Price, pno, with comments by Effie Scott.
Dallas, September 29, 1929

| DAL-465 | Nasty But Nice | Br 7136 |

Sammy Price and His Four Quarters: prob. Douglas Finnell, tp; Bert Johnson, tb; Sammy Price, pno Percy Darensbourg, bj.
Dallas, September 29, 1929

| DAL-464 | Blue Rhythm Stomp | Br 7136 |

Effie Scott, vcl, acc by Sam Price, pno; Percy Darensborough, gtr; Bert Johnson, tb on first title only.
Dallas, September 19, 1929

| DAL-468 | Lonesome Hut Blues | Vo 1461 |
| DAL-469 | Sunshine Special | Vo 1461 |

Monette Moore, vcl, acc by her Swing Shop Boys: possibly Sam price, pno, unknown gtr, sb, d
New York, February 19, 1936

| 60520-B | Rhythm for Sale (Swing Shop Swing) | De 7161 |

| 60521-A | Two Old Maids in a Folding Bed | De 7161 |

Charles "Cow Cow" Davenport, acc by Joe Bishop, fh; Sam Price, pno; Teddy Bunn, gtr; Richard Fullbright, sb.
New York, May 8, 1938

63763-A	Don't You Loud-Mouth Me	De 7486
63764-A	I Ain't No Iceman	De 7462
63765-A	The Mess Is Here	De 7813
63766-A	Railroad Blues	De 7462
63767-A	That'll Get It	De 7486

Ebony Three, vcl trio, acc by Buster Bailey, cl; Sam price, pno; Richard Fullbright, sb; O'Neil Spencer, d.
New York, May 25, 1938

63862	Swing Low, Sweet Chariot	De 7527
63863	Go Down Moses	De 7527
63864	Heartbroken Blues	De 7503
63865	Mississippi Moan	De 7503

Trixie Smith, vcl, acc by Charlie Shavers, tp; Sidney Bechet, cl, as; Sam Price, pno; Teddy Bunn, gtr; Richard Fullbright, sb; O'Neil Spencer, d.
New York, May 26, 1938

63866-A	Freight Train Blues	De 7489
63867-A	Trixie Blues	De 7469
63868-A	My Daddy Rocks Me, Part 1	De 7469
63869-A	My Daddy Rocks Me, Part 2	De 7617
63870-A	He may Be Your Man, But He Comes to See Me Sometimes	De 7528
63871-A	Jack, I'm Mellow	De 7528
63872-A	Lady Be Good	AH 158 (LP)
63877-A	My Unusual Man	De 7489

Leola B. Wilson, vcl, acc by Charlie Shavers, tp; Sidney Bechet, cl, as; Sammy Price, pno; Teddy Bunn, gtr; Wellman Braud, sb; O'Neil Spencer, d.

63873-A	Uncle Joe	De 7500
63874-A	I Am a Woman	Rejected
63875	Toot It Brother Armstrong (instrumental)	Rejected
63876-A	Blue Monday on Sugar Hill	De 7500

Blue Lu Barker, vcl, acc by Danny Barker's Fly Cats: Benny Carter, tp; Buster Bailey, cl; Sam Price, pno; Danny Barker, gtr; Wellman Braud, sb.
New York, August 11, 1938

64432-A	You're Going to Love the Hold Home, Jim	De 7560
64433-A	New Orleans Blues	De 7538
64434-A	He Caught the B&O	De 7506
64435-A	Don't You Make Me High	De 7506

Add unknown d.
New York, November 22, 1938

64767-A	I Feel Like Lying in Another Woman's Husband's Arms	Rejected
64768-A	Give Me Some Money	Rejected
64769-A	I Got Ways Like the Devil	De 7560
64770-A	That Made Him Mad	De 7538

Acc by Danny Barker's Fly Cats: Charlie Shavers, tp; Chu Berry, ts; Sam price, pno; Danny Barkers, gtr; unknown sb, d.
New York, April 20, 1939

75433-A	Scat Skunk	De 7813
75434-A	Nix on Those Lush Heads	De 7588
75435-A	Buy Me Some Juice	Rejected
75436-A	Georgia Grind	De 7588

Acc by Henry Allen, tp; Sam Price, pno; Danny Barker, gtr; Wellman Braud, sb; unknown d.
New York, November 17, 1939

66893-A	Blue Deep Sea Blues	De 7709
66894-A	Never Brag about Your Man	De 7683
66895-A	He's So Good	De 7695
66896-A	I Don't Dig You, Jack	De 7770

New York, December 13, 1939

66956-A	Handy Andy	De 7709
66957-A	Jitterbug Blues	De 7713
66958-A	You Been Holding Out Too Long	De 7695
66959-A	Lu's Blues	De 7770

Lether [sic] McGraw, vcl, acc by Sam Price's Fly Cats: Charlie Shavers, tp; Buster Bailey, cl; Sam Price, pno; possibly Wellman Braud, sb; O'Neil Spencer, d.
New York, March 24, 1939

65267-A	Do Your Duty	De 7580
65268-A	Low Down Dirty Groundhog	De 7580

Ollie Shepard, vcl, acc by Sam Price, pno; unknown d; and possibly Chu Berry, ts.

New York, April 18, 1939

65420-A	Now Low Down Dirty Shame	De 7585
65421-A	The Numbers Blues	De 7585
65422-A	Sweetest Thing Born	De 7629
65423-A	Shepard Blues (Pig Latin Blues)	De 7602
65424-A	Outdoors Blues	De 7613
65425-A	Sugar Woman Blues	De 7602
65426-A	Hell Is So Low Down	De 7716
65427-A	My Dripping Blood Blues	De 7613
65428-A	Blues 'Bout My Gal	De 7639

Harlem Stompers: Sam Price, pno; unknown gtr, sb, d; Hester Lancaster, vcl.

New York, April 27, 1939

65486-A	The Monkey Swing	De 7600
65487-A	Jammin' in Gerogia	De 7616
65488-A	My Understanding Man	De 7600
65489-A	Serenada to a Jitterbug	De 7616

Georgia White, vcl, acc by Sammy Price, pno; Teddy Bunn, gtr; possibly John Lindsay, sb.

New York, May 18, 1939

65597-A	The Way I'm Feelin'	De 7596
65598-A	Married Woman Blues	De 7596
65599-A	How Do You Think I Feel?	De 7562
65600-A	Fire in the Mountain	De 7608
65601-A	When the Red Sun Turns to Gray, I'll Be Back	De 7608

Sam Price and His Texas Blusicians: Joe Brown, Ed Mullens, tp; Don Stovall, as; Ray Hill, ts; Sam Price, pno, vcl; Duke Jones, sb; Wilbert Kirk, d.

New York, March 13, 1940

67304-A	Fetch It to Me	De 7781
67305-A	Cow Cow Blues	De 7732
67306-A	Sweepin' the Blues Away	De 7781
67307-A	Swing out in the Groove (vcl, SP)	De 7732

New York, September 25, 1940

68149-A	How 'Bout That Mess	De 8505
68150-A	Oh Red (vcl, SP)	De 8505
68151-A	Oh Lawdy Mama (vcl, SP)	De 7811
68152-A	The Dirty Dozens (vcl, SP)	De 7811

Johnnie Temple, vocal, acc by Buster Bailey, cl; Sam Price, pno; Albert Casey, gtr; Hert Cowens, d.
New York, April 4, 1940

67489-A	Good Woman Blues	De 7735
67490-A	Skin and Bones Woman	De 7750
67491-A	I'm Cuttin' Out	De 7772
67492-A	Fireman Blues	De 7782
67493-A	Lovin' Woman Blues	De 7772
67494-A	Roomin' House Blues	De 7782
67495-A	Sugar Bowl Blues	De 7735
67496-A	Stick Up Woman (Let Me Make This Trip with You)	De 7750

Sam Price and His Texas Blusicians: Lem Johnson, cl, vcl; Sam Price, pno, vcl; unknown sb, d, wb.
New York, December 6, 1940

68457-A	Thinking (vcl, SP)	De 8515
68458-A	Queen Street Blues (vcl, LJ)	De 7820*
68459-A	Jumpin' the Boogie	De 8515
68460-A	Louise Louise (vcl, LJ)	De 7620

*DE 7820 released as Lem Johnson and His Washboard Band

Shad Collins, Bill Johnson, tp; Don Stovall, as; Lester Young, ts; Sam Price, pno, vcl; Duke Jones, sb; Harold West, d; Yack Taylor, Spo-De-O Sam (presumably Price), vcl.
New York, April 3, 1941

68920-A	The Good Drag (GoneWid De Goon)	De 8547
68921-A	Things 'Bout Coming My Way (vcl, YT)	De 8557
68922-A	Lead Me Daddy Straight to the Bar (vcl, SP)	De 8649
68293-A	Just Jivin' Around	De 8557

Sam Price, pno, vcl; unknown gtr, d; Yack Taylor, vcl.
New York, April 8, 1941

68951	My Mellow Man	De 7836*
68952	Knockin' Myself Out	De 7836
68953-A	You're Gonna Go Your Way and I'm Gonna Go Mine	De 7850*
68954-A	I Lost Love (When I Lost You)	De 8547

*De 7836 and 7850 released as Yack Taylor records

Chester Boone, tp; Floyd Brady, tb; Don Stovall, as; Skippy Williams, ts; Sam Price, pno, vcl; Ernest Hill, sb; Herb Cowens, d.
New York, June 13, 1941

69365-A	Do You Dig My Jive?	De 8575
69366-A	I Know How to Do It	De 8566
69367-A	Valetta (vcl, sp)	De 8566
69368	Boogie Wood Moan	De 8575

Joe Turner, vcl, acc by Sam Price, pno; Leonard Ware, gtr; Billy Taylor, sb.
New York, July 17, 1941

69523-A	Nobody in Mind	De 7868
69254-A	Somebody's Got to Go	De 7856
69525-A	Ice Man	De 7856
69526-A	Chewed Up Grass	De 7868

Emmett Berry, tp; Ray Hogan, tb; Fess Williams, cl, as; Don Stovall, as; Sam Price, pno; Billy Taylor, sb; J.C. Heard, d; Ruby Smith, Jack Meredith, vcl.
New York, December 10, 1941

70029-A	Why Don't You Love Me Any More?	De 8609
70030-A	Harlem Gin Blues	De 8609
70031 A-B	My Name Is Jim	Rejected
70032-B	Match Box Blues	De 8624

Herman Autrey, tp; David Young, ts; Sam Price, pno; William Lewis, gtr; Vernon King, sb; O'Neil Spencer, d; Mabel Robinson, vcl.
New York, January 20, 1942

70187-A	Me and My Chauffeur	De 8601
70188-A	I've Got Too Many Blues	De 8601
70189-A	It's All Right, Jack	De 8649
70190-A	Blow, Katy, Blow	De 8624

Instrumentation and personnel unknown.
New York, July 25, 1942

71195-A	Teed Up	De 8642
71196-A	Frantic	De 8642

Mabel Robinson, vcl, acc by Sam Price's Blusicians: Herman Autrey, tp; David Young, ts; Sam Price, pno; William Leiws, gtr; Vernon King, sb; O'Neil Spencer, d.
New York, January 20, 1942

70187	Me and My Chauffeur	De 8601
70188-A	I've Got Too Many Blues	De 8601

Nora Lee King, vcl, acc by Sam Price, pno; unknown gtr, sb.
New York, September 11, 1941

69740-A	Love Me	Rejected
69741-A	Love You Rock You Home	De 7883
69742-A	Yup Da Da Da	Rejected
79743-A-B	Why Don't You Do Right?	De 7866

New York, October 8, 1941

69793-B	Love Me	De 7870
69794-A	Yump Da Da Da	De 7870

Pete Brown and His Band: Dizzy Gillespie, tp; Jimmy Hamilton, cl; Pete Brown, as; Sam Price, pno; Charlie Drayton, sb; Ray Nathan, d; Helen Humes, Nora Lee King, vcl.

New York, February 9, 1942

70229-A	Mound Bayou (vcl, HH)	De 8613
70300-A	Unlucky Woman (Unlucky Blues) (vcl, HH)	De 8613
70301-A	Gonna Buy Me a Telephone (vcl, HH)	De 8625
70302-A	Cannon Ball (vcl, NLK)	De 8625

Lem Johnson, vocal, acc by Sam Price, pno; George van Eps, gtr; Haig Stevens, sb.

New York, May 19, 1942

70760-A	Goin' Down Slow	De 7895
70761-A	Candy Blues	De 7895

WILLIE REED

Vcl, acc by own gtr.

Dallas, December 8, 1928

147600-2	Dreaming Blues	Co 14407-D
147601-1	Texas Blues	Co 4407-D

Dallas, 5 Dec. 1929

149544-1	Leavin' Home	Historical Records ASC 17
149545-1	Goin' Back to My Baby	Co unissued

Note: 149544 issued on LP only

Dallas, September 26, 1935

DAL-166-	Some Low Down Groundhog Blues	Vo 03093
DAL-167-2	White House on the Hill Blues	Vo unissued

Dallas, September 27, 1935

DAL-168-2	Lay My Money Down Blues	Vo unissued
DAL-169-2	Changing Time Blues	Vo unissued
DAL-170-	All Worn Out and Dry Blues	Vo 03093
DAL-171-2	Boogie Woogie Mama Blues	Vo unissued

Dallas, September 28, 1935

DAL-176-2	Central Avenue Blues	Vo unissued
DAL-177-2	Rachel Lee Blues	Vo unissued

Dallas, September 30, 1935

DAL 189-1	Heart-Breakin' Mama Blues	Vo unissued
DAL-190-1	Whose Muddy Shoes Are These?	Vo unissued

SHELTON BROTHERS (BOB & JOE) (see also Lone Star Cowboys)

Note: Also known as Shelton Brothers & Curley Fox (SB & CF), Joe Shelton (JS), Joe Shelton & Curley Fox (JS & CF). When Joe and Bob Attlesey began playing on radio in 1934, they adopted the surname "Shelton" and were subsequently called the Shelton Brothers. All of their recordings in 1933 were under the name Attlesey, but from 1934 onward they were identified as the Shelton Brothers.

Bob Shelton, gtr, harmony vcl; Joe Shelton, md, lead vcl.
Chicago, February 22, 1935

C-9809	Deep Elem Blues	DE 5099
C-9810	A Message from Home Sweet Home	DE 5135
C-9811	The Coupon Song (JS vcl, gtr)	DE 5087
C-9812	Hang out the Front Door Key	DE 5099

February 23, 1935

C-9813	Just Because	DE 5100
C-9814	Who Wouldn't Be Lonely	DE 5100
C-9815	Nothin'	DE 5161
C-9816	Beautiful Louisiana	DE 5079
C-9817	Will There Be Any Cowboys in Heaven?	DE 5135
C-9818	Stay in the Wagon Yard (JS, vcl, gtr)	DE 5087
C-9819	Johnson's Old Grey Mule	DE 5161
C-9820	'Neath the Maple in the Lane	DE 5079

Bob Shelton, b, vcl; Joe Shelton, gtr, vcl; Curley Fox, fid, lead vcl.

August 19, 1935

C-90251	Sal Let Me Chew Your Rosom Some (SB & CF)	DE 5137
C-90252	Gonna Raid That Chicken Roost Tonight (SB & CF)	
		DE 5137
C-09253	by Curley Fox	
C-90254	Deep Elem Blues No. 2	Unissued
C-90255	missing master; no information	

Bob Shelton, harmony vcl, gtr; Joe Shelton, md, lead vcl; Curley Fox, fid
August 20, 1935

C-90256	When It's Night Time in Nevada	Unissued
C-90257	Bury Me Beneath the Willow (JS & CF)	Unissued
C-90258	Lover's Farewell (JS & CF)	Unissued
C-90259	by Curley Fox	
C-90260	Budded Roses	Unissued
C-90261	New John Henry Blues (SB & CF)	Unissued
C-90262	Sittin' on Top o'the World	DE 6079
C-90263	Cheatin' on Your Baby	Unissued
C-90264	Match Box blues (SB & CF)	Unissued
C-90265	Daddy Don't 'Low No Low Down Hangin' Round	
		Unissued

Joe Shelton, md, vcl; Curley Fox, gtr.
August 21, 1935

C-90266	Black Sheep	Unissued
C-90267	by Curley Fox	
C-90268	Sweet Evalina	Unissued

Joe Shelton, gtr, vcl; Curley Fox, fid.
New York City, December 18, 1935

60242	Match Box Blues (JS)	DE 5177

Bob Shelton, vcl, jug; Joe Shelton, lead vcl, md, gtr; Curley Fox, fid, vcl
December 19, 1935

60243	Budded Roses	DE 5180
60244	I'm Sitting on Top of the World	DE 5190
60245	When It's Night Time in Nevada	DE 5219
60246	I'm Thinking Tonight of My Blue Eyes (JS & CF)	
		DE 5184
60247	Bury Me Beneath the Willow (JS & CF)	
		DE 5184
60248	The Black Sheep (JS)	DE 5219

60257	'Leven Miles from Leavenworth	DE 5180
60258	Daddy Don't 'Low No Low Down Hangin' Round	
		DE 5198
60259	Deep Elem Blues No. 2	DE 5198
60260	(by Curley Fox)	
60261	New John Henry Blues* (SB & CF)	DE 5173
60262	At the Shelby County Fair (JS)	DE 5177
60263	Ridin' on a Humpback Mule* (SB & CF)	DE 5173

*Curley Fox, lead vcl

Bob Shelton, gtr, vcl; Joe Shelton, md, lead vcl
December 20, 1935

60264	Sweet Evelina	DE 5261
60265	Answer to Just Because	DE 5170
60266	(by Curley Fox w/vcl by Joe Shelton)	
	Bob Shelton, harmony vcl, Joe Shelton,	
	lead vcl, gtr, Curley Fox, fid.	
60267	Lover's Farewell	DE 5261
60268	That's a Habit I've Never Had	DE 5170
60269	Four or Five Times	DE 5190

Bob Shelton, harmony vcl; Joe Shelton, lead vcl, md; Leon "Lonnie" Hall, fid; Grundy "Slim" Harbert, sb; Harry Sorenson, acd; Gene Sullivan, gtr.
February 13, 1935

C-9813	Just Because	DE 5100
C-9814	Who Wouldn't Be Lonely	DE 5100
C-9815	Nothin'	DE 5161
C-9816	Beautiful Louisiana	DE 5079
C-9817	Will there Be Any Cowboys in Heaven?	DE 5135
C-9819	Johnson's Old Grey Mule	DE 5161
C-9820	'Neath the Maple in the Lane	DE 5079

Bob Shelton, harmony vcl; Joe Shelton, lead vcl, md; Leon "Lonnie" Hall, fid; Grundy "Slim" Harbert, sb; Harry Sorenson, acd; Gene Sullivan, gtr, harmony vcl.
Dallas, February 17, 1937

61820	Answer to Blue Eyes	DE 5440
61821	I'm Gonna Fix Your Wagon	DE 5471
61822	The Story of Seven Roses	DE 5353
61823	I'm Here to Get My Baby Out of Jail	DE 5409
61824	Way Down in Georgia	DE 5471
61825	Aura Lee	DE 5533

61826	Givin' Everything Away	DE 5367
61827	Cinda Lou	DE 5409
61828	New Cinda Lou	DE 5456
61829-61831	by Jimmie Davis	
61832	Hard Hearted Mama	Unissued

Bob Shelton, b, vcl; Joe Shelton, gtr, vcl; Curley Fox, fid, lead vcl.
February 18, 1937

61839	Deep Elem Blues No. 3	DE 5422
61840	New Trouble in Mind Blues	DE 5339
61841	That Golden Love (My Mother Gave to Me)	DE 5468
61842	She Was Happy Till She Met You	DE 5381
61843	A Prisoner's Dream	DE 5381
61844	Answer to a Prisoner's Dream	DE 5468
61845	Someone to Love You When You're Old	DE 5440
61846	Goodness Gracious Gracie	DE 5397
61847	Nobody But My Baby Is Getting My Love	DE 5397
61848	Uncle Eph's Got the Coon*	DE 5456
61849	A Dollar Down and a Dollar a Week	DE 5339

*Gene Sullivan, harmony vcl on trio

February 19, 1937

61862	Just Because No. 3	DE 5367
61863	All Night Long	Unissued
61864	Alone with My Sorrows*	DE 5353
61865	Go Long Mule	DE 5422

*accompanied by gtr only, played by Joe Shelton

Bob Shelton, gtr, harmony vcl; Joe Shelton, lead vcl, md; Leon "Lonnie" Hall, fid; Grundy "Slim" Harbert, b; Howard Oliver, bj; Harry Sorensen, acd; Gene Sullivan, gtr.
December 12, 1937

63022	When You Think a Whole Lot About Someone	
DE 5508		
63023	Who Calls You Sweet Mama Now	DE 5519
63024	I Told Them All About You	DE 5484
63025	As Long As I Have You	DE 5519
63026	Blue Kimono Blues	DE 5475
63027	I'm Gonna Let the Bumble Bee Be	DE 5545
63028	Eight More Years to Go	DE 5496
63029	My Gal Is Mean	DE 5475
63030-63039	by Leon's Lone Star Cowboys	

63040	Seven Years with the Wrong Woman	DE 5484
63041	Take Me Back to Renfro Valley	DE 5545
63042	You're Standing on the Outside Now	DE 5568
63043	The Old Mill's Tumbling Down	DE 5585
63044	The Pig Got Up and Slowly Walked Away	Unissued
63045	No Foolin'	DE 5568
63046	Down on the Farm (They All Ask for You)	DE 5533
63047	If You Want Me You Got to Run Me Down	Unissued
63048	By the Stump of the Old Pine Tree	DE 5496
63049	Far over the Hill	DE 5585
63050	Jealous	DE 5508

Bob Shelton, harmony vcl; Joe Shelton, lead vcl, amp md; Grundy "Slim" Harbert, b; Felton "Preacher" Harkness, fid; Howard Oliver, tbj; Gene Sullivan, gtr.
San Antonio, September 18, 1938

64534	You Can't Put That Monkey on My Back	DE 5609
64535	Thankful and Thankful Again	DE 5609
64536	On the Owl-Hoot Trail	DE 5630
64537	She's Somebody's Darling Once More	DE 5630
64538	Knot Hole Blues	DE 5653
64539	Meet Me Somewhere in Your Dreams	DE 5653
64540	Those Dusty Roads	DE 5717
64541	Let a Smile Be Your Umbrella on a Rainy Day	DE 5606

September 19, 1938

64542	Wednesday Night Waltz	DE 5621
64543	Someday Baby	DE 5645
64544	My Own Sweet Darling Wife	DE 5723
64545	Ace in the Hole	DE 5661
64546	Lita	DE 5621
64547	I'm Savin' Saturday Night for You	DE 5661
64548	My Girl Friend Doesn't Like Me Anymore	DE 5645
64549	Mandy	DE 5669
64550	She Gave It All Away	DE 5678
64551	Lost Woman	DE 5606

Bob Shelton, harmony vcl; Joe Shelton, lead vcl; Grady Hester or Preacher Harkness, fid; Hezzie Bryant, b; Bob Dunn, amp stg; Dickie McBride, gtr; Leo Raley, amp md; Joe Thames, bj.
Houston, Texas, March 4, 1939

| 65130 | You Can't Put That Monkey on My Back No. 2 | DE 5665 |

65131	Just Because You're in Deep Elem	DE 5665
65132	That's No Way to Treat the Man You Love	DE 5678
65133	She's My Gal (Right or Wrong)	DE 5700
65134	I Just Don't Care Anymore	DE 5669
65135	Bye Bye Baby Bye Bye	DE 5706
65136	(Aye, Aye) On Mexico's Beautiful Shore	DE 5709
65137	That's Why I'm Jealous of You	DE 5706

March 5, 1939

65146	The Pretty Little Girl with a Smile	DE 5700
65147	Hallelujah I'm Gonna Be Free Again	DE 5717
65148	You Can't Fool a Fool All the Time	DE 5723
65149	You Gotta Quit Cheatin' on Me	DE 5709
65150	How Times Have Changed	DE 5690
65151	You Can't Do That to Me	DE 5690

Bob Shelton, harmony vcl; Joe Shelton, lead vcl; Cliff Bruner, fid; Hezzie Bryant, b; Bob Dunn, amp stg; Dickie McBridge, gtr; Aubrey "Moon" Mullican, pno; Leo Raley, amp mandola.

September 3, 1939

66380	Lay Your Hand in Mine	DE 5755
66381	Old Age Pension Blues	DE 5811
66382	My Grandfather's Clock	DE 5739
66383	Don't Leave Me All Alone	DE 5795
66384-66385	See listings for September 4, 1939	
66386	Shoutin' in the Amen Corner (A Rhythmic Sermon)	
		DE 5760

September 4, 1939

66384	Dig Me a Grave in Missouri	DE 5739
66385	Silver Dollar	Unissued
66386	See listing for September 3, 1939	
66387	Ain't No Use to Worry Anymore	DE 5811
66388	I Wish It Wasn't So	DE 5795
66389	Parking Meter Blues	DE 5755
66390	If You Don't Like My Peaches (Leave My Tree Alone)	
		DE 5787
66391	You Can't Get Love (Where There Ain't No Love)	
		DE 5776
66392	No Matter What They Say	DE 5760
66393	Don't Take My Darling Away	DE 5787
66394	I Have My Bed	DE 5776

Bob Shelton, harmony vcl; Joe Shelton, amp md; Merle Shelton, gtr; Grundy "Slim" Harbert, b; Billy McNew ("Billy Mack"), amp stg; Jimmy Thomason, fid.

April 6, 1940

92023	You Can't Get Me Back When I'm Gone	DE 5826
92024	Doggone Crazy Blues	DE 5844
92025	Coo See Coo	DE 5833
92026	I'll Be Seein' You in Dallas Alice	DE 5844
92027	Tell Me with Your Blue Eyes	DE 5855
92028	Somebody Stole My Little Darling	DE 5855
92029	It's Hard to Love and Not Be Loved	DE 5865
92030-92035	by Rice Brothers' Gang	
92036	I'm a Handy Man to Have Around	DE 5833
92037	What's the Matter with Deep Elem	DE 5898

April 7, 1940

92038	There'll Always be a Maple on the Hill	DE 5826
92039	It's a Weary World without My Blue Eyes	DE 5865
92040	Henpecked Husband Blues	DE 5898
92041	Beautiful Brown Eyes	DE 6079

Bob Shelton, harmony vcl; Joe Shelton, lead vcl, md; Grundy "Slim" Harbert, b; Bruce Pierce, bj; Merle Shelton, gtr; Jimmy Thomason, fid.

Dallas, Texas, April 25, 1941

93659	Ida Red	DE 5946
93660	Rompin' and Stompin' Around	DE 5964
93661	Who's Gonna Cut My Baby's Kindling	DE 5964
93662	Love Me Easy (Or Leave Me Alone)	DE 5975
93663	I'll Never Get Drunk Anymore	DE 6021
93664	Choo Choo Blues	DE 6071
93665	I'm Driftin' and Shiftin' My Gears	DE 6047
93666	I Just Can't Go	DE 5996
93667	Weary	DE 6021

April 26, 1941

93668	I Just Dropped in to Say Goodbye	DE 6071
93669	When It Rains It Really Pours	DE 6047
93670	South	DE 5946
93671	Sittin' on Your Doorstep	DE 5996
93672	Old Fashioned Locket	DE 5975

HENRY "BUSTER" SMITH

Walter Page's Blue Devils: Walter Page, bb, sb, dir; James Simpson, Hot Lips Page, tp; Dan Minor, tb; Buster Smith, cl, as; Ted Manning, as; Reuben Roddy, ts; Charlie Washington, pno; Reuben Lynch or Thomas Owens, gtr; Alvin Burroughs, d; Jimmy Rushing, vcl.
Kansas City, November 10, 1929

KC-612	Blue Devil Blues (vcl, JR; bb)	Vo 1463
KC-613	Squabblin' (sb)	

Count Basie and His Orchestra: Count Basie, pno, dir; Buck Clayton, Ed Lewis, Bobby Moore, tp; George Hunt, Dan Minor, tb; Earl Warren, as, vcl; Buster Smith, a; Jack Washington, as, bar; Herschel Evans, Lester Young, cl, ts; Freddy Green, gtr; Walter Page, sb; Joe Jones, d; Jimmy Rushing, Billie Holiday, vcl.
Savoy Ballroom, New York, July 7, 1937

62332-A	One O'Clock Jump	De 1363

Count Basie and His Orchestra: Count Basie, pno, dir; Buck Clayton, Ed Lewis, Harry Edison, tp; Dicky Wells, Benny Morton, Dan Minor, tb; Earl Warren, as; Jack Washington, as, bar; Herschel Evans, Lester Young, ts; Freddy Green, gtr; Walter Page, sb; Joe Jones, d; Jimmy Rushing, Helen Humes, vcl; Buster Smith, a.
New York, November 16, 1938

64748-A	The Blues I Like to Hear (vcl, JR)	De 2284

Pete Johnson and His Boogie Woogie Boys: Hot Lips Page, tp; Buster Smith, as; Pete Johnson, pno; Lawrence Lucie, gtr; Abe Bolar, sb; Eddie Dougherty, d; Joe Turner, vcl.
New York, June 30, 1939

25023-1	Cherry Red	Vo/OK 4997
25024-1	Baby, Look At You	Vo/OK 4997
25025-1	Lovin' Mama Blues	Vo/OK 5186

Harlan Leonard and his Rockets: Harlan Leonard, cl, as, bar, dir; Edward Johnson, William H. Smith, tp; James Ross, tp; Fred Beckett, Richmond Henderson, tb; Darwin Jones, as; Henry Bridges, cl, ts; Jimmy Keith, ts; William Smith, pno; Winston Williams, sb; Jesse Price, d; Stan Morgan, gtr; Ernie Williams, vcl; Buster Smith, a.
New York, March 11, 1940

047797-1	Ride My Blues Away	BB B-11032

Stan Morgan, gtr, replaces Ware; Myra Taylor, Ernie Williams, vcl.

New York, March 11, 1940

047796-1	I Don't Want to Set the World on Fire (vcl, MT; as, ED)	
		BB B 10919
04797-1	Ride My Blues Away (vcl, EW; as, BS)	BB B 11032
047798-1	I'm in a Weary Mood (vcl, DJ)	BB B 10736
047799-1	Parade of the Stompers (as, RC)	————

Bon Bon and his Buddies: Joe Thomas, tp; Eddie Durham, tb, gtr; Buster Smith, cl; Jackie Fields, as; James Phipps, as; Al Hall, sb; Jack Parker, d; Bon Bon Funnell, vcl.

New York, July 23, 1941

69557-A	I Don't Want to Set the World on Fire	De 3980
69558-A	Blow, Gabriel, Blow	De 8567
69559-A	Sweet Mama, Papa's Getting Mad	De 3980
69560-A	All That Meat and No Potatoes	Dec 8567

Hot Lips Page and His Band: Hot Lips Page, tp, vcl; Buster Smith, cl, as; Jimmy Powell, as; Sam Davis, ts; Jimmy Renolds, pno; Abe Bolar, sb; Ed McConney, d; Romayne Jackson-the Harlem Highlanders, vcl.

New York, January 23, 1940

67091-A	I Would Do Anything For You (vcl, HLP)	De 7699
67092-A	I Ain't Got Nobody (vcl, HH)	De 7714
67093-A	A Porter's Love Song to a Chambermaid (vcl, RJ)	
		De 7757
67094-A	Gone with the Gin	De 7714
67099	Walk It To Me (Call of the Wild)	De 7757
67100	I Won't Be Here Long (vcl, HLP)	De 7699

(See also 1939 Joe Turner session under Buster Smith.)

Don Redman and His Orchestra: Don Redman, cl, ss, as, vcl, dir; Tom Stevenson, Otis Johnson, Al Killian, tp; Claude Jones, Gene Simon, tb; Scoville Brown, Tapley Lewis, Edward Inge, as; Robert Carroll, ts; Nicholas Rodriguez, pno; Bob Lessey, gtr; Bob Ysaguirre, sb; Manzie Johnson, d; Bootsie Garrison, vcl. This personnel is from the Victor files; Johnny Simmen claims Buster Smith was present and played the as solo.

New York, January 17, 1940

045946-1 or 2	You Ain't Nowhere (vcl, DR, ch)	BB B 10615

Boone's Jumping Jacks: Chester Boone, tp, vcl; Buster Smith, cl; George Johnson, as; Chauncey Graham, ts; Lloyd Phillips, pno; Vernon King, sb; Shadrack Anderson, d.

New York, October 16, 1941

69827-A	Messy (vcl, CB & ch)	De 8644
69828	I'm Fer It (vcl, CB)	De 8590
69829-A	Please Be Careful (If You Can't Be Good) (vcl, CB)	
		De 8644
69830-	Take Me Back (vcl, CB)	De 8590

Snub Mosley and His Band: Courtney Williams, tp; Snub Mosley, slide s, tb, vcl; Willard Brown, Buster Smith, as; Hank Duncan, pno; John Brown, sb; Joe Smith, d; Hazel Diaz, The Tampa Boys, vcl.

New York, February 11, 1942

70305-A	'Deed I Do (vcl, HD)	De 8626
70307-A	Case of the Blues (vcl, HD)	De 8626
70308-A	Blues at High Noon (as, HS)	De 8614
70309-A	Between You and the Devil (vcl, Sm)	De 8614

Eddie Durham and His Band: Joe Keyes, tp; Willard Brown, Buster Smith, a; Lem Johnson, ts, vcl; Conrad Frederick, pno; Eddie Durham, gtr, as; Averil Pollard, sb; Arthur Herbert, d.

New York, November 11, 1940

68336-A	I Want a Little Girl	De 18126
68337-A	Moten's Swing	De 18126
68338-A	Fare Thee Honey, Fare Thee Well (vcl, LJ)	De 8529
68339-A	Magic Carpet	De 8529

Buster Smith's Band: Buster Smith, dir, as, gtr; Charles Gillum, tp; Clinton Smith, tb; Leroy Cooper, bar; Herman Flowers, or, pno; Eddie Cadell, ts; Boston Smith, pno; Josea Smith, sb; Robrt Cobbs, Jr., d.

| *The Legendary Buster Smith* | Atlantic |
| | 1323 (LP) |

Fort Worth, June 7, 1959

Buster's Tune
E-Flat Boogie
September Song
King Alcohol
Kansas City Riff
Late Late
Organ Grinder's Swing

J. T. "FUNNY PAPER" SMITH (THE HOWLING WOLF)

Smith also recorded a number of unissued sides for Vocalion in Fort Worth in 1935: matrix numbers FW 1175-81, FW 1189-95 and FW 1202-06. As "Howling Smith," he accompanied Black Boy Shine, Magnolia Harris, Bernice Edwards and Dessa Foster on a number of recordings. (See "Blues & Gospel Records, 1890-1943."

Smith, vcl, gtr; unknown pno.
Chicago, September 18, 1930

C-6397	Hobo Blues	Vo unissued
C-6398	Old Rounder's Blues	Vo unissued

vcl, gtr.
Chicago, September 19, 1930

C-6404-A	Howling Wolf Blues- No.1	Vo 1558
C-6405-A	Howling Wolf Blues- No.2	Vo 1558

vcl, gtr.
Chicago, c. September 20, 1930

C-6408	Heart Bleeding Blues	Vo 1590
C-6409	Good Coffee Blues	Vo 1590

Vcl, gtr; unknown gtr, pno.
Chicago, c. October 26, 1930

C-6451	Hobo Blues	Vo 1582
C-6452	Old Rounder's Blues	Vo 1582

Note: apparently unissued or withdrawn immediately.

vcl, gtr.
Chicago, c. November 5, 1930

C-6494-A	Hard Luck Man Blues	Vo 1679
C-6495	God Bless Her Sweet Heart (gtr)	Vo unissued

Magnolia Harris, Howling Smith, vcl duet
Chicago, c. late December 1930

C-7100	Mama's Quittin' and Leavin'- Part 1	Vo 1602
C-7101	Mama's Quittin' and Leavin'- Part 2	Vo 1602

vcl, gtr.
Chicago, January 10, 1931

C-7209-A	Howling Wolf Blues- No. 3	Vo 1614

| C-7210-A | Howling Wolf Blues- No. 4 | Vo 1614 |

Dessa Foster, Howling Smith, vcl duet; acc. Howling Smith, gtr.
Chicago, January 19, 1931

| C-7238-A | Tell It To the Judge- No. 1 | Vo 02699 |
| C-7239- | Tell It To the Judge- No. 2 | Vo 02699 |

"Funny Paper" Smith, vcl, gtr.
Chicago, February 12, 1931

| VO-126 | Honey Blues | Vo 1633 |
| VO-127 | Corn Whiskey Blues | Vo 1633 |

"Funny Paper" Smith, vcl, gtr.
Chicago, March 10, 1931

VO-130-A	Wiskeyhead Blues	Vo 1664
VO-131-A	Forty-Five Blues	Vo 1664
VO-132-A	County Jail Blues	Vo 1679

"Funny Paper" Smith, vcl, gtr.
Chicago, July 10, 1931

VO-165-A	Hungry Wolf	Vo 1655
VO-166-A	Hoppin' Toad Frog	Vo 1655
VO-167-A	Fool's Blues	Vo 1674
VO-168-A	Seven Sisters Blues- Part 1	Vo 1641
VO-169-A	Seven Sisters Blues- Part 2	Vo 1641
VO-170-A	Before Long	Vo 1674

SOUTHERN SANCTIFIED SINGERS

(poss. a Rev. D. C. Rice Group) Vocal group; acc unknown, tp; unknown, tb; unknown pno; unknown, gtr, unknown, d.
Chicago, c. April 16, 1929

| C-3296 | Soon We'll Gather at the River | Br 7074 |

(poss. a Rev. D. C. Rice Group) Vocal group; acc unknown, tp; unknown pno; unknown, gtr, unknown, d.
Chicago, c. April 16, 1929

| C-3297 | Where He Leads Me I Will Follow | Br 7074 |

DICK STABILE AND HIS ORCHESTRA

Dick Stabile, cl, as, dir; Bunny Berrigan, Eddie Farley, tp; Mike Riley, tb;
Chauncey Gray, pno; Billy Wilson, vcl; unknown gtr, sb, d.
New York, January 29, 1936

60413-A	Deep Elem Blues	De 716

TEXAS JUBILEE SINGERS

Vocal group; acc. prob. Arizona Dranes, pno, vcl.
Dallas, December 8, 1928

147604-2	He's the Lily of the Valley	Co 14445
147605-2	He's Coming Soon	Co 14445

JESSE "BABYFACE" THOMAS

vcl, gtr.
Dallas, August 10, 1929

55324-	Down in Texas Blues	Vi 23381
55325-	My Heart's A Rolling Stone	Vi 23381
55326-1	Blue Goose Blues	Vi V38555
55327-2	No Good Woman Blues	Vi V38555

(WILLIAM) RAMBLIN' THOMAS

vcl, gtr.
Chicago, c. February, 1928

20334-2	So Lonesome	Pm 12637
20335-3	Hard To Rule Woman Blues	Pm 12670
20336-3	Lock and Key Blues	Pm 12637
20337-2	Sawmill Moan	Pm 12616
20338-2	No Baby Blues	Pm 12670
20339-2	Ramblin' Mind Blues	Pm 12616
20343-2	No Job Blues	Pm 12609
20344-2	Back Gnawing Blues	Pm 12609

vcl, gtr.
Chicago, c. November 1928

21017-4	Jig Head Blues	Pm 12708

21018-2	Hard Dallas Blues	Pm 12708
21019-4	Ramblin' Man	Pm 12722
21020-4	Poor Boy Blues	Pm 12722
21027-1	Good Time Blues	Pm 12752
21028-2	New Way of Living Blues	Pm 12752

vcl, gtr.
Dallas, February 9, 1932

70666-1	Ground Hog Blues	Vi 23332
70667-1	Shake It Gal	Vi 23332
706687	Ground Hog Blues No. 2	Vi 23365
70669-1	Little Old Mama Blues	Vi 23365

ALPHONSO TRENT (also known as Alphonse Trent)

Alphonso Trent and His Orchestra: Alphonso Trent, pno, dir; Chester Clark, Irving Randolph, tp; Leo "Snub" Mosley, tb, vcl; James Jeter, Charles Pillars, Lee Hilliard, as; Hayes Pillars, ts, bar; Leo "Stuff" Smith, vn; Eugene Crooke, bj, gtr; Robert "Eppie" Jackson, bb; A. G. Godley, d; John Fielding, vcl.
Richmond, Indiana, October 11, 1928

| 14327-B | Louder and Funnier (vcl, SM, SS, JF) | Gnt 6664 |
| 1428 | Gilded Kisses (v, JF) | Gnt 6664 |

Richmond, Indiana, December 5, 1928

14518	Black and Blue Rhapsody	Gnt 5710
14519	Nightmare	Gnt 5710
14520,-A	Adorable Dora	Rejected

Alphonso Trent and His Orchestra: Alphonso Trent, pno, dir; Chester Clark, Irving Randolph, George Hudson, Peanuts Holland, Tp; Leo "Snub" Mosley, tb; James Jeter, Charles Pillars, Lee Hilliard, as; Hayes Pillars, ts, bar; Leo "Stuff" Smith, vn, vcl; Eugene Crooke, bj, gtr; Robert "Eppie" Jackson, bb; A. G. Godley, d.
Richmond, Indiana, March 5, 1930

| 16349-A | After You've Gone (vcl, SS) | Gnt 7161 |
| 16350-A | St. James Infirmary | Gnt 7161 |

Richmond, Indiana, March 24, 1933

| 19080 | Clementine (vcl, PH) | Ch 16587 |
| 19081 | I've Found a New Baby (vcl, PH) | Ch 16587 |

BESSIE TUCKER

vcl; acc by K. D. Johnson, pno.
Memphis, August 29, 1928

45436-2	Bessie's Moan	Vi V38526
45437-1, -2	The Dummy	Vi 21708
45440-1,-2	Fort Worth and Denver Blues	Vi 21708
45441-2	Penitentiary	Vi V38526
45444-1	Fryin' Pan Skillet Blues	Vi unissued
45445-1, -2	My Man Has Quit Me	Vi 21692

Note: Matricies 45438/9 and 45442/3 are all by Ida May Mack. 45440-2 and 45444-1 were issued on Vi XLP LVA 3016 only.

vcl; acc by K. D. Johnson, pno.
Memphis, August 30, 1928

45448-1, -2	Got Cut All To Pieces	Vi V38018
45449-2	Black Name Moan	Vi 21692

Dallas, August 10, 1929

55328-1, -2	Better Boot That Thing-1	Vi V38542
55329-1, -2	Katy Blues	Vi V38542
55330-1	Mean Old Jack Stropper Blues	Vi V38538
55331-1	Old Black Mary	Vi V38538

K. D. Johnson, pno; Jesse Thomas, gtr.
Dallas, October 17, 1929

56404-2	Key to the Bushes Blues	Vi 23385
56405-1	Bogey Man Blues	Vi 23385
56406-1, -2	Mean Old Master Blues	Vi 23392
56407-2	Pick on Me Blues	Vi unissued

Dallas, October 21, 1929

56447-1	Whistling Woman Blues	Vi unissued
56448-2	T.B. Moan	Vi 23392

BLACK ACE (BUCK TURNER)

Babe Kyro Lemon Turner, vcl, gtr.
Fort Worth, April 5, 1936

FW-1260-1	Bonus Man Blues	ARC unissued
FW-1261	Black Ace Blues	ARC unissued

Vcl, gtr; unknown 2nd gtr.
Dallas, February 15, 1937

61789-A	Trifling Woman	De 7281
61790-A	Black Ace	De 7281
61791-A	You Gonna Need My Help Some Day	De 7340
61792-A	Whiskey and Women	De 7340
61793-A	Christmas Time Blues (Beggin' Santa Claus)	De 7387
61794-A	Lowing Heifer	De 7387

PAUL VAN LOAN AND HIS ORCHESTRA

Paul van Loan, tv, a, dir; musicians prob. Allen McAllister, George Hall, tp; George Vaughn, Tom Kraus, Glen Wakeman, cl, ss, as, ts; Joe Cirina, pno; Whitey Campbell, bj; Ed Grier, bb; George Sterinsky, d.
New York, September 25, 1935

1623-C	Deep Elm (You Tell 'Em I'm Blue)	Cam 820

AARON "T-BONE" WALKER

Oak Cliff T-Bone: Vcl, acc by own gtr; Douglas Finnell, pno.
Dallas, December 5, 1929

149548-1	Trinity River Blues	Co 14506-D
149549-2	Wichita Falls Blues	Co 14506-D

T-Bone Walker featured vcl with Les Hite and His Orchestra: Les Hite, as, dir; Paul Campbell, Walter Williams, Forrest Powell, tp; Allen Durham, tb; Les Hite, Floyd Turnham, as; Quedellis "Que" Martyn, Roger Hurd, Sol Moore, bar; Nat Walker, pno; Frank Pasley, gtr; Al Morgan, sb; Oscar Bradley, d.
New York, c June 1940

US-1852-1	T-Bone Blues	Vs 8391

Note: Remaining titles from this session do not feature Walker.

T-Bone Walker, gtr, featured with Freddie Slack and His Orchestra: Charles Gifford, Clyde Hurley, John Letman, Bill Morris, tp; Bruce Squires, Gerald Foster, Bill Lawlor, tb; Barney Bigard, cl, ts; John Huffman, Willie Martinez, as; Ralph Lee, Les Baxter, ts, bar; Freddie Slack, pno, dir; George M. "Jud" De Naut, sb; Dave Coleman, d; Ella Mae Morse, Johnny Mercer, Gay Jones, vcl.
Hollywood, July 20, 1942

50	He's My Guy	Cap 113
51-A	Mister Five by Five	Cap 115
52-A	The Thrill Is Gone	Cap 115
53	Roiffette	Cap 129

T-Bone Walker, vcl, gtr; Freddie Slack, pno, dir; George M. "Jud" De Naut, sb; Dave Coleman, d.

| 54-A | I Got a Break Baby | Cap 10033 |
| 55-A | Mean Old World | Cap 10033 |

T-Bone Walker, gtr, featured with Freddie Slack and His Orchestra; same personnel as on July 20, 1942, except that vocalists are Ella Mae Morse, Johnny Mercer, Margaret Whiting and the Mellowaires.

Hollywood, July 31, 1942

70	That Old Black Magic	Cap 126
71	Old Rob Roy	Cap 133
72	Waitin' for the Evening Mail	Cap 137
73	Wreck of the Old 97	Cap 122
74	Hit the Road to Dreamland	Cap 126
75-A	Get on Board, Little Children	Cap 133
76	I Lost My Sugar in Salt Lake City	Cap 122

This artist recorded extensively after 1943.

HERB WIEDOEFT'S CINDERELLA ROOF ORCHESTRA

Herb Wiedoeft, tp, dir; Joseph Nemoli, c, vcl; Jesse Stafford, tb, bh; Larry Abbott, Gene Siegrist, Fred Bibesheimer, cl, as, ts, o; Vincent Rose, pno; Jose Sucedo, bj; Guy Wiedoeft, bb, sb; Adolph Wiedoeft, d, x; Clyde Lucas, tb, vcl; Dubbie Kirkpatrick, unknown instrument.

| E-16701 | Deep Elm (You Tell 'Em I'm Blue) | Vri 504 |

OSCAR "BUDDY" WOODS

gtr; Jimmie Davis (white artist), vcl; acc. poss. "Dizzy Head" (Ed Schaffer), gtr.

Memphis, May 20, 1930

| 59952-2 | She's a Hum Dum Dinger (From Dingersville) Vi V40286 |

Shreveport Home Wreckers: Ed Schaffer, gtr, vcl, k; Oscar Woods, gtr.

Memphis, May 21, 1930

59965-2	Fence Breakin' Blues	BB B5341
59966-2	Home Wreckin' Blues	BB B5341

Gtr; Jimmie Davis (white artist), vcl; acc poss. "Dizzy Head" (Ed Schaffer), gtr.
Memphis, November 29, 1930

64760-2	Bear Cat Mama From Horner's Corners	Vi 23517

Jimmie Davis, Oscar Woods, vcl duet; acc Ed Schaffer, gtr; Oscar Woods, gtr.
Dallas, February 8, 1932

70656-1	Saturday Night Stroll	Vi 23688

Gtr; Jimmie Davis (white artist), vcl; acc poss. "Dizzy Head" (Ed Schaffer), gtr.
Dallas, February 8, 1932

70657-1	Sewing Machine Blues	BB B5751
70658-1	Red Nightgown Blues	BB B5699
70659-1	Davis's Salty Dog	Vi 23674

(The Lone Wolf), vcl, gtr.
New Orleans, March 21, 1936

60847-	Evil Hearted Woman Blues	De 7904
60848-A	Lone Wolf Blues	De 7219
60849-	Don't Sell It—Don't Give It Away	De 7219

Buddy Woods with the Wampus Cats: Oscar Woods, vcl, gtr; unknown pno, sb, d.
San Antonio, October 30, 1937

SA-2844-1	Muscat Hill Blues	Vo 03906
SA-2845-1	Don't Sell It (Don't Give It Away)	Vo 03906

Buddy Woods (Acc. by "Wampus Cats"): Oscar Woods, vcl, gtr; prob. Herb Morand, tp; unknown, pno, 2nd gtr, sb, d.
Dallas, December 4, 1938

DAL-702-1	Jam Session Blues	Vo 04604
DAL-703-1	Low Life Blues	Vo 04745
DAL-704-1	Token Blues	Vo 04604

Buddy Woods (Acc. by "Wampus Cats"): Oscar Woods, vcl, gtr; unknown, pno; unknown 2nd gtr; unknown, sb; unknown, d.
Dallas, December 4, 1938

DAL-707-1	Come on Over to My House Baby	Vo 04745

* * *

Abbreviations of instruments and roles in recording

a—arranger
acc—accompanied
acd—accordion
ah—alto horn
amp—amplified
as—alto saxophone
b—bass (unspecified)
bb—brass b (sousaphone/tuba)
bcl—b clarinet
bd—b drum
bh—baritone horn
bj—banjo
bsn—boon
bsx—b saxophone
c—cornet
ca—cor anglais (English horn)
cel—celeste
cl—clarinet
Cm—C-melody saxophone
d—drums (except washboard and wood blocks)
db—doubling
dir—director
elg—electric guitar
elo—electric organ
eu—euphonium
f—flute
fh—flugelhorn
fid—fiddle
gfs—goofus/cuesnophone
gtr—guitar
h—harmonica
har—harmonium
hfp—hot fountain pen (miniature clarinet)
k—kazoo
ldr—leader
md—mandolin
mel—mellophone

o—oboe
oc—ocarina
or—(pipe) organ
pac—piano accordion
pic—piccolo
pno—piano
q.v.—quo vides (Latin, "which you may see")
sb—string b
sd—snare drum
ss—soprano saxophone
stg—steel (Hawaiian) guitar
sw—swanee (slide) whistle
tb—trombone
tbj—tenor banjo
th—tenor horn
tp—trumpet
ts—tenor saxophone
u—ukulele
vc—violincello (cello)
vcl—vocalist
vib—vibraphone
vl—viola
vn—violin
vtb—valve trombone
w—whistling
wb—washboard
x—xylophone

Abbreviations of record labels

AH—Ace of Hearts
ARC—American Record Company
Ban—Banner
BB—Bluebird
Br—Brunswick
Cam—Cameo
Cap—Capitol
CC—Collectors' Corner
Ch—Champion
Cl—Clarion
Col—Columbia
Com—Commodore Music Shop
CQ/cq—Claxtonola

DA—Documentary Arts
DE/De—Decca
Do—Domino
Ed—Edison Diamond Disc
El—Electrola
Ele—Electradisk
Gnt—Gennett
HJC—Hot Jazz Clubs
HJCA—Hot Jazz Clubs of America
HMV—His master's voice
JA—Jazz Archives (LP)
JCI—Jazz Classic
JP—Jazz Panorama (LP)
Od—Odeon
OK—Okeh
Par—Parlophone
PC—Palm Club
Ph—Philips
Pm—Paramount
Pol—Polydor
TR—Top Rank
TT—Timely Tunes
Van—Vanguard
Vi—Victor
Vo—Vocalion
Vri—Variety (absorbed by Vocalion)
Vs—Varsity

Appendix 2
Light Crust Doughboys Recording Sessions
1936–1948

Compiled 1989 by Marvin "Junior" Montgomery, known since 1948 as "Smokey" Montgomery.

Over the years I have seen many miscues on record jackets, magazine articles, etc., regarding the Doughboy Recording sessions—who played what, sang what, yelled what, or just plain old what—I decided (with a lot of prodding from Bob Pinson and some back-up from Muryel "Zeke" Campbell, Kenneth "Abner" Pitts, Jim "Bashful" Boyd, Joe Frank "Bashful" Ferguson, Frank Reneau and Leroy Millican) to put the record straight. As Zeke, Abner and Junior (yours truly) are the only living members who played on all of these sessions it stands to reason that this is as correct as the record will ever get.

April 4, 1936, Fort Worth, Texas
A & R (producer): "Uncle" Art Satherley. Musicians: Dick "Bashful" Reinhart, rhythm gtr, vcl; Bert "Buddy" Dodson, b, vcl; Clifford "Doctor" Gross, fid and b vcl on quartets; Kenneth "Abner" Pitts, fid, acd, baritone vcl on trios and quartets; Muryel "Zeke" Campbell, acoustic lead gtr; Marvin "Junior" Montgomery, tbj, tgtr and a vcl now and then. (My first recording session with the Doughboys along with Reinhart, Dodson and Campbell.)
Eddie Dunn was our radio announcer and boss; he was not a musician.

On all twin fid work, Gross played the lead part and Pitts the harmony part. Each song discographed in order of performance.

FW-1250. I'm a Ding Dong Daddy from Dumas
1. Twin fids, Gross-Pitts
2. Vcl, Reinhart
3. Acoustic gtr solo, Campbell
4. Tbj solo, Montgomery
5. Vcl
6. Acoustic gtr solo, Reinhart
7. Vcl
8. Hot fid solo, Pitts

FW-1251. My Buddy. Unissued.

FW-1252. I Like Bananas (Because They Have No Bones)
1. Twin fids
2. Vcl unison, Dodson, Reinhart, Pitts, Montgomery, Gross
3. Verse: lead vcl, Dodson; background vcl, Pitts, Reinhart, Montgomery, Gross
4. Chorus trio: Dodson, lead; Reinhart, tenor; Pitts, baritone
5. Twin fids
6. Vcls: Dodson, group; Pitts group; Montgomery (one line); Reinhart (one line); group
7. Gtr solo, Campbell; fid solo, Pitts; tag-group

FW-1253. The Wheel of the Wagon Is Broken. Unissued.

April 5, 1936 (same place, same musicians)
FW-254. Little Hillbilly Heart Throb. Unissued.

FW-1255. Did You Ever Hear a String Band Swing? (Composer Marvin Montgomery)
1. Intro-fid, Pitts
2. Vcl lead, Montgomery group, Pitts, Reinhart, Dodson, Gross
3. Fid, Pitts
4. Talk, Montgomery; Pitts, fid; talk, Montgomery; Dodson, acoustic b solo
4. Gtr solo, Campbell
5. Bj solo, Montgomery
6. Fid, Pitts

FW- 256. Tonight I Have a Date (Composer, Marvin Montgomery). Unissued.

FW-1257. Saddle Your Blues to a Wild Mustang
1. Intro twin fids, Gross, Pitts
2. Vcl, Dodson
3. Twin fids
4. Vcl

FW-1258. Gloomy Monday. Unissued.

FW-1259. Memories. Unissued.

Notice: As you read on you'll find that on a lot of the songs Gross did not play, due to the fact that he couldn't read music and was a slow learner. On the recording sessions we didn't like to waste time waiting for him to learn a song, and so Pitts (who acted as leader on the sessions) and I would leave him out. Gross would go to the corner and sulk.

May 26 & 29, 1936. Los Angeles.
We were in Hollywood at Republic Studios to make the movie *Oh, Susannah* with Gene Autry. Pitts remembers that "Uncle" Art Satherley was *not* at those sessions, but thinks the producer's name was Gray.

Musicians: Reinhart, Vcl, rhythm gtr and md (the one I have and intend to send to The Country Music Foundation in Nashville soon). You'll hear it on "My Buddy." Dodson, vcl, b; Pitts, fid; Gross, fid; Campbell, lead acoustic gtr; Montomgery, tbj & tgtr.

May 26, 1936
LA-1121. Little Hill-Billy Heart Throb
1. Twin fids, Gross, Pitts
2. Vcl, Reinhart (Dick had a sore throat and sang this in a key almost too low for him)
3. Twin fids
4. Vcl 5. Gtr solo, Campbell
6. Vcl.

LA-1122. My Buddy.
1. Twin fids, Gross, Pitts—Fills; Montgomery, tgtr
2. Vcl trio: Dodson, lead; Reinhart, tenor; Pitts, baritone.
3. Md solo, Reinhbart
4. Vcl trio.

LA-1123. The Wheel of the Wagon Is Broken
1. Intro, tgtr, Montgomery
2. Vcl, Reinhart; tgtr fills, Montgomery
3. Twin fids, Gross, Pitts
4. Vcl, tgtr ending.

LA-1124. Tonight I Have a Date. Unissued. (Uncle Art still didn't like my song, and I don't blame him.)

LA-1125. Lost
1. Twin fids, vcl, Dodson; fills on tgtr, Montgomery; fid fills, Pitts; twin fid, gtr

283

solo, Campbell; vcl. Pitts remembers he played both 2nd and 3rd harmony notes part of the time.

May 29, 1936 Los Angeles.

LA-1126. Sweet Uncle Zeke. This song was composed by Freddy Casares, fid player with the old Wanderers fid band which Dodson, Reinhart and I played with before we joined the Doughboys. This song was also used as background music in the movie *Oh, Susannah.*

1. Gtr solo, Reinhart
2. Fid solo, Pitts
3. Gtr solo, Campbell
4. Bj solo, Montgomery
5. Gtr and fid duet, Reinhart and Pitts.

LA-1127. All My Life
1. Twin fids, Gross, Pitts
2. Vcl, Dodson, tgtr fills, Montgomery
3. Twin fids
4. Vcl

LA-1128. Jig in "G." Unissued.

LA-1129. When the Moon Shines on the Mississippi Valley
1. Twin fids
2. Vcl, Reinhart
3. Fiddle, Pitts
4. Vcl.

LA-1131. It's Been So Long
1. Fid, Pitts
2. Vcl, Dodson
3. Gtr solo, Campbell
4. Vcl.

LA-1132. Cross-Eyed Cowboy from Abilene (Composer, Marvin Montgomery) Notice: I wrote these terrible songs and I couldn't get anybody to sing them so I had to sing them myself.
1. Fid, Pitts
2. Vcl, Montgomery
3. Gtr solo, Campbell
4. Vcl

September 10, 1936, Fort Worth, Texas
Producer (A & R) "Uncle" Art Satherley, Don Law. Musicians: Reinhart, rhythm gtr, vcl; Dodson, b, vcl; Pitts, fid, acd; Gross, fid; Campbell, solo acoustic gtr; Montgomery, tbj. Notice: Along about this time Uncle Art asked me to play 4/4 time on the bj. Up until then I played mostly 2/4. You'll hear me doing 4/4 from now on.

FW-1262. I'd Love to Live in Loveland (With a Girl LIke You). Unissued.

FW-1263. Happy Cowboy. (Notice: We met the Sons of the Pioneers and played on their radio show while we were in Hollywood. When we got back to Texas we started doing a lot of their songs.)
1. Twin fids
2. Vcl, Dodson. Trio: Dodson, lead; Reinhart, tenor; Pitts, baritone
3. Twin gtrs, Reinhart, Campbell; Twin fids; Trio.

FW-1264. Blue Guitar. Unissued.

FW-1265. A Mug of Ale. Unissued.

FW-1266. Sweet Georgia Brown. Unissued.

FW 1267 Oh, Susannah
1. Bj, Montgomery
2. Vcl, Dodson. Quartet: Dodson, lead; Reinhart, tenor; Pitts, baritone; Gross, b. Solo gtr, Campbell; fid, Gross; Bj, Quartet. Rhythm acd played by Pitts.

FW-1268. The Strawberry Roan. Unissued.

FW-1269. The Big Corral. Unissued.

FW-1270. I Want a Girl (Just Like the Girl That Married Dear Old Dad). Unissued.

FW-1271. When You Wore a Tulip (and I Wore A Big Red Rose). Unissued.

June 12, 1937 Dallas, Texas
A & R Producer, Art Satherley, Don Law. Musicians: John "Knocky" Parker, pno, acd, first recording session with the Doughboys. Raymond "Snub" DeArman, slap b, rhythm gtr, vcl (his second time as a Doughboy—he left the first time to join Cecil Brower in Columbus, Ohio to make transcrip-

tions, shortly before Reinhart, Dodson and I joined the Doughboys. He replaced Dodson in the band playing slap b.) Pitts, Gross, Campbell, Reinhart, Montgomery. From now on most of the yells, etc., on the records will be DeArman. Campbell plays electric gtr for first time.

DAL-268. Emaline
1. Pno intro, Parker
2. Fid, Pitts
3. Vcl, Reinhart
4. elg, Campbell; bridge & fid to end of chorus, Pitts
5. Pno, full chorus to end, Parker.

DAL-269. Let Me Ride By Your Side in the Saddle. Unissued.

DAL-270. Tom Cat Rag. Unissued.

DAL-271. Blue Guitars
1. Pno intro, Parker
2. Elg, Campbell
3. Pno
4. Gtr
5. Fid, Pitts
6. Gtr

DAL-272. Dusky Stevedore
1. Twin fids, Gross, Pitts
2. Vcl duet: DeArman, lead, Reinhart, tenor
3. Bj solo, Montgomery
4. Acd, Parker; Pitts plays pno rhythm
5. Vcl duet

DAL-273. If I Don't Love You (There Ain't a Cow in Texas)
1. Twin fids, Gross, Pitts
2. Vcl, Reinhart
3. Elg, Campbell
4. Acd, Parker; Pitts to pno

DAL-274. Roll Along, Jordan
1. Twin fids, Gross, Pitts
2. Vcl verse, DeArman
3. Quartet: DeArman, lead; Reinhart, tenor; Pitts, baritone; Gross, bass
3. Gtr, Campbell

4. Twin acds, Parker, Pitts
5. Vcl verse, Quartet chorus.

DAL-275. One Sweet Letter from You. Unissued.

DAL-276. Song of the Saddle. Unissued.

DAL-277. Anna Lou. Unissued.

DAL-278. Avalon
1. Twin fids
2. Pno: four hands, Pitts on bass end and Parker on high end
3. Bj
4. Gtr
5. Acd, Parker; Pitts stays on pno rhythm

June 20, 1937 Dallas.
Same musicians. Notice: The jump in record numbers means that between our recording sessions Uncle Art and Don Law recorded several other groups.

DAL-385. Gig-a-Wig Blues (Composer, Marvin Montgomery)
1. Fid, Pitts
2. Bj, Montgomery
3. Pno, Parker
4. Gtr, Campbell
5. Acd, Parker; Pitts to pno

DAL-386. In a Little Red Barn
1. Twin fids, Gross, Pitts
2. Vcl, DeArman
3. Pno, Parker
4. Gtr, Campbell
5. Fid, Pitts

DAL-387. Beaumont Rag
1. Fid, Gross
2. Bj, Montgomery
3. Fid, Gross
4. Gtr, Campbell
5. Fid, Gross

(Rhy gtr, Reinhart; rhy acd, Pitts; yells and slap bass, DeArman—he yelled a lot didn't he? More than Bob Wills?)

DAL-388. The Eyes of Texas
1. Twin fids, Gross, Pitts
2. Vcl quartet: DeArman, lead; Reinhart, tenor; Pitts, baritone; Gross, bass
3. Gtr, Campbell
4. Pno, Parker
5. Quartet

DAL-389. Washington and Lee Swing
1. Twin fids, Gross, Pitts
2. Bj, Montgomery
3. Acd, Pitts
4. Gtr, Campbell
5. Pno, Parker
6. Twin fids

DAL-390. Stay on the Right Side Sister. Unissued.

DAL-391. Just Once Too Often
1. Gtr intro, Reinhart
2. Fid, Pitts
3. Vcl, Reinhart
4. Gtr, Campbell.

DAL-392. Stay Out of the South. Unissued.

May 14, 1938, Dallas, Texas
Parker Willson is now our M.C. and boss-man. He sang b with the quartet and now and then sang a solo. The Doughboys also have a mascot, Charles Burton, eleven or twelve years of age, who sang on the radio show several times a week and went on some of our personal appearance shows. His real name was Willson. Parker Willson had Charles use Burton as a last name because Parker Willson didn't want the public to think that Charles was his son. Musicians: Same as last session. Fids, Gross, Pitts; gtrs, Reinhart, Campbell; pno, Parker; Bj, Montgomery; b, DeArman. Producer: A & R, Uncle Art Satherley, Don Law.

DAL-529. Sitting on Top of the World
1. Elg, Dick "Bashful" Reinhart

2. Vcl, Reinhart
3. Fid, Pitts
4. Vcl, Reinhart
5. Elg, Reinhart. Campbell played rhy gtr.

DAL-530. Weary Blues
Fid, Pitts; elg, Campbell; pno, Parker; Bj, Montgomery; Rhy gtr, Reinhart; Slap b and yells, DeArman. Notice: All harmony parts played on elg, fid and pno. Gross went to his corner on this one.

DAL-531. Gulf Coast Blues
1. Pno ntro, Parker
2. Fid, Pitts
3. Vcl, Reinhart
4. Pno, Parker
5. Gtr, Campbell
6. Vcl

DAL-532. The Budded Rose
1. Twin fids, Gross, Pitts
2. Vcl, DeArman
3. Gtr, Campbell
4. Vcl

DAL-533. I'll Get Mine
1. Twin fids, Gross, Pitts
2. Vcl verse, Reinhart; quartet, DeArman takes lead, Reinhart goes to tenor, Pitts, baritone, Gross, b
3. Gtr, Campbell
4. Pno, Parker 5. Fid solo, Pitts
6. Vcl verse, quartet

DAL-534. Blue Hours
1. Twin fids, Gross, Pitts; steel gtr, Reinhart; Parker on pno to bridge then puts on acd
2. Acd, Parker with steel background
3. Steel played in harmony (Bridge) steel plays single string lead
4. Tag, fids and steel; bowed B, DeArman; tgtr, Montgomery; Rhy gtr, Campbell.

DAL-535. Three Shif-less Skonks.
1. Twin fids, Gross, Pitts

2. Vcl solo, DeArman; quartet, DeArman, lead; Reinhart, tenor; Pitts, baritone; Gross, b
3. Fid Solo, Pitts
4. Pno, Parker
5. Vcl solo, quartet
6. Elg, Campbell
7. Vcl solo, quartet

DAL-536. Kalua Loha. Unissued.

DAL-537. Slow Down, Mr. Brown
1. Fid, Pitts
2. Vcl, Reinhart
3. Gtr, Campbell
4. Pno, Parker
5. Vcl out

DAL-538. Beautiful Ohio
1. Twin fids, Gross, Pitts
2. Vcl, Charles Burton (Doughboy Mascot)
3. Elg lead, Campbell, twin fid background
4. Vcl.

DAL-539. Waiting for the Robert E. Lee
1. Twin fids, Gross, Pitts
2. Vcl, Reinhart
3. Acd, Parker, Pitts to pno
4. Gtr, Campbell
5. Vcl

DAL-540. Hills of Old Wyomin'
1. Fid, Pitts
2. Vcl, Charles Burton
3. Unison hum, Parker Willson (MC), DeArman, Pitts, Reinhart
4. Vcl, hum
5. Vcl quartet, Reinhart, tenor; DeArman, lead; Pitts, baritone; Wilson, b
6. Vcl with hum

DAL-541. Tom Cat Rag (Composer, Marvin Montgomery)
1. Fid, Pitts
2. Vcl, DeArman; lead, Reinhart; tenor, Pitts, baritone
3. Gtr, Campbell

4. Pno, Parker
5. Bj, Montgomery
6. Vcl

DAL-542. Gig-a-Wig Blues (Composer, Marvin Montgomery)
Notice: Gig-a-Wig Blues is also number 385. I do not know which version they released but I would think that it would be the last one we cut (542).

DAL-543. Knocky-Knocky (Composer, Knocky Parker)
1. Pno
2. Fid, Pitts
3. Pno
4. Gtr, Campbell
5. Pno

DAL-544. The Birth of the Blues
1. Gtr intro, Reinhart
2. Twin fids, bridge, pno, twin fids
3. Vcl, Reinhart
4. Gtr, Campbell; pno, Parker
5. Fid solo, Pitts; vcl out

DAL-545. Rockin' Alone (In an Old Rockin" Chair). Unissued.

DAL-546. Pretty Little Dear
1. Twin fids
2. Vcl, DeArman
3. Gtr, Campbell
4. Vcl
5. Twin fades, Pitts solo at bridge; twin fids
6. Vcl.

DAL-547. Sweeter Than an Angel
1. Fid, Pitts
2. Vcl. Reinhart
3. Gtr
4. Pno
5. Fid solo, Pitts
6. Vcl

DAL-548. Stumbling
1. Tgtr lead, Montgomery; 2nd gtr (acoustic), Campbell; 3rd gtr (acoustic), Pitts

2. Acoustic gtr solo, Campbell
3. Pno, Parker
4. Fid, Pitts

DAL-549. Clarinet Marmalade
1. Fid, Pitts
2. Elg, pno & fid in harmony (Campbell, Pitts, Parker)
3. Fid, Pitts
4. Gtr, Campbell
5. Pno, Parker
6. Harmony parts
7. Fid, Pitts

We recorded twenty-one songs on this session all in one day. The longest session we ever had in one day.

November 30, 1938, Dallas, Texas
Producer (A & R) Art Satherley, Don Law. Musicians: "Buck" Buchanan, fid replacing "Doctor" Gross (who left before getting fired after pulling a knife on Parker Willson, our boss-man). Jim "Bashful" Boyd replacing Dick "Bashful" Reinhart who left because Burrus Mill hired Parker Willson as MC and boss instead of him. Reinhart joined Gross and they formed the Universal Cowboys for Universal Flour Mills. Boyd states that he joined the Doughboys in August of 1938. Buchanan joined about one month earlier. Ken "Abner" Pitts, fid; "Zeke" Campbell, elg; "Junior" Montgomery, bj and kazoo; "Knocky" Parker, pno, acd; "Snub" DeArman, slap b.

DeArman and Boyd changed off between b and rhythm gtr. You can identify DeArman's b playing because he slapped it more than Boyd, also he was inclined to play a lot of backward b. Example: to play a C chord in 2/4 time you should play C then G. DeArman would reverse the rule and play G then C: Hence the term "Backwar B." This was very upsetting to some of the musicians in the band, most especially "Knocky" Parker. Notice on this session that Boyd did all the solo vcl. For some reason DeArman was left out. Also Uncle Art (or Parker Willson) calmed him down on the yells.

DAL-641. It Makes No Difference Now (Boyd's first record as a Doughboy. On the following recordings I also have input coming from Boyd. He believes it is his younger brother, John Boyd, who is playing steel on this song. Pitts and I both agree with this. John recorded several songs under his own name for Uncle Art during this session. Not long after these sessions, John was killed in a motorcycle accident.)

1. Elg, Campbell, steel fills (John Boyd)
2. Vcl, Boyd
3. Campbell & steel
4. Vcl, Boyd
5. Twin fids, Pitts, lead; Buchanan, harmony
6. Vcl, Boyd; tgtr, Montgomery; B, DeArman; rhy gtr, Boyd

Notice: While Buchanan was on the band Pitts played lead and Buchanan played the harmony parts.

DAL-642. Blue-Eyed Sally
1. Twin fids, Pitts, Buchanan
2. Vcl, Boyd
3. Elg, Campbell
4. Pno, Parker
5. Twin fids
6. Vcl, Boyd, rhythm; DeArman, b; bj, Montgomery.

DAL-643. You're the Only Star (In My Blue Heaven). The Columbia release has DeArman listed as the vclist, NOT TRUE. It was Jim Boyd.
1. Twin fids, Pitts, Buchanan
2. Vcl, Boyd
3. Two gtrs: tgtr lead, Montgomery; Acoustic standard gtr, Campbell; harmony twin fids (Bridge) twin gtrs
4. Vcl, Boyd; DeArman, b

DAL-644. Baby, Give Me Some of That (Composer, Marvin Montgomery)
1. Twin fids, Pitts, Buchanan
2. Vcl, Boyd
3. Pno, Parker; Elg, Campbell
4. Twin fids, hot solo fid, Buchanan; vcl, DeArman, b

DAL-645. Dirty Dishrag Blues (Composer, Zeke Campbell)
1. Acoustic gtr intro, Boyd
2. Elg, Campbell
3. Vcl, Boyd
4. Pno, Parker
5. Fid solo, Pitts
6. Vcl
7. Elg
8. Vcl, DeArman b; Montgomery, bj

DAL-646. (New) Jeep's Blues
1. Pno intro, Parker
2. Twin fids, Pitts, Buchanan
3. Elg, Campbell
4. Pno
5. Elg
6. Twin fids

DAL-647. Zenda Waltz
1. Twin fids, Pitts, Buchanan
2. Elg, Campbell
3. Twin fids, tgtr, Montgomery; Bowed b, DeArman; rhy gtr, Boyd

DAL-648. Grey Skies. Unissued.

DAL-649. Thousand Mile Blues
1. Twin fids
2. Fid solo, Buchanan
3. Vcl, Boyd
4. Elg, Campbell
5. Pno, Parker; Kazoo, Montgomery
6. Vcl; slap b by DeArman

DAL-650. Gin Mill Blues
1. Pno, Parker
2. Elg, Campbell; twin fid, background, Pitts, Buchanan
3. Pno, Parker
4. Pno, twin fid, BG
5. Fids and pno, bowed b, Boyd; tgtr, Montgomery; rhy gtr, DeArman

DAL-651. Yancy Special. Unissued.

DAL-652. The Farmer's Not in the Dell
1. Elg, Campbell
2. Vcl, Boyd
3. Pno, Parker; hot fid, Buchanan, pno
4. Twin fids, Pitts, Buchanan; DeArman, B; Boyd, rhy gtr

DAL-653. Foot Warmer
1. Twin fids, Pitts, Buchanan
2. Elg (Campbell) in harmony with fids
3. Pno, Parker

4. Elg
5. Fid solo, Buchanan
6. Elg
7. B, Boyd; rhy gtr, DeArman; bj, Montgomery

DAL-654. Troubles
1. Twin fids, Pitts, Buchanan
2. Vcl, Boyd
3. Humming trio: Boyd, tenor; DeArman, lead; Pitts, baritone
4. Elg, Campbell
5. Vcl
6. Hum trio. (Boyd thinks Willson sang baritone on this one; Pitts thinks it was he; take your pick.)

DAL-655. Pussy, Pussy, Pussy (Composer, Marvin Montgomery)
1. Vamp-Girl Voice, Montgomery
2. Group Voices, Pitts, Boyd, DeArman, Montgomery
3. Elg, Campbell
4. Fid, Buchanan
5. Pno, Parker
6. Cat, DeArman; Girl, Montgomery; male voice, DeArman
7. Group voices
8. Elg, fid background. Boyd on b. (This record got on more juke-boxes than any other song I ever wrote.)

Dallas, June 14, 1939
Producer (A & R) Art Satherley, Don Law. Musicians: Cecil Brower, fid, re-placing Buchanan. Pitts, Campbell, Parker, DeArman, Boyd, Montgomery. Charles Burton, our mascot, did some vcl as well as Parker Willson, our MC and boss-man. Musically, this is probably the best session we ever did. We recorded in the old Brunswick Warehouse with no air conditioning, and it was hot. We played with our shirts off and I suspect the bottle was passed around a few times among some of the band members as well as the boss-man—why hide it—Willson, Brower, DeArman and Don Law and maybe a swig or two by Boyd.

DAL-803. Let's Make Believe We're Sweethearts
1. Elg, Campbell
2. Vcl, Boyd
3. Twin fids: Brower lead, Pitts Harmony 4. Elg, fids in unison, vcl. Boyd on b; DeArman, rhythm gtr; Parker on pno; Montgomery, bj.

Notice: After Brower joined the Doughboys he played lead fid and Pitts played the harmony fid.

DAL-804. Thinking of You
1. Twin fids, Brower, Pitts
2. Vcl, DeArman
3. Elg, Campbell
4. Accordian, Parker (Pitts switched to rhythm pno)
5. Vcl. Boyd, b; DeArman, rhythm

DAL-805. If I Didn't Care
1. Intro, unison fids
2. Vcl, Charles Burton
3. unison fids, tgtr fills, Montgomery; Boyd on b

DAL-806. Mary Lou
1. Elg, Campbell
2. Vcl, Charles Burton
3. Twin fids, Brower, Pitts
4. Elg, vcl. tgtr, Montgomery; b, Boyd; rhy, DeArman

DAL-807. In Ole' Oklahoma
1. Twin fids, Brower, Pitts
2. Vcl, Parker Willson
3. Twin fids, vcl. Boyd, b; Montgomery, tgtr; DeArman, rhythm
I might mention the Parker Willson, Charles Burton vcl recordings did not sell very well—Uncle Art recorded and released them as a favor to Parker Willson.

DAL-808. She Gave Me the Bird (Composer, Marvin Montgomery)
1. Twin fids, Pitts, Brower
2. Vcl, Boyd
3. Elg, Campbell
4. Fid solo, Brower
5. Girl Voice, Montgomery (sound effects, Boyd & DeArman)
6. All Sing (Voices), Pitts, Montgomery, DeArman, Boyd, Willson, the Bird, Willson.

DAL-809. Three Naughty Kittens (Composer, Marvin Montgomery)
1. All sound effects, Parker Willson. Voices: Willson, Boyd, DeArman, Pitts, Montgomery
2. Little girl, Parker Willson

3. Pno, Parker
4. Little Girl, Willson
5. Low voice, Willson: Vcl Group
6. Gtr, Campbell
7. Little Girl, Willson

DAL-810. We Must Have Beer (Marvin Montgomery)
1. Twin fids, Pitts, Brower
2. Vcl Group, Pitts, Boyd, DeArman, Willson
3. Acd, Parker; Twin fids
4. Acd, Twin fids
5. Interlude
6. Acd
7. Twin fids
8. Interlude, Twin fids
9. Gtr Solo
10. Vcl Group
11. Pno, Parker
12. Twin fids & gtr

DAL-811. Tea for Two
1. Twin fids, Pitts, Brower
2. Pno, Parker
3. fids & pno
4. Gtr, Campbell; pno; twin fids (rhy gtr, DeArman; b, Boyd; tgtr, Montgomery)

DAL-812. Little Rock Get-a-Way
1. Pno, Parker
2. Pno, twin fids, Pitts, Brower, pno
3. Elg, Campbell
4. Harmony, gtr, fids, pno; harmony, pno, fids (b, Boyd; tgtr, Montgomery; rhy gtr, DeArman)

DAL-813. We Found Her Little Pussy Cat (Marvin Montgomery)
1. Vamp, Cats, DeArman, Willson; Girl Voice, Montgomery
2. Voices: DeArman, Pitts, Willson, Boyd, Montgomery
3. Elg, Campbell
4. Pno, Parker
5. Fid, Brower
6. Vamp, Cats, Male Voice, DeArman; Girl, Montgomery
7. Vcl Group

8. Gtr & fids; tag, voices, cat, Willson (b, Boyd, Rhy. Gtr, DeArman, tgtr, Montgomery)

DAL-814. Old November Moon (Marvin Montgomery). Unissued.

DAL-815. The Cattle Call
1. Twin fids, Pitts, Brower
2. Vcl, Boyd; Trio: Boyd, high; DeArman, middle; Willson, low voice
3. Elg, Campbell
4. Vcl, Boyd, twin fids
5. Vcl, Boyd; Trio: DeArman, Boyd, Willson

DAL-816. Texas Song of Pride (Marvin Montgomery)
1. Twin fids, Pitts, Brower
2. Vcl group, DeArman, Pitts, Boyd, Willson
3. Gtr, Campbell
4. Pno, Parker
5. Vcl group, quartet ending: Boyd, tenor; DeArman, lead; Pitts, baritone; Willson, b

June 15, 1939
DAL-827. Two More Years (And I'll Be Free)
1. Gtr, Campbell (playing two part harmony)
2. Vcl, Boyd
3. Gtr
4. Twin fids, Pitts, Brower
5. Vcl
6. Gtr
7. Vcl

DAL-828. Mama Won't Let Me (Campbell, Parker, Montgomery; I wrote the fid parts only)
1. Gtr (Campbell) & pno (Parker) intro
2. Gtr
3. Pno
4. Twin fids, Pitts, Brower
5. Gtr lead, pno harmony: Bridge, Pno lead, gtr harmony: gtr lead, pno harmony; Boyd, b.

DAL-829. All Because of Lovin' You
1. Gtr, Campbell

2. Vcl, DeArman
3. Twin fids, Pitts, Brower
4. Vcl

Notice: This is the worst performance of any song we had recorded so far—the Doughboys always played the same chords at the same time up until this song. I don't know how the mixed-up chords and bass got by Uncle Art and Pitts. Campbell and Pitts had the best ears in the band, not counting Parker.

DAL-830. Oh Baby Blues
1. Twin fids, Pitts, Brower
2. Vcl, Boyd
3. Gtr, Campbell, vcl out

DAL-831. Beer Drinkin' Mama (Marvin Montgomery)
1 Gtr, Campbell
2. Vcl, Boyd
3. Pno, Parker
4. Twin fids, Pitts, Brower
5. Bj, Montgomery
6. Vcl
7. Gtr (DeAman played b and Boyd rhy gtr)

DAL-832. Mama Gets What She Wants (Knocky Parker)
1. Pno, Parker
2. Vcl, Boyd
3. Gtr, Campbell
4. Vcl
5. Fid, Brower
6. Vcl (Yells, Parker; he felt so good about the way Boyd was singing his song he couldn't hold it in)
7. Gtr

DAL-833. My Gal's with My Pal Tonight (Marvin Montgomery)
1. Twin fids, Pitts, Brower
2. Vcl, Boyd
3. Twin fids
4. Vcl

DAL-834. I Had Someone Else Before I Had You
1. Twin fids, Pitts, Brower
2. Vcl, Boyd
3. Gtr, Campbell; pno, Parker
4. Vcl, Boyd, b

DAL-835. You Got What I Want (Marvin Montgomery)
1. Twin fids, Pitts, Brower
2. Vcl, Boyd
3. Gtr, Campbell
4. Pno, Parker, vcl out; Boyd, b

DAL-836. Jazzbo Joe (Marvin Montgomery)
1. Kazoo, Montgomery
2. Vcl, Boyd
3. Kazoo, twin fid background, Pitts, Brower
4. Gtr, Campbell
5. Fid solo, Brower
6. Pno, Parker
7. Gtr
8. Fid solo, Pitts
9. Kazoo fid background
10. Vcl with kazoo ending, Boyd, b

DAL-837. If I Had My Way
1. Gtr, Campbell
2. Vcl, Boyd
3. Pno, Parker; Twin fids, Pitts, Brower
4. Vcl out; Boyd, b

We recorded 25 songs in two days, eleven of which I wrote. In hindsight I think that if I'd been serious about my songwriting, instead of doing the off-beat stuff, I might have come up with something worth listening to.

Early September 1939, Fort Worth (At our broadcasting studio at the Burrus Flour Mill in Saginaw, Texas). Uncle Art Satherley sent us "I'll Keep on Loving You" and wanted it in a hurry—we cut it and "Little Rubber Dolly" and sent the master to New York. Musicians: fids, Pitts, Brower; b, DeArman; acoustic gtr, Boyd; bj, Montgomery; Elg, Campbell. Knocky Parker (pno) was not on this session. Engineer, our own radio engineer, Jerry (Snag) Stewart. Boss-Man, Parker Willson.

25317. I'll Keep on Loving You
1. Elg, Campbell
2. Vcl, DeArman
3. Twin fids, Pitts, Brower
4. Vcl out; Boyd, b

25318. Little Rubber Dolly
1. Fid, Brower
2. Vcl: DeArman, lead; Boyd, high, high tenor
3. Fid
4. Vcl
5. Fid; acoustic gtr fills played by Boyd. Campbell played acoustic rhythm.
Question: What did Pitts play? Answer: Pitts says he didn't play anything.

Late Oct. 1939, Fort Worth In our Saginaw Studio. Uncle Art wanted a quick "Truck Driver Blues." Same musicians plus Parker back on pno.

25525. Horsie Keep Your Tail Up
Horse, Boyd
1. Vcl: DeArman, lead; Boyd, tenor
2. Bj, Montgomery
3. fids, Pitts, Brower
4. Vcl
5. Gtr, Campbell; vcl: quartet ending, Boyd, tenor; DeArman, lead; Pitts, baritone; Willson, b voice

25526. Truck Driver's Blues
1. Gtr, Campbell
2. Vcl, Boyd
3. Fids, Pitts, Brower
4. Vcl out: Boyd, rhy; DeArman, b

Early December 1939, Fort Worth (Saginaw)
The two previous sessions worked out fairly well and so Parker Willson talked Uncle Art Satherley into letting us produce our own session, picking our own songs. Outside of "Green Valley Trot" we didn't pick very commercial songs. Same musicians.

25594. Green Valley Trot (Another mislabeled record. Joe "Bashful" Ferguson did not come down from Bob Wills's band until the first of January 1940 to replace Boyd, who left to join Governor W. Lee O'Daniel and His Hillbilly Boys in Austin, Texas. Joe Frank Ferguson is the only musician to come from the Bob Wills band to the Doughboys. All the other musicians left the Doughboys to join Wills.)
1. Gtr, Campbell, full chord lead (no steel gtr)
2. Vcl: DeArman, lead; Boyd, tenor; Pitts, baritone

3. Fid, Brower
4. Vcl solo, Boyd
5. Gtr
6. Vcl, duet
7. Gtr, trio out

25595. Marinita (I think we did this song in order to get our picture on the music.)
1. Acoustic gtr intro, Boyd
2. Fid, Pitts, Brower
3. Vcl, Boyd
4. Acd, Parker; Pitts to rhythm pno
5. Three gtrs, tgtr, Montgomery; standard acoustic gtrs, Boyd, Campbell (Parker back on pno)
6. Vcl out

25596. Careless
1. Gtr, Campbell
2. Vcl, Boyd, fid and steel gtr fills
3. Pno, Parker; steel, Campbell; fids, Pitts, Brower
4. Vcl out. Parker Willson had been on Campbell to play some steel gtr. Campbell played it on this song although he really didn't want to and didn't especially like it when he heard it.

25597. Listen to the Mockingbird. Unissued.

April 24, 1940, Fort Worth (Our Saginaw Studio)
Untold Tales Til Now: Uncle Art Satherley didn't seem to like what we were doing on our own and so he, along with Don Law, came down to Saginaw to produce some sessions. At the same time he recorded several other groups, which probably included the Bob Wills band. The real reason, however, was due to the fact that all of the major record labels had just signed contracts with the American Federation of Musicians and could not record non-union musicians. At that period in time Local 72, AF of M did not seem to want C & W musicians in their union, although Kenneth Pitts, Knocky Parker and I were attending Texas Christian University at the time as part-time students studying every music class available and probably knew more about music history, etc. than a good percentage of the union members. (This is the feeling I had at the time.)

Brower, having traveled with Ted Fiorito's Orchestra, belonged to the L. A. Local. Joe (Bashful) Ferguson, who joined the Doughboys in January

1940, replacing Jim Boyd, came off the Bob Wills Band and was a member of the Tulsa Local. I had belonged to the AF of M local in Newton, Iowa, before I came to Texas, but was not a member at the time of this session. Uncle Art decided to let me play on the session anyhow, as there was not a union banjo player available. I don't know whether he listed me as playing on the session or not. I suppose that if the AF of M had found out that Uncle Art had done such a dastardly deed as to let a non-union banjo player play with union musicians on a recording session they would have taken him out and hung him by his thumbs. But until now, this fact has never been written down.

And so, for this session only, some of the regular Doughboys had to be replaced by union pickers. Leroy Millican, Local 72, replaced Campbell on electric guitar; Babe Wright, Local 72, faced up to the pno in Parker's place' Paul Waggoner, Local 72, picked the rhythm gtr; hence, the band consisted of Wright, pno; Brower, fid; Ferguson, b; Millican, Elg; Waggoner, rhy gtr and non-union Montgomery bj. Singing and arranging was not yet controlled by the union and so Pitts, DeArmand, Willson and Campbell could get in on the singing. Also, Pitts wrote all the lead parts for the electric guitar to make the band sound as much like the Doughboys as possible. Although these records were given DAL numbers, they were recorded at our studio in Saginaw, Texas. Neither Pitts, Ferguson nor I could remember Millican playing on these sessions and so I located Millican, alive and retired in Dallas, and sent him a tape. He called back and said that he was playing the lead guitar on these sessions. Thanks, Zeke Campbell, for remembering about Millican.

DAL-1054. Goodbye Little Darling
1. Elg, Leroy Millican
2. Vcl: DeArman, lead; Ferguson, tenor; Pitts, baritone
3. Fid, Brower
4. Vcl
5. Fid, gtr duet, Brower, Millican
6. Vcl
7. Gtr
8. Vcl

DAL-1055. I Want a Feller (Marvin Montgomery)
1. Fid, Brower
2. Vcl, DeArman
3. Gtr, Millican
4. Vcl
5. Fid
6. Vcl
7. Fid

DAL-1056. Rainbow
1. Gtr, Millican
2. Fid, Brower
3. Fid
4. Gtr lead, fid harmony
5. Fid
6. Gtr and fid duet

DAL-1057. Alice Blue Gown
1. Fid, Cecil
2. Vcl, Ferguson
3. Gtr, Milliccan
4. Pno, Babe Wright
5. Vcl

Up to now the pno was not featured on a solo, due to the fact Willson and Uncle Art were afraid that people would realize that it was not Knocky Parker playing, but unto this day, none of the music historians, or anybody else, has ever questioned me on who the musicians were on this session. It seems Pitts did a good job arranging the music in the Doughboy fashion, regardless of the players. And we non-union musicians who swore on a stack of old broken Doughboy 78s to keep the secret from our radio fans, did, until now! I will, however, mention the fact that Bob Pinson noticed that Pitts was not playing fid on these sessions.

April 26, 1940. Same place, same musicians and singers.
DAL-1070. South (Uncle Art sent an old original record of this song down and Pitts wrote the parts out to sound like the Doughboys. It turned out to be one of our best juke-box sellers.) Notice: Some group cut twelve songs on April 25th—could have been Bob Wills.

DAL-1071. She's Too Young (To Play with the Boys) (Pitts, Campbell, Parker)
Vamp, voices: Pitts, DeArman, Willson, Ferguson
2. Fid, Brower
3. Vcl solo, DeArman, voices
4. Gtr, Millican
5. Vcl
6. Fid
7. Vcl
8. Pno, Wright
9. Vcl

DAL-1072. Mean, Mean Mama (From Meana) (Pitts, Campbell, Parker)
1. Gtr, Millican
2. Vcl, Ferguson
3. Fid, Brower
4. Vcl

DAL-1073. Cripple Creek (Pitts wrote lyrics to this old Breakdown. Pitts states that he thinks it was me. Come on, Ken, it's not that bad, go ahead and take credit for it.)
1. Fid, Brower; voice, Parker, Willson
2. Fid
3. Vcl solo, DeArman; quartet: Ferguson, Tenor; DeArman, Lead; Pitts, baritone; Willson, b
4. Fid
5. Vcl
6. Fid, yells, Willson, DeArman
7. Vcl

DAL-1074. Little Honky Tonk Headache (Marvin Montgomery)
1. Gtr, Millican
2. Vcl, Ferguson
3. Pno, Wright
4. Fid, Brower
5. Vcl

DAL-1075. Good Gracious Gracie (Marvin Montgomery)
1. Fid, Brower
2. Vcl, Ferguson
3. Gtr, Millican
4. Pno, Wright
5. Vcl

DAL-1076. If You'll Come Back (Marvin Montgomery)
1. Gtr, Millican
2. Vcl, DeArman
3. Fid, Brower
4. Gtr, vcl to end

DAL-1077. Snow Deer
1. Fid, Brower, playing double stops
2. Gtr, Millican in harmony with fid
3. Fid

4. Gtr and fid
5. Fid

The union musicians on these sessions were paid union scale. Ferguson, Brower and I put the money we got in the pot and it was divided equally between Pitts, Campbell, Parker, DeArman, Brower, Ferguson and yours truly.

February 27, 1941, Fort Worth in the old WBAP radio studios on top of the Blackstone Hotel. The Doughboys all belong to Local 72 AF of M now. For some reason or other Uncle Art gave these records Dallas numbers. Bob Wills and numerous other bands recorded here during this same series of sessions. I remember having a long talk with Tommy Duncan at the studio right after we finished our session. Producer: Art Satherely, Don Law. Musicians: J. B. Brinkley, rhy gtr and vcl, replacing DeArman who was accidentally burned to death. Frank Reneau, pno, replacing Ted Druer who replaced Knocky Parker when Knocky left to finish his college education. Plus Campbell, Pitts, Brower, Ferguson and Montgomery.

DAL-1184. Too. Late
1. Gtr, Campbell; steel gtr fills, Ted Daffan
2. Vcl duet, Brinkley, lead; Ferguson, harmony
3. fids, Brower, Pitts
4. Vcl, duet
Notice: Ted Daffan had just finished a session or was waiting to do a session, or was hoping Uncle Art would let him do a session. Daffan kept pestering Uncle Art to let him play on a Doughboy record, and so, with Parker Willson's approval, Daffan played on two songs with us on this session: "Too Late," and "Five Long Years." This is the only time Daffan ever played with the Doughboys.

DAL-1185. The Little Bar Fly (Marvin Montgomery)
1. Gtr, Campbell
2. Vcl, Brinkley
3. Fids, Brower, Pitts; pno, Reneau, fids
4. Vcl

DAL-1186. It's Your Worry Now (Marvin Montgomery)
I got the idea for this song while we were playing a personal appearance in Pine Bluff, Arkansas when I overheard a young couple having an argument. As she walked away she heatedly said, "It's your worry, now." I've often wondered what he had to worry about.
1. Gtr, Campbell

2. Vcl, Brinkley
3. Fids, Brower, Pitts
4. Gtr
5. Vcl
6. Vcl

DAL-1187. Zip Zip Zipper (Marvin Montgomery)
1. Vamp, vcl group, Willson, Pitts, Ferguson, Brinkley
2. Vcl group
3. Gtr, Campbell
4. Pno, Reneau
5. Fid solo, Brower
6. Vcl chorus
7. Gtr and fids

DAL-1188. The Bartender's Daughter (Marvin Montgomery)
1. Gtr, Campbell
2. Vcl, Brinkley
3. Fids, Brower, Pitts
4. Vcl

DAL-1189. Don't Lie To An Innocent Maiden (Marvin Montgomery)
1. Gtr, Campbell
2. Vcl, Ferguson
3. Fids, Brower, Pitts
4. Vcl

DAL-1190. Little Honky Tonk Heartthrob (Marvin Montgomery). Unissued.

DAL-1191. Five Long Years (Brinkley)
1. Elg lead, Campbell; steel gtr fills, Ted Daffan
2. Vcl, Brinkley
3. fids, Brower, Pitts
4. Vcl

DAL-1192. Sweet Sally (Campbell, Pitts, Parker)
1. Gtr lead in, J. B. Brinkley, with fids, Brower, Pitts
2. Vcl, Brinkley
3. Gtr, Campbell
4. Pno, Reneau
5. Fid solo, Brower
6. Vcl

Notice: On this session we begin to lose our Doughboy rhythm style—due somewhat to the fact that on some of the songs the bj is almost out of the picture and we missed the 2/4 beat of Parker's pno. Reneau's pno (to me) seems over-balanced, I think because they ("they" being Parker Willson?") wanted to get the many, many, many b runs Reneau added (and there goes the rhythm.) J. B. Brinkley played good rhythm but again, most of it was lost due to the poor balance of the instruments.

DAL-1193. Slufoot on the Levee (Frank Reneau)
1. Pno vamp, Reneau
2. Gtr, Campbell with fids, Brower, Pitts
3. Gtr
4. Gtr and fids
5. Fid solo, Brower
6. Gtr and fids
7. Pno
8. Gtr and fids
9. same

DAL-1194. Honky Tonk Shuffle (Campbell)
1. Gtr, Campbell
2. fids, Brower, Pitts
3. Pno, Reneau
4. Gtr

March 3, 6, 14, Fort Worth.
These sessions were recorded at the old WBAP radio studios on top of the old Blackstone Hotel. In order to confirm this, I called Joe Frank Ferguson, and he remembers that when we finished one of our sessions, Bob Wills was waiting to record. Bob told Joe to go home and get his saxophone as they were going to record some big band numbers and needed Joe's sax to help out. (Big Beaver.) I also called Frank Reneau who now lives in Temple, Texas. Frank remembers doing all these sessions at WBAP, including the religious songs. He recalls that we had trouble with Campbell's electric amp, as it was picking up police calls. I remember that Uncle Art became somewhat upset due to the fact that it was messing up some of our cuts. No tape recording in those days and the acetates cost money. These were our last sessions before going off to fight WWII. Producer; Uncle Art Satherly, Don Law. Musicians: "Cecil" Brower (Coast Guard), fid; Kenneth "Abner" Pitts (Army inspector at American Manufacturing Company producing shells), fid, acd; Muryle "Zeke" Campbell, (Bookkeeper at vital food company), elg; Joe "Bashful"

Ferguson (Coast Guard), b, vcl; "Frank" Reneau (Army - Italy), pno; "J. B." Brinkley (4F), rhy gtr, vcl; Marvin "Junior" Montgomery (Swing Shift Supervisor at Crown Machine & Tool producing six inch shells for the Navy), bj, tgtr, sometimes vcl; "Dolores Jo" Clancy, Little Light Crust Sweetheart, eleven or twelve years of age.

March 3, 1941.
Still using Dallas numbers, but recorded in Fort Worth. I think Uncle Art did this just to confuse future music historians, because some of them have sure been confused about where these sessions took place and who played on them.

DAL-1207. Be Honest with Me
1. Fids, Brower, Pitts
2. Vcl, Brinkley
3. Gtr, Campbell
4. Vcl
5. fids, gtr fills, vcl ending

DAL-1208. Bear Creek Hop (Marvin Montgomery, the old "Bear Creek Hop" breakdown; I wrote the words and the melodies that go with the words.)
1. Voice: Parker Willson; fid, Brower
2. Vcl, Brinkley
3. Quartet: Ferguson, tenor; Brinkley, lead; Pitts, baritone; Willson, b
4. Fid, Brower
5. Vcl
6. Quartet
7. Fid, Brower
8. Vcl
9. Quartet. All yells by Parker Willson (his version of Bob Wills).

DAl-1209. It's Funny What Love Will Make You Do. Unissued.

DAL-1210. Do You Ever Miss Me? Unissued.

DAL-1211. Won't You Wait Another Year (Marvin Montgomery. The tour of duty was two years in the Armed Forces, this poor guy had one year to go hoping not to get a "Dear John" letter.)
1. Gtr, Campbell
2. Vcl, Brinkley
3. Fids, Brower, Pitts

4. Vcl
5. Gtr
6. Vcl, two fids

DAL-1212. I Want a Waitress (Marvin Montgomery)
1. Vcl Group, Brinkley, Ferguson, Pitts, Willson, Montgomery
2. Vcl solo, Montgomery
3. Gtr, Campbell
4. Pno, Reneau
5. Vcl
6. Fid solo, Brower
7. Gtr
8. Vcl
9. Gtr & two fids. Due to the fact that I had to stand close to the mike to sing, I played the tgtr because the bj would have been too loud.

DAL-1213. Can't Ease My Evil Mind
1. Gtr, Campbell
2. Vcl, Brinkley
3. Fids, Brower, Pitts
4. Vcl
5. Pno, Reneau
6. Vcl. A very sloppy ending on this one

DAL-1214. After You Said You Were Leaving (Marvin Montgomery)
1. Gtr, Campbell
2. Vcl, Dolores Jo (Clancy) Little Light Crust Sweetheart
3. Pno, Reneau
4. Fids, Brower, Pitts
5. Vcl. Montgomery played tgtr

March 6, 1941.
DAL-1229. Big House Blues. Unissued.

DAL-1230. We Just Can't Get Along. Unissued.

DAL-1231. Have I Lost Your Love Forever (Little Darling)
1. Gtr, Campbell
2. Vcl, Ferguson
3. fids, Brower, Pitts
4. Vcl

5. Gtr
6. Fids
7. Vcl

DAL-1232. Why Did You Lie to Me?
1. Gtr, Campbell
2. Vcl, Brinkley
3. Gtr & twin fids, Brower, Pitts
4. Vcl

DAL-1233. I'll Never Say Goodbye (Marvin Montgomery). Unissued.

DAL-1234. Salvation Has Been Brought Down. Unissued.
Parker Willson talked Uncle Art into letting the quartet do some religious songs because during this time we were doing two programs a week (Tuesday and Thursday) of all religious songs. The quartet was made up of Joe "Bashful" Ferguson, tenor; J. B. Brinkley, lead; Kenneth "Abner" Pitts, baritone; and Parker Willson, bass. Frank Reneau played the pno. Campbell and I went home. These songs would never get on the juke boxes (our biggest market at that time), hence Uncle Art was reluctant to release them. Besides, The Chuck Wagon Gang and the Stamps-Baxter Quartets had that market sewed up.

DAL-1235. I Shall See Him By and By. Unissued.

DAL-1236. I Know I'll See Mother Again. Unavailable.

DAL-1237. Beyond the Clouds. Unavailable.

March 16, 1941.
DAL-1323. This Life Is Hard to Understand

DAL-1324. In the Morning
Last song recorded by this group of Light Crust Doughboys

POST WWII

September 1947, King Records, Session at Sellers Studio, Dallas, Texas
The Post-World War II Light Crust Doughboys. Mel Cox (Jack Perry), MC, vcl and fid; Wilson Perkins (Lefty), lead elg and steel gtr; Charles Godwin

(Knocky), accordion; Hal Harris (Bashful), rhy gtr and vcl; Red Kidwell (Sleepy), b and vcl; Carroll Hubbard (Ezra), fid and vcl; Marvin Montgomery (Junior), tbj, rhy gtr and arranger; Sid Nathan (owner of King Records), producer.

K2563. The New Sow Song (words by Mel Cox)
Intro
1. Vcl verse, Cox; chorus, all sing
2. Acd, Godwin
3. Vcl
4. Elg, Perkins
5. Vcl
6. Twin fids: Cox, lead; Hubbard, Harmony
7. Bj, Montgomery; b, Kidwell; Rhythm gtr, Harris; vcl out, sound effects, Cox and Hubbard.

K2564. Pappy's Banjo Boogie (Mel Cox, words; Marvin Montgomery, music)
Intro, acd
1. Bj, Montgomery
2. Vcl, Cox
3. Bj
4. Vcl
5. Elg lead, Perkins; accordian, Godwin; fid, Hubbard
6. Vcl
7. Bj
8. Vcl, out

K2565. No Suh (Marvin Montgomery)
Fid intro, Hubbard
1. Vcl, Cox, all sing answers
2. Acd, Godwin
3. Vcl
4. Elg, Perkins
5. Vcl
6. Fid, Hubbard
7. Vcl
8. Fid and acd ending

K2566. Guitar Jump (Wilson Perkins)
Acd, Godwin; fid, Hubbard, intro
1. Steel gtr, Perkins

312

2. Acd, Godwin
3. Steel
4. Twin fids, Cox & Hubbard
5. Steel

K2567. Fisherman's Polka (Wilson Perkins)
1. Acd, Godwin; Twin fids, Cox, Hubbard
2. Twin fids
3. Elg, Perkins
4. Twin fids
5. Acd
6. Twin fids

K2568. It's a Dirty Shame (Marvin Montgomery)
Intro acd, Elg, twin fids
1. Vcl, Hal Harris; quartet BG, Hubbard, Kidwell, Cox, Godwin
2. Acd, gtr, twin fids
3. Vcl
4. Gtr
5. Vcl

K2569. Slow Down My Darling (Cox). Unissued.

K2570. Oh My Aching Back (Marvin Montgjomery)
Intro, acd, fid, Hubbard
1. Vcl (talking), Mel Cox; vcl chorus, Cox, Hubbard, Harris, Kidwell
2. Acd & fid, Hubbard
3. Vcl
4. Acd, elg, acd & fid, Hubbard
5. Vcl

K2571. Ezra's Waltz (Carroll Hubbard, music; Mel Cox, words)
1. Twin fids, Cox & Hubbard
2. Vcl, Cox; vcl chorus, Cox, Hubbard, Kidwell, Harris
3. Whistle, Cox
4. Vcl, vcl chorus
5. Twin fids, vcl out; steel gtr, Perkins; md, Montgomery

K2572. Oklahoma Waltz (Marvin Montgomery, music; Mel Cox, words)
1. Twin fids
2. Vcl, Kidwell
3. Twin fids

4. Vcl
5. Band, out; steel, Perkins; md, Montgomery
Notice: Starting with K2573 you will hear no more acd. The foregoing songs
were recorded on Thursday night and on Friday Charley (Knocky) Godwin
left town due to wife trouble. And so on Friday night we recorded with no
acd. Godwin, an ex-Marine pilot, later died when he crashed his own plane.

K2573. I'm Gonna Be Gone, Gone, Gone (Mel Cox)
Intro fid, Hubbard
1. Talk & vcl, Cox
2. Steel, Perkins; bj, Montgomery; vcl, out

K2574. Just a World of Heartaches (Montgomery). Unissued.

K2575. Hook, Line and Sinker (Cox). Unissued.

K2576. Wedding Ring for Sale (Montgomery). Unissued.

K2577. I Cried and Cried and Cried (Montgomery)
1. Fid, Hubbard
2. Vcl, Cox with Hubbard
3. Elg, Perkins
4. Vcl
5. Fid, Hubbard
6. Vcl
7. Elg
8. Vcl

K2578. After We've Been in Love (Montgomery). Unissued.

Session, Sellers Studio.
Sid Nathan Producer. Sid sat in the control booth and talked with Mr. Sellers while I played the bj with Wilson (Lefty) Perkins playing rhy gtr and Red Kidwell picking the b.

K2579. Hear Dem Bells (arr. Montgomery)
(also released on Federal 10014, album)

K2580. Ring Ring De Banjo (arr. Montgomery)

K2581. Blue Bells Of Scotland/Sweet And Low (arr. Montgomery)

K2582. My Old Kentucky Home (arr. Montgomery)
(also released on Federal 10014, Album)

K2583. Raggin' on the Banjo (Marvin Montgomery)
Released on the back side of Cowboy Copas/Grandpa Jones record K2955
The Feudin' Boogie.
Last song recorded on this three-day recording session.

Session recorded at Seller's Studio, Dallas, in early part of 1948. Mel Cox
signed a contract with Sid Nathan to record as The Flying X Ranchboys so
that he could collect all the royalties from the record sales. As The Light
Crust Doughboys, we shared the record roalties equally. This under the table
act by Mel made some of the band members very unhappy. By the end of
1948 Mel was no longer with us. I took over as leader after Mel left. Hal
Harris left before we did this session. Mel Cox, fid, leader; Carroll Hubbard,
fid; Red Kidwell, b; Wilson Perkins, elg and steel; Marvin Montgomery, rhy
gtr, arranger.

K2805. Tears in My Heart (Marvin Montgomery). Unissued.

K2806. Honolulu Lou (Music, Perkins; words, Cox)
Intro: Steel, Perkins
1. Vcl trio, Mel Cox, Carroll Hubbard, Red Kidwell
2. Steel
3. Vcl trio, out (rhy gtr, Montgomery; fids, Hubbard, Cox; b, Kidwell; steel,
   Perkins). Five members in band.

K2807. I Cried My Last Tear over You (Montgomery). Unissued.

K2808. Starlight Waltz (Mel Cox)
1. Twin fids, Cox, Hubbard
2. Vcl, Red Kidwell
3. Twin fids
4. Vcl, out; steel, Perkins; rhy gtr, Montgomery

K2809. Billy Goat Rag (Montgomery)
Intro, twin fids, goat, Carroll Hubbard
1. Twin fids
2. Elg turn around, Perkins
3. Vcl trio, Cox, lead; Kidwell, tenor; Hubbard, baritone and goat
4. Elg, Perkins

5. Hot fid, Hubbard
6. Elg
7. Vcl trio, out

K2810. I'm Moving You Right Out of My Heart (Cox). Unissued.

K2811. She's a Backwoods Woman (Cox). Unissued.

K2812. I'd Never Cry Again (Montgomery). Unissued.

This completes the list of commercial recordings made by the Light Crust Doughboys until 1979 when we recorded an album for Burrus Mills. Then in 1981 we recorded *50 Years of Texas Style Music* (Golden Anniversary) and in 1986 we recorded the album *150 Years of Texas Country Music* which Burrus Mills still sells by placing coupons in the Light Crust Flour packages.

From April 4, 1936, through March 14, 1941, the Doughboys recorded 163 cuts. We had two cuts on seven songs. We recorded 156 songs. Of these, twenty-eight titles were never released. We had 128 titles released.

I had thirty-four songs recorded of which four ("Tonight I Have a Date," "Old November Moon," "Little Honky Tonk Heartthrob," and "I'll Never Say Goodbye") were never issued. Most of the songs not issued were cowboy songs. Re: "The Big Corral," "Strawberry Roan," etc., and barbershop quartet type songs such as: "When You Wore a Tulip," "I Want a Girl (Just Like the Girl That Married Dear Old Dad)," etc. Uncle Art Satherley was looking for danceable, juke box type songs and we were giving him the stuff that we played on our daily radio programs. I think the reason Uncle Art took so many of my songs was because I was writing trash that we could never play on the air, but which the juke box operators liked, such as: "Pussy, Pussy, Pussy," "You Got What I Want," "Baby, Give Me Some of That," "She Gave Me the Bird," etc.

After WWII in 1945 all MCs of The Light Crust Doughboys were called Jack Perry after Jack Perry Burrus, founder of the Burrus Mil and Elevator Company. To name a few who were called Jack Perry: Mel Cox, Jimmy Jeffreys, Paul Blunt, Walter Hailey.

Quotes from Kenneth Pitts's letter to me after listening to the tapes of the Light Crust Doughboy recordings:

> My first general observation of this entire effort is that the bank might have been better off under the leadership of someone other that me. I failed in many instances to exhibit any imagination and foresight musically—all I wanted was to hear what I thought was good from a group

with the ability that group had. My judgment, business-wise, and in the matter of dealing with other people, was very minus—I needed to be much more "political" than I was. On the other hand, I realize that it is easy to make great "hindsights" about anything.

My second general observation is that Mr. Satherley should have really taken us to task as to repertoire and style on the recordings. Possibly he was trying to let our natural inclinations lead us to some sound that would have been distinctive. As it was, the only distinctive sounds we had were Zeke (Campbell), you, Knocky (Parker) and the twin fiddle sound. But none of these four ever seemed to get together and really jell. However, I don't want these acid criticisms to be interpreted to mean the entire effort was a complete loss.

Back in those days, most everybody was in a sort of terror that he might have found himself suddenly without a job. I think it is to the credit of Bob Wills, Gross, and even "Snag" (Jerry Stewart, our radio engineer) that they at least drew some sort of line in their defense. It's hard to say which course might have been wise for us—probably the one we stuck to. Of course, Bob Wills's success is acknowledged. Gross, in case you didn't know, had some success after he went to Louisville (Kentucky) and organized his own band.

Excerpts from "Zeke" Campbell's letter to me after listening to the Doughboy recordiings.

Here are some things that might interest you. When I first joined the Doughboys in October 1935, they had seven men. I made the eighth. All the guys had either gone with O'Daniel or Bob Wills. Pitts and Gross were the only original ones left. Pitts and Gross on fiddles, Bruce (Roscoe) Pierce on guitar, Hubert Barham on bass, Doc Eastwood on banjo, Matt Welch on accordion, and a guy named Leonard Grider as vocalist. He didn't play any instrument. Ramon DeArman and Cecil Brower had gone to Columbus, Ohio, to make transcriptions for some cereal company. I don't remember whether Curly Perrin had gone with them or joined O'Daniel. You and Dick (Reinhart) and Bert (Dodson) joined the band exactly two weeks after I did. You three guys replaced five men.

I have been unable to find a picture of this group. Pierce states that they were Doughboys for such a short time no picture was made. Cecil Brower was not a Doughboy at that time. He left Milton Brown and the Musical Brownies to make the move to Ohio. He joined the Doughboys, replacing Buchanan, some time after returning from Ohio.

Thanks to Kenneth "Abner" Pitts (1934–1941), Muryel "Zeke" Campbell (1935–1941), Jim "Bashful" Boyd (1938–1940), Joe Frank "Bashful" Ferguson (1940–1942), Frank Reneau (1941–1942), and Leroy Millican (a Doughboy for a few hours during the month of April, 1940) for their assistance in compiling this Discography.

There are a few minor points that may not be exactly right, but this is as close as it's ever going to get.

Marvin "Junior" Montgomery (1935-1989), I've been Leader of the Doughboys since 1948. I lost "Junior" and became "Smokey" in September of 1948 when we went on WBAP TV, Channel 5, Fort Worth, Texas.

Appendix 3
Deep Elem on Record
(for full discographical information on these recordings, see Appendix I)

Note: the following recordings are all in the Sound Thinking Music Research library (1534 N. Moorpark Rd., Suite 333, Thousand Oaks CA 91360) and are available for dubbing or auditioning purposes. Studio time is $70 per hour.

Elm Street Blues, Ida May Mack, Victor V-38030 (August 29, 1928)

Deep Elm Blues, Lone Star Cowboys, Bluebird B-6001 (August 4, 1933)

Deep Elem Blues, Shelton Brothers, Decca 5099 (February 22, 1935)

Deep Elm Blues, Prairie Ramblers, ARC 5-11-51 (August 15, 1935)

Elm Street Woman Blues, Dallas Jamboree Jug Band, Vocalion 03092 (September 20, 1935)

Deep Elem Blues, Rhubarb Red (Les Paul), Montgomery Ward M-8012 (May 20, 1936)

Deep Elem Blues #2, Rhubarb Red, Montgomery Ward M-8013 (May 20, 36)

Daddy's Got the Deep Elm Blues, Jimmie Revard & His Oklahoma Playboys, Bluebird B-7061 (February 27, 1937)

Just Because You're in Deep Elem, Shelton Brothers, Decca 5665 (March 4, 1939)

Deep Elm Swing, Texas Wanderers, Decca 5775 (August 28, 1939)

What's the Matter with Deep Elem, Shelton Brothers, Decca 5898 (April 6, 1940)

Deep Elm Boogie Woogie Blues, Shelton Brothers, King 660 (1947)

Deep Elem Blues, Wilburn Brothers, Decca 29887 (January 18, 1956)

Appendix 4
Deep Ellum Blues

    This cassette was recorded by Alan Govenar in the early 1980s and released by Documentary Arts in 1986. While it does not include historical .recordings, it focuses on performers who started their careers during the heyday of Deep Ellum in the 1920s and 1930s and who were still active in Dallas during the 1980s. Govenar presented Buster Smith with the idea of forming a band called "The Heat Waves of Swing" and Smith organized the group, which was featured at the 1981 Downtown Dallas Traditional Music Festival, and later renamed "Dallas Jazz Greats," at the Dallas Folk Festival in 1983, 1984, 1986 and 1988. Alex Moore, Hal Baker and the Gloomchasers, Lavada Durst, Robert Shaw and Bill Neely were recorded for Govenar's "Masters of Traditional Music" radio series.

Dallas, 1981-1985
The Deep Ellum Blues, DA1 101
Hal Baker and the Gloomchasers: Hal Baker, cl and unknown acc.
    At the Jazz Band Ball
Heat Waves of Swing: Buster Smith, elg; Herbert Cowens, d; Benny "Chops" Arrandondo, tp; Boston Smith, pno; James Clay, sax
    Kansas City
    Monkey Jump
    Walkin' to New Orleans
Lavada Durst, vcl, pno.
Austin, 1984
    How Long
    Pinetop Boogie
Alex Moore, vcl, pno.
Dallas, 1981–1985
    Central Tracks Blues
Bill Neely, vcl, gtr
Austin, 1983–1984
    Deep Ellum Blues
    Graveyard Blues
    Matchbox Blues (Blind Lemon Jefferson)
    Blues on Ellum
Robert Shaw, vcl, pno.
Austin, 1984
    Hurry Down Santa Fe

Bibliography

Books and Articles

Barlow, William. *Looking up at Down: The Emergence of Blues Culture.* Philadelphia: Temple University Press, 1989.

Basie, Count, as told to Albert Murray. *Good Morning Blues: The Autobiography of Count Basie.* New York: Random House, 1985.

Brakefield, Jay F. "Birthday of a Bluesman: A Look Back at Life, Music of Blind Lemon Jefferson." *The Dallas Morning News.* September 23, 1993. 5C.

Brewer, J. Mason. *Heralding Dawn: An Anthology of Verse.* Dallas: June Thompson Printing, 1936.

Brown, Roger S. "Recording Pioneer Polk Brockman." *Living Blues* 23 (1975): 31.

Carr, Patrick, ed. *The Illustrated History of Country Music.* New York: Doubleday, 1979.

Charles, Ray and David Ritz. *Brother Ray: Ray Charles' Own Story.* New York: The Dial Press, 1978.

Charters, Samuel. *The Bluesmen.* New York: Oak Publications, 1968.

_____. *The Country Blues.* New York: Rinehart, 1959.

Dance, Helen O. *Stormy Monday: The T-Bone Walker Story.* New York: Da Capo Press, 1990.

Dixon, Robert and John Goodrich. *Recording the Blues, 1902–1940.* New York: Stein and Day, 1970.

Driggs, Frank. "Budd Johnson, Ageless Jazzman." *Jazz Review* (November 1960).

Enstam, Elizabeth York, ed. *When Dallas Became a City: Letters of John Milton McCoy, 1870–1881.* Dallas: Dallas Historical Society, 1982.

Evans, David. "Ramblin'." *Blues Revue Quarterly* 9 (Summer 1933): 16–18.

Foreman, Ronald Clifford. "Jazz and Race Records, 1920–32: Their Origins and Their Significance for the Record Industry and Society." PhD dissertation, University of Illinois, 1968.

Fox, Ted. *Showtime at the Apollo.* New York: Holt, Rinehart and Winston, 1983.

Gazzaway, Don. Conversations with Buster Smith." *Jazz Review.* Parts I, II, and III. (December 1959–February 1960).

Ginell, Cary. *Milton Brown and the Founding of Western Swing.* Urbana: University of Illinois Press, 1994.

Govenar, Alan. "Buster Smith: Dallas Jazz Patriarch." *Parkway* (April 1983): 34–35.

_____. *Daddy Double Do Love You.* Chicago: Jubilee Press, 1993.

_____. "Hal Baker and the Gloomchasers." *Parkway* (May 1983): 31.

_____. "Herbert Cowens: USO Drummer, Extraordinaire." *Legacies* 4 (Spring 1992): 32–36.

_____. "The History of Deep Ellum." In program booklet for the Dallas Black Dance Theatre production of *Deep Ellum Blues.* December 4–6, 1986.

_____. *Meeting the Blues.* Dallas: Taylor Publishing, 1988.

_____. *Portraits of Community: African-American Photography in Texas.* Austin: Texas State Historical Association, 1996.

_____. "That Black Snake Moan: The Music and Mystery of Blind Lemon Jefferson." In Pete Welding and Toby Byron, ed. *Bluesland: Portraits of Twelve Major American Blues Masters.* New York: Penguin Books, 1991. 16–37.

_____. "Them Deep Ellum Blues: A Street, a Sound, and a Time." *Legacies* 2 (Spring 1990): 4–9.

_____. "Variants of Texas Blues." *Texas Humanist* 7 (July–August 1985): 28–31.

_____, Francis E. Abernethy, and Patrick B. Mullen. *Juneteenth Texas: Essays in African-American Folklore.* Denton: University of North Texas Press, 1996.

Greene, A. C. *Dallas U.S.A.* Austin: Texas Monthly Press, 1984.

_____. *The Dallas Morning News.* January 16, 1994. 44A.

Harlan, Louis R. *Booker T. Washington: The Wizard of Tuskegee, 1901–1915.* New York: Oxford University Press, 1983.

Heilbut, Tony. *The Gospel Sound: Good News and Bad Times.* New York: Simon and Schuster, 1971.

Hester, Mary Lee. "Texas Jazz Heritage." *Texas Jazz* (June 1979):

"Honest Joe Goldstein, Pawn Shop Owner, Dies." *Dallas Morning News* (September 4, 1972).

"Interview with Houston Stackhouse." *Living Blues* 17 (1974): 20–21.

Jones, G. William. *Black Cinema Treasures: Lost and Found.* Denton: University of North Texas Press, 1991.

Lederer, Katherine. "And Then They Sang a Sabbath Song." *Springfield* (April–June 1981): 26–36.

Lindsley, Philip. *History of Greater Dallas and Vicinity.* Volume 1. N.P.: Lewis Publishing, 1909.

Lippman, Laura. "Blind Lemon Sang the Blues: Wortham Man Recalls His Memories of Musician." *Waco Herald-Tribune.* June 2, 1983. 11A.

Lornell, Kip and Charles Wolfe. *The Life and Legend of Leadbelly.* New York: HarperCollins, 1992.

McDonald, William L. *Dallas Rediscovered: A Photographic Chronicle of Urban Expansion 1870–1925.* Dallas: Dallas Historical Society, 1978.

Malone, Bill C. *Country Music U.S.A.* Austin: University of Texas Press, 1985.

Minutaglio, Bill. "The Buried Past." *Dallas Life Magazine, Dallas Morning News.* September 5, 1993.

Nixon, Bruce. "The Sounds of Deep Ellum." *Dallas Times Herald.* September 23, 1983.

Oakley, Giles. *The Devil's Music.* London: Ariel Books, 1976.

Oliphant, Dave. *Texas Jazz.* Austin: University of Texas Press, 1996.

Oliver, Paul. *Blues Off the Record.* New York: DaCapo Press, 1988.

Payne, Darwin. *Dallas, An Illustrated History.* Woodland Hills, California: Windsor Publications, 1982.

Pearson, Nathan W., Jr. *Goin' to Kansas City.* Urbana: University of Illinois Press, 1987.

Pittman, Ophelia. *Por Você, Por Mim, Por Nós.* N.P.: Editora Record, 1984.

Price, Sammy. *What Do They Want? A Jazz Autobiography.* Urbana: University of Illinois Press, 1990.

Rogers, John William. *The Lusty Texans of Dallas.* New York: E. P. Dutton, 1951.

Russell, Ross. *Jazz Style in Kansas City and the Southwest.* Berkeley: University of California Press, 1971.

Sampson, Henry T. *Blacks in Blackface: A Source Book on Early Black Musical Shows.* Metuchen, New Jersey, 1980.

Sanders, Barrot Steven. *Dallas, Her Golden Years.* Dallas: Sanders Press, 1989.

Schuller, Gunther. *The Swing Era: The Development of Jazz, 1930–1945.* New York: Oxford University Press, 1989.

Schuller, Tim. "The Buster Smith Story." *CODA* (December–January 1987–88), 4.

Soltes, William. "A Little Story of My Life in America." Unpublished manuscript, 1967.

Spivey, Victoria. "Blind Lemon Jefferson and I Had a Ball." *Record Research.* 78 (May 1966): 9.

Steinberg, Richard U. "See That My Grave Is Kept Clean." *Living Blues* 83 (1982): 24–25.

"T-Bone Walker in His Own Words." *Record Changer* (October 1947): 5–6+.

Townsend, Charles R. *San Antonio Rose: The Life and Music of Bob Wills.* Urbana: University of Illinois Press, 1986.

Uzzel, Robert L. "Music Rooted in Texas Soil." *Living Blues* 83 (1982): 24–25.

Willoughby, Larry. *Texas Rhythm, Texas Rhyme: A Pictorial History of Texas Music.* Austin: Texas Monthly Press, 1984.

The WPA Dallas Guide and History. Denton: University of North Texas Press, 1992.

Interviews and Letters

Albert, Don. Interview with Nathan Pearson and Howard Litwak, April 17, 1977.

Bedford, Louis. Interview with Jay Brakefield, December 5, 1992.

Boyd, Jim and Marvin Montgomery. Interview with Alan Govenar and Jay Brakefield, January 29, 1992.

Bruner, Cliff. Interview with Jay Brakefield and Allan Turner, June 7, 1981.

Callahan, Walter. Interview with Jay Brakefield, December 6, 1993.

Cody, Joe. Interview with Jay Brakefield, June 18, 1992.

Cokes, Curtis. Interview with Jay Brakefield, August 7, 1992.

Conley, Anna Mae and Lucile Bosh McGaughey. Interview with Jay Brakefield and Alan Govenar, October 3, 1992.

Cowens, Herbie. Interview with Alan Govenar, January 20, 1992 and February 5, 1992.

Cox, Quince. Interview, March 18, 1987.

Doran, Ed. Interview with Jay Brakefield, April 24, 1992.

Edwards, C. W. "Gus." Interview with Jay Brakefield, May 1, 1992.

Emory, Emerson. Interview with Jay Brakefield, December 5, 1992.

Feldman, Label. Interview with Jay Brakefield, May 20, 1992.

Fields, Jimmy. Interview with Alan Govenar, January 23, 1994.

Freed, Joe. Interview with Jay Brakefield, May 6, 1992.

Gimble, Johnny. Interview with Alan Govenar, September 22, 1994.

Goldstein, David and Isaac. Interview with Jay Brakefield, March 22, 1992.

Goldstein, Dora. Interview with Jay Brakefield, February 28, 1992; May 1, 1992.

Goldstein, Eddie. Interview with Jay Brakefield, April 3, 1992.

Goldstein, Isaac. Interview with Jay Brakefield, March 22, 1992.

Goldstein, Rocky. Interview with Jay Brakefield, March 22, 1992.

Howard, Theaul. Interviews with Jay Brakefield, October and November 1993.

Howze, William. Interview with Harmon Howze, October 10, 1984.

Hurd, Charlie. Interview with Jay Brakefield, November 1993.

Kirkes, Walker. Interview with Alan Govenar, June 9, 1994.

Lipscomb, Mance. Interview with Glen Myers, Center for American History Center Collection, Austin, Texas.

Luterman, Sam. Interview with Jay Brakefield, August 19, 1992.

McCormick, Mack. Interview with Jay Brakefield, July 29, 1989.

McGowan, Alto. Interview with Jay Brakefield, April 15, 1992.

McMillan, Rudolph. Interview with Jay Brakefield, April 9, 1993.

Montgomery, Marvin. Interviews with Alan Govenar, July 31, 1996; August 1, 1996; August 2, 1996; August 8, 1996; March 12, 1998; March 18, 1998.

_____. Interview with Jay Brakefield and Alan Govenar, July 15, 1996.

Moore, Alex. Interviews with Alan Govenar, April 9, 1982, November 5, 1988, and November 8, 1988.

Moss, John H. Interview with Alan Govenar, August 12, 1993.

Neely, Bill. Interview with Alan Govenar, August 29, 1984.

_____. Interview with Jay Brakefield, June, 1989.

Parker, John "Knocky." Interview August 28, 1963. Reel 1, pp.2–4. Hogan Jazz Archive, Howard-Tilton Memorial Library, New Orleans.

Pittman, Eliana. Interview with Jay Brakefield, August 8, 1996.

Porte, Masha. Interview with Alan Govenar, March 4, 1992.

Price, Sammy. Interview with Jay Brakefield, June 7, 1991.

Prince, Robert. Interview with Jay Brakefield, January, 1993.

Putnam, Ernestine. Interview with Alan Govenar, September 10, 1993.

Richardson, Jack. Interview with Jay Brakefield, May 23, 1992.

Sampson, Albert. Interview in Hogan Jazz Archive, Howard-Tilton Memorial Library, Tulane University.

Smith, Henry "Buster." Interviews with Alan Govenar, December 14, 1982; January 10, 1983.

Smith, Junious and Jay. Interview with Jay Brakefield, July 11, 1992.

Stillman, Sam. Interview with Jay Brakefield, March 2, 1992.

Stout, Bret. Interview with Jay Brakefield, June, 1993.

Tuck, Sam. Interview with Jay Brakefield, June 15, 1992.

Wackwitz, Hank. Letter to Alan Govenar, March 1992.

Walker, Julius. Interview with Jay Brakefield, August 1, 1992.

Watson, Willard. Interview with Jay Brakefield, July 16, 1992.

Williams, Danny. Letter to Alan Govenar, September 30, 1996.

Wilson, Will. Interview with Jay Brakefield, May, 1993.

Wright, Margaret. Letter to Alan Govenar, March 20, 1992.

Wyll, Max. Interview with Jay Brakefield, March 25, 1992.

Newspapers

Brotherhood Eyes. (Dallas, Texas.)
The Dallas Express. (Dallas, Texas.)
The Dallas Morning News. (Dallas, Texas.)
Dallas Times Herald. (Dallas, Texas.)
The Freeman. (Indianapolis, Indiana.)

Albums, Tapes, CDs, Films

Alex Moore: Then and Now. Audiocassette. Dallas: Documentary Arts, DA 105.

Black on White/White and Black. Documentary film. Dallas: Documentary Arts, 1989.

Briggs, Keith. Liner notes to *Jesse Thomas, 1948–1958.* Document BDCD-6044.

Calt, Stephen. Liner notes to *Blind Lemon Jefferson, King of the Country Blues.* Yazoo 1069.

_____, Woody Mann, and Nick Perls. Liner notes to *Funny Papa Smith: The Original Howling Wolf.* Yazoo L-1031.

Charters, Sam. Liner notes to *The Complete Blind Willie Johnson.* Columbia 52835.

Doering, Teddy. Liner notes to *J. T. "Funny Paper" Smith, 1930–1931.* Document BDCD-6016.

Evans, David. Liner notes to *Blind Willie Johnson: Sweet As the Years Go By.* Yazoo 1078.

Funk, Ray. Liner notes to *Preachin' the Gospel: Holy Blues.* Columbia Legacy CK 46779.

Garon, Paul. Liner notes to *Texas Blues: The Complete Recorded Works of Coley Jones, "Bo" Jones, "Little Hat" Jones, Willie Reed, Oak Cliff T-Bone Walker 1927–1935.* Document DOCD-5161.

Govenar, Alan. Liner notes to *Alex Moore: Wiggle Tail.* Rounder 2091.

Groom, Bob. Liner notes to *"Ramblin" Thomas & The Dallas Blues Singers: Complete Recorded Works 1928–1932.* Document DOCD-5107.

Lornell, Kip. Liner notes to *Gene Campbell: Complete Recorded Works 1929–1931.* Document DOCD-5151.

_____. Liner notes to *Texas Black Country Dance Music, 1927–1935.* Document DOCD-5162.

_____. Liner notes to *Texas Slide Guitars: Complete Recorded Works 1930–1938, Oscar Woods and Black Ace.* Document DOCD-5143.

McCormick, Mack. "Biography of Henry Thomas: Our Deepest Look at Roots." Liner notes to album, *Henry Thomas: Ragtime Texas.* Herwin 209.

Oliver, Paul. Liner notes to *Whistlin' Alex Moore: From North Dallas to the East Side.* Arhoolie CD 408.

Romanski, Ken. Liner notes to *Arizona Dranes: Complete Recorded Works in Chronological Order 1926–1929.* Document BDCD-6031.

_____. Liner notes to *The Complete Recorded Works of Reverend F. W. McGhee in Chronological Order 1927–1929.* Document BDCD-6031.

Shaw, Malcolm. Liner notes for *Arizona Dranes, 1926–1928.* Herwin 210.

Index

Italicized page references refer to illustrations.
"DE" refers to Deep Ellum.

J

musicians influenced by, 146
on Texas fiddle, 153
western movie influence, 162
Wills Fiddle Band, 159
Wilson, Will, 171, 176–178, 189
Woodmen of the World Brass Band,
33
Woods, Oscar "Buddy," 92–93
"World is Waiting for the Sunrise,
The," 140, 145
World War II, 176
WPA Dallas Guide and History, 184,
185, ix, xiii
Wright, Margaret, 122

Wyll, Issie, 47
Wyll, Max, 45

Y

"Yellow Briches," xvi
"You Are My Sunshine," 93
Young, Lester, 126
YWCA, 181

Z

zither, 102